South China Sea and Its Affiliated Islands and Reefs in History

Li Baotian, Zhang Dan and Wu Liang

Translated by You Ying

CHICAGO ACADEMIC PRESS

South China Sea and Its Affiliated Islands and Reefs in History
Authors: Li Baotian, Zhang Dan and Wu Liang
Translator: You Ying
Language: English
Word Count (for Space of All Pages): 289 thousand words
Publisher: Chicago Academic Press
Number of Pages: 318
ISBN: 978-1-965890-30-1

Publishing	Chicago Academic Press
	5923 N Artesian Ave
	Chicago IL 60659
Email	contact@chicagoacademicpress.com
Website	http://chicagoacademicpress.com/
Book Size	6X9 inches
First Edition	August, 2025

About the Translator

You Ying, the translator of this book, is a lecturer at the School of Foreign Studies of Guangdong Ocean University. A native of Zhanjiang, Guangdong, she earned her bachelor's degree from theSchool of Translation Studies of Jinan University and a master's degree in Applied Translation Studies from the University of Leeds, UK. Her research focuses on translation technology, localization services, and English-Chinese translation theory and practice.

As an accomplished academic, she has led several significant projects including Humanities and Social Sciences Project of Guangdong Ocean University(2021) and the Industry-Academia Collaborative Education Program of the Ministry of Education of China(2024). She has collaborated with Guangzhou Huayan Cultural Communication Co. Ltd. as a co-editor.

This book is published as one of You's project deliverables of the Industry-Academia Collaborative Education Program of the Ministry of Education of China in 2024 (No.2410314249).

Contents

Chapter 1
Regional Environment of the South China Sea

Section 1 Geographical Location and Range of the South China Sea

The South China Sea, the southernmost and largest of China's four marginal seas, is situated at 23°27'-3°57' N latitude, and 99°10'-122°10' E longitude in the western Pacific Ocean. With an average water depth of 1,212 meters and a maximum depth of 5,559 meters, the South China Sea covers an area of 3.5 million square kilometers, of which 2.1 million square kilometers encircled by the "Nine-dash Line" are within the range of China's territorial sea. To the north of this region are various Chinese provinces such as Guangdong, Guangxi, Fujian, Hainan and Taiwan; to its west are Vietnam, Cambodia and Thailand on the Indo-China Peninsula; to its south Malaysia, Indonesia and Brunei; and to its east the Philippines. It is about 1,380 kilometers from east to west and 2,380 kilometers from north to south.

The northern, central and southern parts of the South China Sea are dotted with four archipelagos: Dongsha Qundao (Dongsha Islands), Xisha Qundao (Xisha Islands), Zhongsha Qundao (Zhongsha Islands) and Nansha Qundao (Nansha Islands). According to *The List of Standard Geographical Names of the South China Sea Islands* published by the China Committee on Geographical Names, there are about 250 islands, reefs, beaches and shoals apart from collective nouns, waterways and non-entity place names. Except for a few volcanic islands and reefs, most of these islands and reefs are composed of corals, viz. biological reefs mainly formed by solidification of stony coral skeletons, which are poles apart from islands and reefs consisting of ordinary rocks (granite, sandstone, basalt, etc.) These reefs are located in tropical sea areas with shallow water in high transparency, proper water temperature (20-30 °C) and appropriate salinity (27-38‰). Thus, corals and other organisms are enabled to coexist at sea peaks, seamounts, sea hills or on top of guyot, continuing to grow, reproduce and die upward, thereby constantly prompting the accumulation and solidification of coral skeletons that gradually approach the sea surface and ultimately forming the said coral reefs. According to their relative position to the sea surface, coral reefs fall into different categories: hidden shoal, deep under the sea surface; ocean bank, shallower in generally small areas; submerged reef, where corals grow upward adjacent to sea surface, submerged at high tide and exposed at low tide; cay - coral reefs that have freshly risen above water at low altitude, covered with coral debris and gravel of shell with little or no vegetation; islands, long been above water, typically small, low and flat, and are covered with lush vegetation and fine sandy soil, some of which are mixed with guano to develop into phosphorous lime soil.

Among South China Sea Islands, there are 35 islands and 13 cays above water, covering a total area of about 12 square kilometers. Among them, Xisha Qundao spans 8 square kilometers, Dongsha Qundao covers 2 square kilometers, and Nansha Qundao also accounts for 2 square kilometers. Whereas most of Zhongsha Qundao is submerged below sea level, with only some small reefs of Huangyan Dao (Huangyan Island) remaining above water.

Section 2 Natural Environment

I. Geological basis

Located at the intersection of Eurasian, Indo-Australian and Pacific plates, the South China Sea is restricted by them during its geological development and evolution. Throughout the long geological history, this region has undergone complex tectonic movements and the mutual transformations between land and oceanic crust, leading to the current tectonic structure there.

The South China Sea and its adjacent waters are part of the continental grabens in this region. Shaped by multiple phases of multi-directional diffusion, shearing, and extension since the disintegration of Cathaysia during the Yanshanian movement, the current tectonic form features a series of giant compound grabens. These are characterized by an asymmetric, diamond-shaped small ocean basin that predominantly trends in a northeast direction.

Under this geological background, several large Cenozoic sedimentary basins rich in oil and gas reserves have formed in the South China Sea, including the Zengmu Basin, Brunei-Sabah Basin, Lile Basin, Northwest Palawan Basin, Wan'an Basin, as well as the Taixi Basin, Pearl River Mouth Basin, Qiongdongnan Basin, Yinggehai Basin and Beibuwan Basin. The Zengmu Basin, Wan'an Basin, Brunei-Sabah Basin, and Northwest Palawan Basin have all been exploited and are currently producing oil and gas.

It is estimated, based on the existing geological data, that the oil and gas reserves in the South China Sea may well reach more than 23 billion tons and 30 trillion cubic meters respectively.

Especially as China's modern equipment for oil extraction has reached advanced international standards, the official launch of the semi-submersible drilling platform "Hai Yang Shi You 981" by CNOOC now enables the country to carry out deep-sea operations at depths of 3,000 meters and drilling up to 10,000 meters. The abundant oil and natural gas resources in the South China Sea are expected to make an even greater contribution to China's modernization efforts.

II.   Geomorphological features

There are three major geomorphic units in the South China Sea: the continental shelf, continental slope, and abyssal basin. The continental shelf covers an area of 1.264 million square kilometers, accounting for 36.11% of the total area, while the abyssal basin spans 430,000 square kilometers. The continental shelf of the South China Sea is divided into four parts—northern, southern, western, and eastern—separated by the central abyssal basin.

The Northern Shelf: Starting from its westernmost point *Beibu Wan* (Northern Bay) to the Taiwan Strait at its easternmost point, the shelf runs northeastward with a length of about 1,650 kilometers and a width of 100-150 kilometers, narrowing eastward. The slope of its outer edge transitions at a depth of 150-200 meters. The northeast and northwest parts of its continental slope are wide and flat at a general depth of 50 meters and a width of 250-300 kilometers. The lower boundary of the continental slope reaches 3,400-3,600 meters deep under the water; while up on its land develops the Dongsha Submarine Plateau where Dongsha Qundao originates. The three-tiered topographic structure of continental shelf, continental slope and abyssal basin in the northern South China Sea is closely related to the formation of the three-tiered trapezoidal terrain of the Chinese mainland.

The southern shelf: Located at latitude 3°50'-12°07' N and longitude 109°-118° E, the shelf extends eastward from the coast of Sarawak to Brunei and Sabah in the northeast direction. Except for Beikang Ansha (North Luconia Shoals), Nankang Ansha (South Luconia Shoals) and Zengmu

Ansha, Nansha Qundao that are located on the continental shelf of Sarawak, the rest of the relevant islands are on its continental slope. In other words, there are more than 230 islands, cays, submerged reefs, ocean banks and hidden shoals scattering on the submarine plateau at the depth from 1,400-2,000 meters in the northeast of the continental slope, all of which are collectively called Nansha Qundao.

The western shelf: Stretching from the mouth of Beibu Wan in the north, the shelf extends to the estuary of Mekong River in the south, forming a narrow, elongated, and straight ribbon-like expanse, which is 40-70 kilometers in width. The continental shelf descends from a steep terrain to a gentle slope, with a depth of approximately 150 meters where the slope transitions. Its continental slope starts from Xisha Trough in the north and reaches Guangyatan Beach (Prince of Wales Bank) in the south. Also, it is bounded by the western edge of the basin in the east, and the east coast of Vietnam in the west. The northern part of the continental slope features an underwater plateau, where the upper slope is home to Xisha Qundao, formed by coral islands, reefs, and shallow banks. In contrast, the lower slope of the plateau is characterized by the vast Zhongsha Qundao, consisting of beaches and submerged reefs.

The eastern shelf: It is composed of the island shelves of Luzon, Mindoro and other islands, extending from north to south. This narrow island shelf, about 1,000 kilometers long and only 50-120 kilometers wide, curves along the island shore and features complex terrain, with Nansha Trough, Palawan Trough and Luzon Trough on its outskirts.

Abyssal basin: Located in the middle of the South China Sea, it constitutes the third tier of the topography of the entire region. With deep-sea trough formed by lithospheric faults on its east and west sides, the abyssal basin here reaches 3,800-4,200 meters below sea level and is filled with deep-sea sediments, featuring abyssal plains and deep-sea hills formed by some isolated single seamounts as its major landforms.

According to field investigation and laboratory analysis, the islands of Dongsha Qundao, Xisha Qundao, Zhongsha Qundao and Nansha Qundao, except for a few formed by volcanic eruptions, are basically moulded by the cementation of the skeletons of hermatypic corals and a small amount of calcareous algae and shells. Apart from a few on the continental shelf (such as Zengmu Ansha, Beikang Ansha and Nankang Ansha), the majority of these islands are spread across the terrace of continental slope.

These coral reefs can be divided into five categories: atolls, platform reefs, barrier reefs, fringing reefs and knoll reefs. According to the analysis and research of the South China Sea Institute of Oceanography, Chinese Academy of Sciences, among the 114 known coral islands and reefs, there are 62 atolls (43 drying reefs and 19 non-drying reefs), 33 platform reefs (8 drying reefs and 25 non-drying reefs), 11 barrier reefs, 5 fringing reef and 3 knoll reefs. Among them, atolls account for 53% and platform reefs 30% of the total reef area.

Specifically, atolls can be further categorized into five main types: open atolls, semi-open atolls, semi-closed atolls, closed atolls and platform-like atolls, which turns out to be the reflection of different stages of atoll evolution. Each atoll is again composed of three major geomorphological units, i.e. seaward slope, reef flat and lagoon, with an entrance channel (absent in closed atolls) that connects the lagoon and the open sea. Lagoons are generally found with patch reefs developed within. Seaward slope refers to the slope of an atoll facing the ocean, which can be classified into two main types: sloping and cliff-like. This classification reflects the strength of hydrodynamic conditions affecting the coral reef. The sloping type experiences stronger hydrodynamic conditions, with its slope within the breaker zone; hence the coverage of living coral is often less than 50%, as observed on the southwestern slope of Ren'ai Jiao (the Second Thomas

Shoal).

The entrance channel is the passage between the atoll lagoon and the open sea. Such channels abound in semi-open atolls, but are found in smaller quantities in semi-closed ones. Most of these channels take a sill-like form, meaning the depth of the channel is greater than that of the lagoon.

A reef flat refers to the part of reef around the atoll that expands along the low water and grows increasingly wider, thereby gradually enclosing a body of water into a lagoon. Reef flats are found in diversified patterns, wide and narrow, some with more reefs above the sea level and others far fewer. In some cases there are even cays developed within.

A lagoon refers to the body of water amid an atoll enclosed by reef flats. Generally, the growth environment on the inner side of the lagoon is inferior to that on the outer edge, leading to faster growth of coral on the reef edge, but slower growth on the inner side of the lagoon. Consequently, negative relief is often formed inside the lagoon rather than on the reef edge. Restricted by the specific environment of the South China Sea, the lagoons of atolls therein are not much deep. For instance, the lagoon in Xinyi Jiao (the First Thomas Shoal) is only 4-12 meters deep, while those in atolls near the Nansha Trough can reach a depth of 30 meters.

Patch reef, or spot reef, refers to a reef that grows on the bottom or slope of a lagoon. The number of patch reefs is generally related to the development of the specific atoll in which they are located. Atolls at the late development stage encompass a greater number of patch reefs that occupy a large part of their lagoons. For example, the patch reef in the lagoon of Meiji Jiao (Mischief Reef) is developed in profusion.

Overall, the absence of uplifted native reefs in the South China Sea indicates that there has been no significant uplift activity in this area since the beginning of the new century. The small reef islands in the South China

Sea are lifted and heaped up by stormy waves. So most of the reef islands or cays in this region are distributed north of latitude 9° N due to frequent impact of typhoons here.

III. Climatic characteristics

Located in low latitudes, the South China Sea experiences a typical tropical oceanic monsoon climate. As an area of perpetual summer and a distinct monsoonal climate without winter, this region also enjoys sunshine, humid air and rainfall in profusion.

The average annual temperature in the South China Sea region stands at 27.8 °C, with a mean minimum temperature of 26.8 °C in January and a mean maximum temperature of 28.9 °C in May. The highest temperature usually occurs in late May at 29.2 °C. The average relative humidity here is 86% throughout the year, with sea level pressure ranging from 1,007. 0 to 1,009.0 hPa during the summer months, and 1,009.0 to 1,011.0 hPa during the winter months. The annual precipitation ranges from 1,500 to 3,500 mm with uneven distribution - up to 3,500 mm in the southern and north-central part, while only 1,500 mm in the west and northwest.

This sea area exhibits prominent monsoon climate characteristics, with the northeast monsoon prevailing in winter (when 75% of the wind is from the northeast). The average wind speed in most parts of the region ranges from 8-9 m/s, but only 3-4 m/s in the south and north-central parts. During the strengthening of the southwest monsoon in summer, monsoon tides often occur, with wind speeds exceeding 8 m/s and gusts reaching Beaufort force 7 to 8. Monsoon tides may sometimes give rise to monsoon depressions, of which about 50% will develop into typhoons.

Apart from the aforementioned monsoon tides and monsoon depressions, there are some other tropical weather systems affecting the South China Sea, such as monsoon convergence zone, subtropical high, tropical cyclone, equatorial buffer zone and equatorial anticyclone.

Composed of the southwest monsoon and the easterly trade winds on the southern side of the subtropical high, the monsoon convergence zone seldom occurs in winter and is more active in other seasons, reaching its peak intensity in June. This zone is often accompanied by strong convective weather such as rainstorms, thunderstorms and gales, and may sometimes trigger the development of tropical depressions.

From mid-March to the end of May and in October every year, the South China Sea is stably dominated by the subtropical high, resulting in hot and mostly clear days. Thus the strong solar radiation that rapidly warms the surface water accumulates substantial thermal energy for both the subsequent northward movement of the convergence zone and the development of summer monsoon in South China Sea and southeastern China.

Tropical cyclones in the region, either from the western Pacific Ocean or the sea south of 16°N latitude, mostly appear during the winter months. Geographically, typhoons in the South China Sea mainly appear in the sea north of 9°N latitude, accounting for 73% of the total number of typhoons and strong winds in the region. In the north-central part of the South China Sea, the maximum wind speed can reach 50 m/s. But tropical cyclones rarely appear south of 8° N latitude - with only nine times in the past 41 years, including only three typhoons as per statistics. The southernmost latitude reached by typhoon center appeared in November, 1971 at 5.1°N latitude.

The equatorial buffer zone is the transition zone that guides the easterly trade winds in the southern or northern hemisphere to turn when they cross the equator. While equatorial anticyclone refers to the anticyclone system in the lower troposphere closely related to the cross-equatorial climate, which are generally associated with fine weather. But the formation and northward movement of equatorial anticyclones are apt to incur and intensify the southwest monsoon in the South China Sea, in turn promoting and reinforcing both monsoon convergence zones and cyclonic vortices in the region, which means heavy rains and strong winds may ensue.

IV. Ocean currents and hydrology

Under the domination of monsoon circulation and weather systems, coupled with the dense islands, reefs, ocean banks and shoals herein, the South China Sea shows extremely complex topographic change, which contributes to special hydrophysical characteristics in the region.

The Nansha sea area is one of the regions with the highest sea surface temperature (SST) in the world. Usually, the SST in the region is around 30 °C, and even up to 31°C in the southern shelf with little seasonal variation. The SST here is higher than the mean air temperature over the sea surface all year round, making this region the most powerful heat source in winter that significantly affects the climate change in South China, Southeast Asia and even the entire world.

The ocean currents in the South China Sea display pronounced features of monsoon currents. When southwest monsoon dominates in summer, the water of the Java Sea in the southern hemisphere is driven by southeast trade winds, flowing into the South China Sea through the Karimata Strait and the Gaspar Strait. After crossing the equator, the southeast trade winds then deflect into the southwest monsoon, driving the seawater to the northeast, passing off the coast of Vietnam and along the west side of Nansha Qundao, ultimately traversing Bashi Channel and Taiwan Strait, with a typical flow velocity of 0.5 m/s, and up to 1 m/s off the southeastern coast of Vietnam. During the domination of northeast monsoon in winter, water from the East China Sea and the Western Pacific flows to the South China Sea, heading southwest from Taiwan Strait and Bashi Channel, passing over the coast of Vietnam and the western side of Nansha Qundao. After crossing the equator, the northeast monsoon deflects into the northwest monsoon in the southern hemisphere, driving seawater into the Java Sea. The velocity of this current is generally 0.8 m/s, reaching 1.5 m/s off the southeast coast of Vietnam. Spring and autumn are periods of seasonal alternation when the currents in the South China Sea change accordingly. In ancient China, fishermen took advantage of ocean currents and sailed into the South China Sea on the northeast current for fishery in autumn and, with a bumper harvest after winter's work, returned home on the southwest current.

The waves in the South China Sea are primarily wind-driven, which mainly emerge as southwest waves during the summer months, and northeast waves during the winter months. The northeast monsoon period generally witnesses higher wave height than the southwest monsoon period, with the maximum figure appearing in typhoon seasons. Contrarily, small waves prevail in spring. Typhoon waves in the South China Sea exert considerable effect on the accumulation and erosion of islands and reefs, serving as the main driving force of the evolution of coral islands to gray sand islands. Therefore, the islands and reefs above surface in the South China Sea lie mostly in the sea north of 9° N latitude.

The salinity of the South China Sea is roughly 32.5-34.25‰ in January, 32.00-34.255‰ in April, 32.25-33.75‰ in July and 32.00-33.25‰ in October. High-salinity tongue is usually observed in the northern part of the South China Sea, with a low-salinity tongue in the southwestern part occasionally. Accordingly, the high-salinity tongue extends westward from Taiwan Province and Bashi Channel, to Dongsha Qundao in September, Xisha Qundao in January, February and March. In April, the high-salinity zone expands to the eastern South China Sea, forming a secondary salinity-tongue that extends outside the Mekong River mouth in Vietnam, with salinity levels reaching 33.5-34.00‰. It gradually contracts thereafter, shrinking to the area from Dongsha Qundao to Taiwan Province by July, and eventually disappearing from the South China Sea in August. The high-salinity tongue waxes in winter and wanes in summer, emerging again in September. In contrast, the low-salinity tongue, appearing in December with salinity below 33.00‰, stretches to most parts of Nansha Qundao and to latitude 16° N during February and March, finally disappearing in April. Specifically, the low-salinity tongue is related to the dilution of seawater due to high precipitation that results in large land runoff in equatorial tropics during autumn and winter, while the high-salinity tongue is associated with the Kuroshio Current, which brings warm, high-salinity Pacific seawater into the South China Sea during winter.

The transparency of water in the South China Sea is affected by multiple factors, including suspended particles in the water, land-based river runoff and sediment concentration, plankton content as well as winds, waves and tides. In general, the turbid coastal seawater displays lower transparency, while water in South China Sea Islands that is far offshore enjoys higher greater transparency. Taking Lizhun Tan (Grainger Bank) for example, despite the general water depth from 18-37 meters therein, the coral bottom can still be clearly seen throughout the bank.

The tide in the South China Sea consists of two major components: the independent tide generated by the tidal forces of celestial bodies and resonant oscillations induced by Pacific tidal waves. The South China Sea sees weaker lunar- or solar-tidal force as it covers a much smaller area than the Pacific Ocean. It is calculated that the amplitude of the spring tide generated by the tidal force on the first and the 15th day of the lunar month is only 8 cm in the South China Sea. The tides in the South China Sea are mainly brought by the resonant oscillations of Pacific tidal waves (including semi-diurnal tidal waves and full-diurnal tidal waves) entering the region. Affected by factors like the land-sea distribution, water depth and Coriolis force during propagation, the tides in the South China Sea are rendered complex in various types such as semi-diurnal tides, diurnal tides, irregular semi-diurnal tides and irregular diurnal tides, with diurnal tidal wave showing significantly larger amplitude than semi-diurnal tidal wave. Specifically, in Nansha Qundao, the amplitude of diurnal tidal wave is 50 cm, and that of semi-diurnal tidal wave is 25 cm; while in Xisha Qundao, these two figures stand at 49 cm and 24 cm respectively. Tides in the South China Sea, especially those near shore, display yet another feature - small tidal range. The general tidal range is 0.5-1.5 meters, with that in Dongsha about 1.5 meters, Nanwei Dao about 1.6 meters, and neap range in Shuangzi Jiao (North Danger Reefs) 0.3-0.6 meters. The average tidal range measured in some specific locations like Meiji Dao is 1.44 meters, with a maximum of 2.32 meters and a minimum of 0.54 meters.

V.   Marine life

Located in the tropics and affected by solar radiation, air temperature, ocean currents, etc., South China Sea Islands and its relevant water provide favorable conditions for the growth and reproduction of tropical marine life due to its warm surface water with a small annual temperature difference. In addition, the complex marine environment in this region encompasses not only wide and deep abyssal basins and troughs, but wide continental shelves and slopesl. Nansha Qundao, in particular, features a submarine plateau with rugged peaks and undulating terrain, where prevailing monsoons lead to significant variations in climate and sea conditions across different seasons. The region also boasts immensely varied ecosystems, hence the substantial diversity of marine   species therein, showing traits as follows:

First, a broad spectrum of marine life. The animals here include coelenterates represented by corals and jellyfishes, echinoderms like sea cucumbers and sea urchins, monoplacophorans or bivalves (gastropods), and cephalopods like octopuses and squids. Also, the region is home to crustaceans like shrimps, crabs and horseshoe crabs, reptiles like turtles and hawksbills, and mammals like dolphins and whales. And fish alone constitutes over a thousand species in Xisha Qundao.

Coral polyps play a unique role in the South China Sea. In particular, the reef-building corals that thrive in warm and shallow waters act as the primary architects of the coral islands and reefs in this region. Growing in tropical oceans, coral polyps have strict requirements for living environment; in this light, the South China Sea provides an ideal natural habitat that is most suitable for their growth and reproduction, wherein the highly transparent surface water has an average annual temperature of 25-28 °C, and is about 20-30 meters deep with high but suitable salinity (32-34‰).

The majority of the species in this region are warm-water tropical organisms, some of which are unique to the South China Sea, such as whitetip sharks, speckled blue groupers, giant clams, etc.

Most organisms experience rapid growth and fast reproduction, but are generally subject to a short life span. Yet some specific species, such as giant calms, can live for more than a hundred years. Some species with short life, precocious puberty and strong fertility, if injured, will soon recover once protective measures are taken.

The variety of marine organisms form a complicated food chain featuring the law of the jungle. Owing to the tense food relationship among species, there is a noticeable alternation of different biological populations.

For instance, the abyssal areas are relatively impoverished in marine life, while the shallow regions with coral reefs are much richer in biodiversity. In this sense, regional environmental characteristics in the South China Sea set the tone for the abundant biological resources here. Marine life in this area can be divided into three groups - plankton, benthos and nekton. Plankton, including phytoplankton and zooplankton, builds the foundation of the marine food chain, and serves as the primary prey for fish, the major resource in oceanic ecosystems, making it the primary productivity of the ocean. The density of plankton reflects the amount of fish prey, which in turn signifies the natural productivity of the ocean, and determines the amount of fish resources and the size of fishing grounds.

Based on geographical location, fishery resources, operating conditions and the fishing practices of generations of fishermen, the State Oceanic Administration (SOA) in China has divided the South China Sea into 23 fishing grounds. Notable ones include the Taiwan Banks fishing ground, the Aodong fishing ground, the Dongsha fishing ground, the Pearl River Estuary fishing ground, the Beibu Wan fishing ground, the Eastern Zhongsha fishing ground, the Western Xisha fishing ground, the Northeastern Xisha fishing ground, and the Southwestern Nansha fishing ground, among others.

There are more than a thousand species of fish in South China Sea Islands, of which 60-80 species are endowed with great economic value, such as yellowfin tuna,, mackerel, goldband fusilier, shark, sailfish, etc. Among them, tuna is a vital fishery resource in South China Sea Islands. Surveys show that there are many areas with dense tuna populations in Xisha Qundao, Zhongsha Qundao and Nansha Qundao that can be explored and exploited.

VI. Organisms and soil unique to South China Sea Islands

The South China Sea typically features low, flat and small islands and cays that stand isolated in the ocean of the tropics far away from the land, and since it has not been long since their formation, the organisms and soil therein are found distinctive.

1.Birds and animals of South China Sea Islands

The myriads of fish and other marine life in South China Sea Islands provide abundant food for seabirds, thus transforming the region into a paradise for birds that has long been crowned as "the realm of birds" since ancient times. Reportedly, about 70 species of birds have been found in Xisha

Qundao alone, which are categorized into residents, winter visitors and summer visitors.

Residents in the region include boobies, frigatebirds, terns, nightingales, barn swallows, etc. As early as the Southern and Northern Dynasties (420-589 AD), there were records of Chinese fishermen working in the South China Sea, among whom Shen Huaiyuan described in his *Nan Yue Zhi* (*A Report on the Southern Yue*): "The gull, also known as the seagull, rises and falls with the high tide in the sea. It typically returns to the islands when the March winds arrive, showing a keen awareness of the changing weather. When a flock flies to the shore, it surely indicates an imminent storm, serving as a sign for the seafarers." The gull mentioned in the text shares similar habits with boobies. Up to now, Chinese fishermen still rely on the behavior of boobies to assess weather changes while fishing in the South China Sea.

In South China Sea Islands, winter visitors like common emerald doves and white-headed ducks will travel from the north to spend the winter here; while summer visitors such as brown noddies and white terns tend to head northward during the summer.

According to the investigation of Chinese scientists, only barn swallows reside in Xisha Qundao. Nonetheless, Vietnam regards countless cubilose in the "Huangsha Islands" described in its ancient books as evidence for their claim on the sovereignty of Xisha Qundao. The fact is, however, that Xisha Qundao is home only to barn swallows, not swiftlets, and the latter is the only species that can build nests on sea cliffs to produce cubilose. Unfortunately, there are no cliffs or swiftlets in Xisha Qundao, thus no cubilose either. Perhaps Vietnam should consider looking for cubilose on its own coastal islands instead.

The colonies of birds represented by boobies in Xisha Qundao produce huge amounts of guano. Over the years, this accumulation has formed valuable phosphate deposits on South China Sea Islands.

Dong Dao (Lincoln Island) in Xisha Qundao is a natural reserve focusing primarily on birds and "wild cattle". The island is home to thousands of boobies, nearly a hundred frigatebirds, as well as other seabirds and various migrants.The so-called "wild cattle" on the island is actually one of the animals (including cattle, sheep, pigs, dogs…) released therein when Li Zhun, the Navy Admiral of Guangdong, visited South China Sea Islands in 1909. While other species did not survive, only cattle persisted due to the suitable conditions.

2. Soil

Living organisms play a decisive role in the formation of soil in South China Sea Islands. Soil experts found that the soil in South China Sea Islands, especially in Xisha Qundao, is obviously different from the tropical soil in other places. The characteristics of coral reef soils in South China Sea Islands are as follows:

The parent material for the soil is biological skeletons. Except for some volcanic islands, all islands in the region are composed of coral limestone (or coral conglomerate) as well as uncemented coral and shell debris, widely different from the soil formed on igneous rocks, metamorphic rocks or weathered sedimentary crusts.

Guano is involved in the formation of soil in this region, making the soil rich in both calcium and phosphorus. The average content of phosphorus pentoxide in soil samples from South China Sea Islands ranges from 28.1% to 29.97% in the surface layer, and reach 28.52% in the deposition layer. Given that the phosphorus content in soils in tropical and subtropical areas of China is generally less than 0.1%, the soil in South China Sea Islands is deemed a crucial source of fertilizer.

Under the influence of guano and plant litter, the decomposition of organic matter in the soil of South China Sea Islands is often outpaced by its accumulation. According to relevant measurement, the organic matter in the topsoil of South China Sea Islands generally ranges from 8% to 10%, with nitrogen typically between 0.4% and 0.6%.

Chapter 2

China's Discovery of the South China Sea and Its Affiliated Islands

Section 1 The prehistoric archaeological civilization of the South China Sea

Backed by the continent and facing the ocean, in addition to the full development of her land-based civilization, China is a country whose maritime-based civilization thrived greatly long before written records. It is no exaggeration that we are one of the earliest people to discover, exploit, and manage the ocean.

There are two main branches of ancestors living on the eastern coast of China - one is the Longshan people who lived on the Shandong coast and created the Longshan culture; the other is branches of the ancient people of Yue who lived on the southeast coast and the Lingnan region, and developed the Baiyue culture.

Typical artifacts of the Longshan culture include half-moon-bladed stone knives, rectangular half-moon-bladed stone adzes, rectangular stone axes, and black fine clay pottery. The representative artifacts of the culture are printed pottery and stepped stone adze. Among them, the half-moon-blade stone adze and the stepped stone adze are both specialized tools for crafting canoes.

The increased maritime activities of the Longshan people and the Baiyue people not only spread their cultures to parts of China's northern and southern coasts but also reached distant overseas areas. Since modern times, archaeologists have discovered perforated stone axes, perforated stone knives, and black keramics from the Longshan culture in locations including the Korean Peninsula, Japan, the eastern coast of the Pacific Ocean, and Alaska in North America. These findings serve as markers of the Longshan people's activities far at sea.

However, the discovery of the stepped stone adze from the Baiyue culture on the islands of Oceania shows that as far back as five or six thousand years ago, the Baiyue people had already ventured onto the ocean. According to the characteristics of the shape of the adze, the development of it is generally divided into three stages. The stepped stone adze is a kind of stone tool with a relatively complex shape; it generally originated in one specific place and then spread with the migration of those who created it. From the perspective of developmental sequence, segments of stone adzes found in China are mostly primary and intermediate utensils, with few advanced ones. However, those found in the Philippines and Polynesian islands are mostly advanced ones, with their birth probably later than those in China. Based on this, archaeologists at home and abroad concluded that the stone adze originated from the southeastern coast of China, and was later carried to various islands in the Pacific Ocean along with the voyage of the Baiyue people. In addition, some in the academia have demonstrated the connection between the ancient culture of the Pacific Islands and their origins in China from anthropology, linguistics, and many other aspects, proving that all islands with stepped stone adzes unearthed are destinations of the Baiyue maritime activities.

Judging from the distribution of the Longshan cultural sites discovered overseas, the Longshan people set off from Shandong across the Bohai Sea, reaching the southern tip of the Korean Peninsula along the northern coast of the Yellow Sea. Then they drifted to northern Japan by a cyclonic flow and passed through the Tsugaru Strait drifting eastward by the warm currents of the North Pacific. The current at 40°N latitude flows westward all year round with prevailing westerlies, with a speed of 20 to 25 nautical miles per day, and can carry vessels to the west coast of North America. In modern archaeology, perforated stone knives, stone axes, and keramics from the Longshan culture have been found in Korea, Japan, the eastern Pacific coast, and Alaska. However, the areas traversed by the current are either uninhabited or accessible by land, which diminishes their significance, resulting in insufficient cultural development in these regions.

On the southeastern coast, the Baiyue could navigate towards the Pacific Ocean through two main currents. One is the North Pacific Current, which is located in the westerlies north of 30°N latitude and flows eastward all year round. This route runs from the Hemudu site near the Qiantangjiang River estuary, passes through Hawaii, and reaches near Guadalupe Island in northern Mexico. The stepped stone adze unearthed on Hawaii Island proves that the Baiyue people did drift here. The other ocean current they took is called the Equatorial Counter Current. It lies between 3°N and 10° N latitude, flowing eastward all year round; while another branch of it heads southward to form the East Australian Current, which then continues eastward as the New Zealand Current. Together with the West Wind in the South Pacific, it continues eastward all the way to Peru in South America. Among the two branches of the Baiyue living on the southeast coast, one crossed the sea from Fujian and Zhejiang to Taiwan, then to the Philippines; while the other drifted straight from Guangdong and Hong Kong to the Philippines. After the two met, they sailed to northern Borneo and Sulawesi Island, whence they drifted eastward along the Equatorial Counter Current. Along this route, a large number of stepped stone adzes have been unearthed in modern times in Mindanao in the Philippines, northern North Borneo, Sulawesi, and the islands of Polynesia, which indicates the frequent activities of the Baiyue in this region during the prehistoric civilization. Living all inseparable from the South China Sea, the Baiyue at that time had been deeply familiar with the South China Sea and South China Sea Islands.

In the early stage of Chinese history, there were no specific records of activities in the South China Sea - yet this is only the infantry of China's navigation activities. This stage spans 1,780 years from the Xia, Shang, and Zhou dynasties to the Spring and Autumn and Warring States periods. This had witnessed the great blending of various ethnic groups, which laid the foundation both for the establishment of the Chinese nation and the further development of maritime civilization in later generations.

To promote marine endeavors, a country must first possess a relatively advanced economic foundation. This includes not only the capability to manufacture equipment and tools for developing maritime activities but also abilities to produce goods for exchange with other countries. So, it can be said that the social and economic development in the early stage of Chinese history provided desirable conditions for the flourishing of its maritime civilization.

According to archaeological evidence, as early as the Xia Dynasty, wooden "ships" as well as large vessels with multiple "cabins" and sails could be built in China. By the Western Zhou Dynasty and the Spring and Autumn and the Warring States, the Chinese realized that ships carried goods without the effort of draft animals, the shipbuilding technology in the country was further improved, which can be seen from the patterns of bronze wares in the Warring States Period. During that time, marine products played an increasingly important role in people's lives. For example, a large number of seashells and whale bones were unearthed in Yinxu ("Ruins of Yin") in Anyang. And there were even tortoise shells produced in the Malay Peninsula for divination.

When discussing China's maritime civilization, one cannot overlook the significance of silk. Originating in China, silk serving as the primary carrier of trade and cultural exchanges between the East and the West, has played a pivotal role in communicating eastern and western civilizations and blazing the Silk Road.

According to archaeological discoveries, as early as over 5,000 years ago during the early Neolithic period, the Chinese began sericulture and silk weaving, making China the cradle of sericulture and silk production in the world. In 1926, half of an artificially split silkworm cocoon shell was found in the Yangshao Cultural Site unearthed in Xiyin Village, Xia County, Shanxi Province, indicating that people at that time had mastered the skill of raising silkworms at home (cf. Li Ji, *Prehistoric Remains of Xiyin Village*).

In Chinese mythology, the legend goes that Leizu, the principal wife of the Yellow Emperor, the ancestor of humanity - had bred silkworms. And words of silkworm, mulberry leaf, and silk can be identified from inscriptions on oracle bones.

The ancient Greeks and Romans, referring to China as "Seres" ("the country of silk"),

regarded the silk from China as a supreme treasure, yet unaware of the true nature of this substance. Pliny (AD 23-79), a Roman naturalist, stated in his work *Natural History*, "Traveling northeast along the coastline of the Caspian Sea and the Scythian Ocean, one arrives at Seres (i.e. China), a land famed for producing silk in forests. Their silk yielded from a tree are extracted, steeped in water, unraveled smoothly, then woven into beautiful brocades that are later transported to Rome."(cf. Zhang Xinglong, *Compilation of Historical Materials About Communications Between China and the West*) Still, it is expounded in some other works that silk is made of bamboo leaves (See **Ishida Mikinosuke**, *Series of Classic Oversea Studies on Modern Chinese Culture*, pp. 17 and 26).

Section 2 Early historical documents

In the Han Dynasty (202 BC-AD 9, AD 25 – 220), Emperor Wu of Han dispatched his envoy Zhang Qian to the outside world of China in the third year of *jianyuan* (138 BC), blazing both the Silk Road on land and the Maritime Silk Road "from Zhangsai of Ri'nan Prefecture, Xuwen, Hepu..." to India via the South China Sea. The establishment of these two routes was mandated by the emperor at that time, representing a decision of the highest power and an action of the government.

According to *The Book of Han: Treatise on Geography*, "From Zhangsai in the Ri'nan Prefecture, Xu Wen, Hepu, it takes about five months by ship to reach Duyuan Kingdom. A continuing voyage for about four months leads to the Kingdom of Ruhmi. Again, after approximately twenty days by ship, one arrives at the Kingdom of Chenli and may reach Pagan Kingdom after walking for over ten days. Setting sail from Pagan Kingdom and traveling for more than two months, one reaches the Kingdom of Huangzhi, where the folklore is slightly similar to Zhuya Prefecture. This vast state is densely populated and abounds with exotic materials, which have frequently been presented as a tribute to Emperor Wu during his reign. A chief translation officer there, who worked in Huangmen (an official office), ventured with all those recruited onto the sea for the purchase of pearls, gemstones, precious stones, and exotic objects, carrying along gold and miscellaneous silk products. The states they arrived in kindly offered food and guides and they were transported by local merchant ships. The team also traded on occasion but robbed and killed others sometimes. Additionally, some of them were unfortunately drowned by storm, while the survivors returned after a few years. The large beads acquired during their voyage were less than two inches in diameter. During the reign of Emperor Ping of Han (9 BC – AD 6), Wang Mang assisted in governance. Seeking to display his prestige and virtue,

Wang generously rewarded the King of Huangzhi and requested envoys to present live rhinoceros as a tribute to the Han court. Starting from Huangzhi, one could arrive in Pizong after an eight-month sail, and reach Ri'nan and Xianglin County after another two months. In the south of Huangzhi lies the Kingdom of Yichengbu, from which the envoy and translator of the Han court returned."

The historical records above indicated that the fleet, affiliated with the Han court, started from Xuwen Port and passed Beibuwan where they turned south. They continued southward along the east coast of the Indo-China Peninsula before going around Cape Cà Mau; then they passed through the Malay Peninsula and entered the Indian Ocean via the Strait of Malacca. On their arrival at the Kingdom of Huangzhi, the crew exchanged the gold and silk (miscellaneous silk products) they brought for pearls, gemstones, precious stones, exotic objects, etc., during which the hardships they suffered are summarized as "unfortunately drowned by storm".

The trading activity mentioned in the text is organized by the government. Prior to this, folk businessmen who had already "ventured into the sea for trade" had grown acquainted themselves with this route and the languages of countries along the route. That is why the government managed to recruit translating officers for the voyage. It can be seen that as early as the pre-Qin period, before the Maritime Silk Road was established, China was already a world leader in the economy. The highly-developed silk production in China provided a material foundation for its foreign trade. Thus, the exported silk garnered admiration overseas, even being equivalent in value to gold in ancient Rome for a time.

The Western Regions and Central Asia are essential for the Silk Road on land. However, due to successive rebellions and continued social unrest in the Western Regions, transportation there was greatly affected, resulting in intermittent disruptions of the overland Silk Road. However, with growing demands for Chinese silk in Rome and other countries, the establishment of the Maritime Silk Road became an urgent need. In AD 166, Anton, Emperor of the Roman Empire (probably Marcus Aurelius Antoninus, AD 121-180), sent envoys to the Han Dynasty, where Roman merchants began to trade directly with China by sea. By the period of Three Kingdoms (AD 220 – 280), Qin Lun, a merchant of Daqin (ancient Rome), visited Sun Quan in AD 226 (i.e. the fifth year of *huangwu* during Sun Quan's reign according to the calendar of the Kingdom of Wu), traveling from Jiaozhi to Jianye (now known as Nanjing) for the interview. At that time, the maritime trade of silk between China and Daqin was already in full bloom.

In the silk trade between China and Daqin, the Kingdom of Tianzhu (present-day India) acted as a transshipment role. As early as the reign of Emperor Augustus (27 BC-AD 14), Rome sent a fleet of 120 ships annually from the Egyptian ports of Hormuz and Berenice to the Malabar coast of India, transporting silk and other goods back and forth. As is stated in Pliny's *Natural History*, "The money of our country that flows into India, Seres (i.e. China) and the Arabian Peninsula every year is no less than a hundred million sestertii (Roman currency)." This shows that there was a huge demand for Chinese silk in Rome at that time. And owing to the enormous cost of this demand, Tiberius even went so far as to issue an edict restricting people from wearing silk during his reign. The Roman philosopher Seneca the Younger (c. 4 BC-AD 65) once exclaimed, "O women, cast off these scarlet garments with golden embroidery! Let the red robes woven by the Tyrians, and the silk gathered from the trees of the distant Seres stay far away from us." All these above are sufficient to prove the influence and importance of Chinese silk to the West at that time, when foreign imports to China, in contrast, were mainly amber, tortoiseshell, pearl, agate, ivory, rhinoceros horn, and other rare products that fed the appetite of the minority living in luxury.

Since the establishment of the Maritime Silk Road by Emperor Wu of Han, China's shipping industry in the South China Sea has been thriving consistently. During the Eastern Han Dynasty (AD 25-220), Guangzhou, as the starting point of the Maritime Silk Road, witnessed not only a large number of Chinese ships sailing overseas but also the endless influx of foreign emissaries and merchants for trading via the South China Sea. For example, Yongyoudiao, the king of the Shan (now known as Myanmar), sent envoys to the Han court to present tribute and brought the "magic man" (i.e. magician) of Daqin in the first year of Emperor An's reign *yongning* (AD 120). In the sixth year of Emperor Shun's reign *yongjian* (AD 131), the Kingdom of Yetiao (now Java) sent envoys to China for trade. In the second year of Emperor Huan's reign *yanxi* (AD 159), the Kingdom of Tianzhu (now India) made frequent tributary visits from beyond the border of Rinan Prefecture. What is worth noting is that in the ninth year of *yanxi* (AD 166), Anton, the king of Daqin (Roman emperor), sent an envoy to the Han court, which was the beginning of direct exchanges between China and European countries. This very envoy came from outside of the border of Ri'nan Prefecture, so it could be that he had taken a boat to Guangzhou via the South China Sea and then transferred to the capital of the Han Dynasty.

Against this background, Yang Fu of the Eastern Han Dynasty expounded in his book *Yi Wu Zhi* (*An Account of Strange Things*), "The water is shallow and abounds with magnets in Zhanghaiqitou (twisted atolls on the rising sea). Therefore, most of the big ships from beyond the border failed to pass because they were fastened by iron sheets." The above-mentioned "Zhanghai (rising sea)" - the historical Chinese name for the South China Sea - comes from the fact that the sea water in this area rises occasionally according to the tidal law. On the other hand, "qitou" (twisted atolls) refers to the many islands, sands, and shoals formed by coral reefs. In this sense, "Zhanghaiqitou" generally refers to the islands and reefs in the South China

Sea. Moreover, the so-called "magnets" refer to a large number of shoals shores and reefs that had not yet been exposed to the sea level at that time. Due to careless navigation, ships ran aground in collision with these hidden shoals' shores or reefs and could not get away, hence the reference to "magnets".

From the latter half of the third century to the fourth century AD, the Chinese not only discovered South China Sea Islands but also had authentic records of them in contemporary Chinese literature. For example, Liu Yuanlin of the Jin Dynasty stated in the annotation of *Wu Du Fu (Rhapsody on the Kingdom of Wu)*, "In the sea of Zhuya stands an islet that measures five hundred miles from east to west, and a thousand miles from north to south, with no water or spring but giant trees. Chop them, and one can drink the sap from them with a basin or a jar." "The sea of Zhuya" means the adjacent sea area of Hainan Island today, which generally refers to the South China Sea; "islet" is what "zhu" means, while "no water or spring" indicates the absence of well water or spring water in this place. To "chop the giant trees, and drink the sap from them with a basin or a jar" means to drink coconut juice. This small islet without well water and spring is located in the sea of Zhuya, spanning five hundred miles from east to west and thousands of miles from north to south. With such a large range, it obviously refers to places like Xisha Qundao (the Xisha Islands) and Nansha Qundao (Nansha Islands) in the South China Sea. And such a vivid and accurate description in the given text could only be made by one who had indeed been to the place in person.

During the periods of the Three Kingdoms, Two Jin dynasties, and the Southern and Northern Dynasties (AD 220-589), while the north was afflicted with successive wars, the relatively stable situation in the south enabled rapid production and development. Additionally, Sun Quan of Wu attached great importance to maritime transportation and trade during the period of the Three Kingdoms, boosting active trade with neighboring countries through the South China Sea at that time. From AD 226 to 231, Sun

Quan sent Zhu Ying, Kang Tai, and others to Fu'nan and other countries. And the embassy stayed in Fu'nan for a long time. During their stay, they traveled to various countries and islands in the Nanyang region, including Nansha Qundao. Returning home, they collaborated to compose *Fu Nan Zhuan* (*An Account of Fu Nan*), saying that "in the rising sea stands a coral island with rocks at its bottom and corals growing on it." We realize, through field investigations, that it is indeed commendable to have such an incisive and accurate understanding of the formation and morphology of Nansha Qundao over 1,700 years ago.

During this period, in addition to business and envoy exchanges, monks also embarked on their scripture-seeking journey from Guangzhou to India through the South China Sea. Among the famous Chinese monks who traveled to India for scriptures, the ones including Dharmodgata from Huanglong in Youzhou traveled to India in the first year of *yongchu* during the Southern Song Dynasty (AD 420) and then returned to Guangzhou. Another notable monk, Faxian from the Eastern Jin, set out from Chang'an in the third year of *long'an* (AD 399), traveled to India overland, and intended to return to Guangzhou by sea. However, due to encountering a storm, he drifted at sea for more than a month before finally reaching Laoshan in Changguang Prefecture, Qingzhou (present-day Laoshan in Qingdao, Shandong province).

Section 3 "Geng Lu Bu" - one of China's essential tools to safeguard sovereignty in the South China Sea

As a major maritime country, there had been Chinese ships navigating the South China Sea long before there were written records. In the Han Dynasty, *The Book of Han: Treatise on Geography* recorded the transportation from China to coastal countries via the South China Sea at that time. During the Tang and Song dynasties (AD 618-906, AD 960-1279), with the improvement of China's shipbuilding and navigation technology, Chinese ships took the lead worldwide in terms of both load capacity and nautical distance.

At the turn of the 11th and 12th centuries, the Chinese had figured out the way to apply compasses to navigation. Ancient sailors traveled back and forth in the boundless sea, acquainted themselves with not only the distance and direction of their voyages, the climate, currents, ebb, and flow in the ocean, but also the sand lines and waterways in various places, the reefs that come in and out of sight, and the depth of the berthing ports as well as that of the seabed. No navigator can sail on the ocean without an in-depth knowledge of the above-mentioned conditions of his route.

It is unknown whether there was any monograph before the Song and Yuan dynasties (AD 960-1279, AD 1271-1368) with specific descriptions of the scenes related to these waterways. However, the definitive historical fact has been that China has used compasses for navigation since the Song Dynasty. For example, as Zhu Yu from the Northern Song Dynasty said in his *Ping Zhou Ke Tan* (*Matters Worth Discussing from Pingzhou*), Vol. II, "The sailors, proficient in geographical law, observe the stars at night and the sun during the day, leveraging the compass when it is overcast or dim." *Meng*

Liang Lu (*Record of a Daydreamer*) added that "relying solely on the compass, one might end up in the belly of a fish even in the event of a minor error." It shows that the sailors in the Song Dynasty acquainted themselves with the geographical situation of the waterway through star observation and compasses.

The Ming Dynasty (AD 1368-1644) was a period of significant advancement of navigation in China when Zheng He made seven expeditions to the West and clearly described the geographical details of his navigation routes in "Zheng He's Navigation Maps". According to the *Flow Record of Shitang in Pingyang County, Wenzhou and Ningbo* (collected by Jimei Navigation School): "In the first year of *yongle* in the Ming Dynasty, Zheng He was dispatched to a foreign country...for the revision of a comprehensive map of astronomical charts, islands, mountains, and water currents, ensuring that those selected could accurately recognize the shapes of mountains and the flow of water, without any errors day or night." This shows that "Zheng He's Navigation Chart" is rectified based on older maps, which means that there were already maps for navigation before the Ming Dynasty. *Geng Lu Bu* (*Manual of Sea Routes*), also known as *Zhen Lu Bu* (*Book of Compass Orientation*) or *Shui Lu Bu* (*Book of Waterway*), is an authentic record of the work and life of Hainan fishermen in the South China Sea and South China Sea Islands. Today, all kinds of documents about *Geng Lu Bu* in the Ming Dynasty tend to note that "the author is hereby ordered to correct the compass course, direction, and measurements, based on the experiences of skilled navigators" (see the manuscript of "*Cheng Zhou Bi Lan* (*A Required Guide for Navigation*)" collected by Xiamen University Museum). This indicates that *Geng Lu Bu* has become more prevailing since the Ming Dynasty. It was widely known among fishermen that *Geng Lu Bu* was handed down from the time when Zheng He lived. For example, there was an old fisherman named Meng Quanzhou from Qifeng Village, Puqian Town of Hainan Province, who was born in 1884 and still able to dictate the compass course to Xisha and Nansha in 1977 (at the age of 93). Besides his oral account about "the waterway record to Xisha and Nansha", he added that his father had been to Nansha during *jiaqing* period in the Qing Dynasty (AD 1636-1912) and had a relevant navigation book at hand. According to Meng, this navigation book has been handed down for ten generations and is said to have originated from Zheng He. Needless to say, the content of the book might have been verified and replenished during the production process of generations of fishermen.

In the early Ming Dynasty when Zheng He sailed to the Western Ocean, his fleet once gave out to all the sailors of the fleet *"The Maps for Direct Voyages to Foreign Lands from the Baochuanchang Shipyard (Departing from Longjiangguan Pass)"*. Gong Zhen, an aide of Zheng He, said in the preface of *Xi Yang Fan Guo Zhi* (*Chronicles of Foreign Countries in the West*), "Initially, they traveled through Fujian, Guangdong, and Zhejiang, selecting experienced sailors who were well-versed in maritime activities, referred to as 'chief navigators,' to serve as crew members. Thus, the compass charts and diagrams were entrusted to the leaders for careful management, as their responsibilities were significant and could not be neglected." Since then, *Zhen Lu Bu* - as the "forerunner of its kind that has guided generations of mariners with detailed knowledge of seas and shores, depths and shallows, islands and reefs, navigational routes, and celestial navigation throughout the ages as an enlightening heritage" - has become a necessity for all seafarers. As is stated in the famous preface of *Shun Feng Xiang Song* (*Fair Winds for Escort*) in the Ming Dynasty, "In the first year of *yongle*, tasked with issuing edicts to Western nations, I repeatedly rectified the compass courses, astronomical charts, the terrain of islands and mountains as well as the pattern of water currents, compiling them into a concise volume. It is essential to select individuals who are well-versed in evaluating the depths of different waters, capable of observing the stars and islands, and able to assess the clarity and depth of the water while on board. To ensure accuracy, those selected must approach this work with diligence, thoroughly and carefully considering every detail, avoiding any superficiality." This clearly mimics Zheng He's tone and might be related to what is recorded in books like *Zhen Wei Pian* (*A Volume on Compass Orientation*) and so on. In the following ages, there were similar records in various versions of compass maps, which indicates that "Zhen Lu Bu" by Zheng He to seafarers during his voyage has been spread far, becoming the master copy of "Zhen Lu Bu" in generations to come, such as *Shun Feng Xiang Song* in the Ming Dynasty, Huang Zhong's *Hai Yu* (*Report on Southeast Asian Countries*), Gu Jie's *Hai Cha Yu Lu* (*Records of Maritime Events*), Zhang Xie's *Dong Xi Yang Kao* (*Studies on the Oceans East and West*), etc.

Fishermen of Hainan in the Qing Dynasty inherited this fine tradition from the Ming Dynasty and provided even more detailed records of navigational routes in "Zhen Lu Bu" of the time. Since the Guangdong Museum collected some "Zhen Lu Bu" dispersed in Hainan Province in 1974, institutions such as the Nanyang Research Institute of Xiamen University and the Geography Department of South China Normal University began systematically gathering various "Zhen Lu Bu" from the public between 1976 and 1981. At present, there are as many as 12 "Zhen Lu Bu" in the three institutions above originating mainly from the Qing Dynasty to the Republic of China. They are generally written by sailors (including fishermen) according to their own sailing experience. Usually, those books recorded no map but compass courses, as well as some common oceanological knowledge, such as omen of typhoons, thunderstorms, rainbows, currents, water depth, reefs, seabed sediments, coastlines, mountain topography, lighthouse location, etc.

The owners of the "Zhen Lu Bu" are fishermen who live and work in the South China Sea and South China Sea Islands. Most of them are from places like Wenchang, Qionghai, Sanya, and Lin'gao in Hainan Province. Surveys show that these fishermen are mainly from Wenchang County and Qionghai County, followed by those from Lin'gao, Lingshui, Wanning, and Sanya. According to fishermen's lore, those from Wenchang County were the first arrivals in the South China Sea and South China Sea Islands in a large number. The fishermen of Qionghai County initially followed Wenchang fishermen to sea but began to surpass the latter from the late Qing Dynasty onwards in number. Fishermen from Qionghai that went to Xisha Qundao and Nansha Qundao outnumbered those in any other county of Hainan. From every winter of November to December (lunar calendar), fishing boats sailed southward with the northeast wind to Xisha Qundao first, where some of them stopped for productive activities, while others stayed for a day or two before continuing southward to Nansha Qundao. After approximately six months of fishing operations during the winter and spring seasons, they returned with the southwest wind during the Qingming and Grain Rain periods of the following year. Owing to equipment limitations, before and shortly after the establishment of the People's Republic of China in 1949, the output of fish in the South China Sea was modest due to preservation challenges. Therefore, fishermen mainly harvested other marine products such as sea cucumbers, trochus, sea turtles, seagrass, etc. In the 1920s, the nacre layer of trochus shell was used as one of the primary raw materials of spray paint for aircraft. Consequently, the price of trochus bounced dramatically, enriching a cohort of fishermen in Hainan. To fish for sea cucumbers, one had to dive 20-30 meters underwater. During my research in Xisha Qundao in 1976, I encountered two elderly men, Su Deliu and Peng Zhengkai, at the dock of Yongxing Island. At that time, they were both around seventy years old and could still dive for sea cucumbers, which was truly admirable.

In the vast expanse of the South China Sea, where emerald waves stretch endlessly, our ancestors traversed these waters through the Song, Yuan, Ming, Qing dynasties, and even the Republic of China. Armed with compasses and "Geng Lu Bu" written based on generations of maritime experience, they sailed across the entire South China Sea. As their descendants, we cannot help but express our heartfelt admiration for their diligence, bravery, and wisdom. With direction being the priority of navigation, fishermen used the 24 characters of Chinese Heavenly Stems, Earthly Branches, and *Bagua* ("eight trigrams") to indicate direction. For example, *Zi* represents the north, *Wu* the south, *Mao* the east, and *You* the west, with a 15° angle between each of the neighboring characters above. In the middle of the compass lies a needle that points south. While the compass needle is generally unaffected by the forward and backward movement during navigation, swaying from side to side may cause errors or even malfunction of the needle. Therefore, each boat carries at least three compasses. "Geng Lu Bu" describes the orientation of each route. In addition to relying on a compass, a sailor should also observe the sun, moon, stars, ocean currents, tides, wind direction, wind speed, etc. as a reference to judge the position and course of the ship. The time and distance of navigation are expressed in *"geng"* (watches). The ancients roughly divided one day and night into ten *geng*, with each *geng* equaling sixty *li (30 kilometers)*. In ancient times when precise measurement methods were absent, there were long-standing disagreements on whether sixty *li* equals one *geng*. Affected by various factors including wind direction and water currents, a typical journey of a ship took about one day and night to cover five *geng* (about 50 nautical miles, or 92.6 km). In "Geng Lu Bu", each route is documented with a corresponding *"geng"* distance. In the 1920s and 1930s, fishing boats rarely used a clock for timekeeping; instead, they lit incense sticks, and several sticks would need to be burned to mark one *geng*. Another unit of measurement was for the depth of seawater. When sailing or entering a port, a long rope with an iron weight would be thrown into the water for depth detection, which is referred to as *"da shui tuo* (water holding)". One "*tuo*" is approximately 1.5 m, that is, the length of a person's extended arms. Though not entirely precise, this approach was easy and accessible. Additionally, the method for detecting water flow involves molding wet ash into a ball and throwing it into the current. If it dissolves slightly and sinks, it is considered normal; if it dissolves rapidly or is swept away, it is deemed abnormal. Xisha Qundao and Nansha Qundao are both coral atolls, where the waters near the islands are relatively deep or consist of rocky bottoms, making it difficult to anchor vessels. Only by thoroughly understanding the surrounding conditions would ships safely anchor. It was in this complicated situation and through the sole reliance on the equipment above that generations of Chinese fishermen lived and carried out productive activities in the South China Sea. The rich heritage left to us by these fishermen is a treasure that deserves the utmost care and development by future generations.

Chinese fishermen have been living and working in the South China Sea for a long time in a large population, taking various courses during navigation. However, through production practice over thousands of years, they have gradually formed the customary route of fishery - or the "optimal routes" - according to the number of resources and the quality of living conditions. "Optimal routes" in different versions vary in terms of the islands traversed; however, the course of three main routes called the Eastward Line, Westward Line, and Southward Line respectively are relatively consistent. Their specific routes are as follows:

The Westward Line is located between many islands (dao) and reefs (jiao) in the southwest of the Nansha Island region, west of the Yongkang Waterway, and south of the Nanhua Waterway. It remains an important fishing ground for China in the South China Sea.

Southern Line	Jiuzhang Atolls (including Jinghong Island (Chenggou), Nanmen Jiao (Nanmen), Ximen Jiao (Ximen), Dongmen Jiao (Dongmen), Anle Jiao, Changxian Jiao (Changxian), Zhuquan Jiao (Empire Reef), Niue Jiao (Niue, or Whitsun Reef), Ranqingdong Jiao (Ross Reef), Ranqing Shazhou (Ranqingzhi, or Grierson Reef), Longxia Jiao (Bamford Reef), Bianshen Jiao (Tetley Reef), Zhangxi Jiao (Jones Reef), Quyuan Jiao (Higgen Reef), Qiong Jiao (Lansdowne Reef), Chigua Jiao (Chiguaxian, or Johnson South Reef), Guihan Jiao (Guihanxian, or Collins Reef), Hua Jiao(Chenggouxian, or Loveless Reef), Jiyang Jiao (Gent Reef) → Liumen Jiao (Alison Reef) → Nanhua Reef (Eluomen, or Cornwallis South Reef) → Maomie Jiao (Maomiexian, or Pigeon Reef) → Siling Jiao (Yanjing, or Commodore Reef) → Yuya Ansha (Shenkuang, or Investigator Shoal) → Boji Jiao (Boji, or Erica Reef) → Nanhai Jiao (Tongzhong) → Bai Jiao (Haikouxian, or Barque Canada Reef) Guangxingzi Jiao (Guangxing Jiao, or Guangxingzi) → Danwan Jiao (Shigongli) → Huanglu Jiao (Wubaier, or Royal Charlotte Reef) → Nantong Jiiao (Danji, or Louisa Reef) → Nanping Jiao (Moguaxian, or Hayes Reef)

The Southward Line refers to the route taken by ancient Chinese fishermen as they navigated southward along the five major atolls arranged in a north-south alignment (Shuangzi Qunjiao, Zhongye Qunjiao, Daoming Qunjiao, Zhenghe Qunjiao, and Jiuzhang Qunjiao). The islands and shoals along the way provided significant convenience for the fishermen's operations. Continuing directly south, one can reach Beikang Ansha and Nankang Ansha, effectively entering the waters of the Zengmu Ansha (James Shoal).

"Chinese fishermen have covered the entire South China Sea area through the aforementioned three operational routes. According to the statistics from the *Compilation of Place Names of Islands in the South China Sea*, "Zhen Lu Bu" by Chinese fishermen had named for up to 285 islands, islets, shoals, cays, and reefs in the South China Sea, which bear little difference from the 287 names in *The List of Standard Geographical Names of the South China Sea Islands* published by the Committee on Geographical Names of China in January 1983.

Chinese fishermen are not only the discoverers and developers of the South China Sea and South China Sea Islands, but also the masters who have lived here for a long time. They sailed southward on the northeasterly monsoon to the South China Sea and relevant waters for fishery activities. From May to November every year, frequent typhoons and violent storms in the South China Sea make it tough for fishermen's offshore fishing. Therefore, they generally reside on various islands, with some staying for one or two years, or even longer. On usual days, fishermen frequently go to the island to collect fresh water, gather firewood, and dry seafood. According to the survey, a fisherman named Fu Hongguang from Wenchang County lived on Nanwei Island for 8 years, while Chen Hongbo from Shangpo Village in the eastern suburb lived on an island for 18 years. At the beginning of the 20th century, Hainan Island witnessed a yearly increase in the population of resident fishermen, with dozens of them in Xisha Qundao and Nansha Qundao respectively. Almost all islands that meet the conditions for habitation (with fresh water, firewood, etc.) are inhabited by Chinese fishermen. The islands with permanent residents include Yongxing Dao (Woody Island), Bei Dao (North Island), Zhaoshu Dao (Tree Island), Ganquan Dao (Robert Island), Shahu Dao (Pattle Island), Jinyin Dao (Money Island), Chenhang Dao (Duncan Island), and Jinqing Dao (Drummond Island) in Xisha Qundao; and Taiping Dao (Taiping Dao), Shuangzi Qunjiao, Zhongye Dao (Thitu Island), Nanyue Island, Hongxiu Dao (Namyit Island), Nanwei Dao, Mahuan Dao, and Xiyue Dao (West York Island) in Nansha Qundao, where fishermen build and live in straw huts. Apart from catching sea turtles, sea cucumbers, oysters, and trochus, fishermen also capture seabirds and collect bird eggs. Those who have lived on the islands for a long time also plant trees and cultivate crops. Specifically, planting coconut trees on islands has become a long-standing tradition among Hainan Fishermen, passed down from generation to generation. The detailed livelihood of Hainan fishermen in South China Sea Islands has been recorded in English, French, Japanese, and other languages. *The China Sea Directory* published in 1868 by the Lords Commissioners of the Admiralty of the United Kingdom, after describing part of the islands and reefs in South China Sea Islands one by one, observed that "Hainan fishermen were found upon most of these islands." In 1918, Japan sent Unosuke Ogura, a veteran naval commander, to Nansha Qundao for "exploration" in an attempt to find uninhabited islands to expand the territory of the Japanese Empire. However, on Beizi Dao (Northeast Cay), Ogura met three fishermen from Wenchang County, Hainan Island, who had lived on the island for two years, thus realizing that it was an "owned island". In April 1933, when France sent ships for aggression to nine islands in Nansha Qundao, including Taiping Dao, Nanyao Dao (Loaita Island), and Anbo Shazhou, it was found that many islands were inhabited by Chinese people, with seven on Nanzi Dao, five on Zhongye Dao and four on Nanwei Dao. Some Chinese fishermen are buried in South China Sea Islands after their deaths. After Japan occupied the Nansha Islands in 1939, they sent investigators to the islands, who reported finding two graves on Beierzi Dao (Northeast Cay). One of the gravestones bore a record as 'Weng Wenqin, the 11th year of Tongzhi's Reign (1872)', and the other with 'Wu XX, the 13th year of Tongzhi's reign (1874)'." In brief, it is readily observable that it is Chinese fishermen, the true discoverers, pioneers, and guardians of the South China Sea and South China Sea Islands, that have left us this precious asset.

Chapter 3

China's Development and Management of the South China Sea and Its Affiliated Islands and Reefs in Hstory

Section 1 Development and management of the South China Sea and its affiliated islands and reefs from Qin and Han dynasties to the Southern and Northern dynasties

As is mentioned before, as early as the prehistoric period with written records, the ancient Chinese had connected with the Malay Islands and the southern part of Indo-China Peninsula by sea. This is strongly indicated by the shouldered stone axes and stepped stone adzes found in the Malay Archipelago and Indo-China Peninsula.

From the 21st century to 771 BC, when China was still in its slave society of the Xia, Shang and Zhou dynasties, the development of the country's navigation industry was in its infancy. Massive maritime activities were intensified by the improvement of social productivity, along with the emergence and development of production technology of bronze, wooden plank ships and sails. Chinese naval vessels not only reached as far north as Alaska, but there is also evidence from archaeological, folkloric, and textual studies suggesting that early Chinese ancestors had sailed to the Americas. By the Spring and Autumn Period and the Warring States Period, Han Feizi, a great Chinese thinker, had argued, "A man tempered by mountains and seas will in turn enrich his country."

In the 26th year of Qin Shihuang's reign (221 BC), the emperor unified China and established the first unified feudal state in China's history. In 214 BC, Qin Shihuang pacified the kingdom Nanyue and expanded his territory to Lingnan, making China a coastal country of the South China Sea, thus strengthening its ties with this sea region.In the second century BC, Emperor Wu of the Han Dynasty initiated the Maritime Silk Road. At that time, although the maritime routes mainly led along the coast, it still seemed reasonable that some ships that deviated from the routes sailed to South China Sea Islands and discovered those islands, which was strongly supported by the results of relevant archaeological investigation. Trapezoidal stone axes, shouldered stone tools and pottery net pendants were found on Ganquan Dao, indicating that as early as the late Neolithic period, residents in the southeast coast of China had reached the island for fishing and hunting, and used pottery retorts in daily life. Moreover, the Chinese ancestors not only lived in Ganquan Dao, but also traveled to islands like Daoming Qunjiao (Loaita Bank and Reefs), Zhenghe Qunjiao (Tizard Bank) and Taiping Dao in South China Sea Islands. Again, this can be testified by archaeological discoveries of daily utensils such as rotated clay pottery and pottery pots, as well as iron production tools and Chinese cash coin Wu Zhu.

From Emperor Wu of the Han Dynasty to the Xin Dynasty (141-23 BC), China sent fleets to the Kingdom of Huangzhi and other countries continuously. Therefore, broken pottery pieces of the Han Dynasty were found in places in the southern tip of present-day Indochina Peninsula (such as the River Johor and Kota Tinggi), which fully proves that Chinese ships were frequent visitors in this sea area at that time.

Meanwhile, people in China had already started to settle   overseas. It is said that ancient stone carvings were found in the Pasemah area of Sumatra, whose style is similar to those in front of Huo Qubing's tomb in Xingping, Shaanxi Province. Moreover, among the funerary objects unearthed from the ancient tomb of Kelinzhi, there is a piece of pottery with Chinese characters meaning "the 4th year of the early Yuan Dynasty" (45 BC), which has become the earliest dated Chinese relic found in the South China Sea.

Collaborating with some fishermen, Chinese archaeologists once salvaged some pieces of embossed pottery from Qin and Han dynasties on the reef of Nanyao Dao, and also found the embossed hard pottery of Han Dynasty on the reef plate and island of Taiping Dao, thus proving that some people in China had indeed set foot on Nansha Qundao in the Han Dynasty.

The South China Sea was called "the Southern Sea" in historical records before the Qin Dynasty, and has been referred to as "Zhanghai" since the Han Dynasty. According to *Shiji* (*Records of the Grand Historian*) written by the famous Chinese historian Sima Qian, after Qin Shihuang unified the whole country in the third century BC, he imposed the system of prefectures and counties and divided the national administrative districts, hence the establishment of Guilin County, Xiangjun County and Nanhai County. As these three counties were all close to the South China Sea, this sea region was then within the sphere of influence of the Qin Dynasty.

In the first year of Qin Er Shi (209 BC), Chen Sheng and Wu Guang lead a peasant uprising against him. At that time, Zhao Tuo, a native of Zhengding, Hebei Province, was appointed as magistrate Nanhai. Taking advantage of the chaos of war throughout the country, he crowned himself king of Nanyue (Guangdong) in Lingnan in 204 BC. After that, Zhao submitted to Liu Bang, Emperor Gaozu of Han, when the latter unified China and established the Western Han Dynasty. Since then, for more than 90 years, Nanyue had become a vassal state of China according to historical records from Vietnam. In the 5th year of Liu Che (Emperor Wu of the Han Dynasty)'s reign *yuanding* (112 BC), Prime Minister Lu Jia of Nanyue planned to revolt against the Han court with others. In the sixth year of *yuanding* (111 BC), Emperor Wu dispatched Lu Bode, General Fubo and Yang Pu, General Louchuan to advance towards Nanyue and counter the rebellion. Lu Jia and others fled into the sea after being defeated and were captured, hence the pacification of Nanyue. Since then, the Western Han Dynasty has re-divided Guilin County, Xiangjun County and Nanhai County of Qin Dynasty into nine counties as Nanhai, Cangwu, Yulin, Hepu, Jiaozhi, Jiuzhen, Ri'nan, Zhuya and Dan'er, with some of them larger than they were in Qin Dynasty. For example, Ri'nan County was located in the area north of Quy Nhon, Vietnam today, while Jiuzhen County and Jiaozhi County are located in the area north of central Vietnam today (including Thanh Hóa, Haiphong, Lao Cai, Meizhou Island).Except for Yulin and Cangwu counties, rest of the nine counties above are all close to the South China Sea, which shows that Emperor Wu of Han has reinforced his management of this sea region, which resulted in the grand establishment of the Maritime Silk Road.

Since the establishment of the Maritime Silk Road by Emperor Wu of Han, communications between China and foreign countries via Zhanghai (i.e. South China Sea) became increasingly frequent. As is mentioned in a historical record, "the seven prefectures of old Jiaozhi relied on maritime routes from Dongye for the transportation of tribute and goods, facing difficulties from turbulent winds and waves, with frequent occurrence of shipwrecks." Hence Yang Fu (Eastern Han Dynasty) remarked in *Yi Wu Zhi* (*An Account of Strange Things*) that "the water is shallow and abounds with magnetic rocks at Zhanghaiqitou. Therefore, most of the big ships from beyond the border failed to pass because they were fastened by iron sheets". From what is stated above, it can be seen that China has gained more specific insight into the South China Sea.

The location and range of Zhanghai (the South China Sea) are clearly recorded in various historical works. For example, *Liang Shu* (the *Book of Liang)* compiled during the Tang Dynasty recorded that" it is also said that the Great Zhanghai is situated at the eastern boundary of Fu'nan (south-central Vietnam today)."Also, *The Old Book of Tang: Treatise on Geography* contains a note of "Nanhai", stating that "Nanhai County is located in the south of the five mountains and north of Zhanghai."

In the following eras, the Chinese gradually deepened their understanding of the South China Sea and South China Sea Islands. For example, Liu Yuanlin of the Jin Dynasty noted in *Wu Du Fu* (*Ode to the*

Capital of Wu), "In the sea of Zhuya stands a *zhu* that measures five hundred miles from east to west, and a thousand miles from north to south, with no water or spring but giant trees. Chop them, and one can drink the sap from them with a basin or a jar." "The sea of Zhuya", i.e. the sea near Hainan Island today, generally refers to the South China Sea which measures five hundred *li* from east to west and a thousand *li* from north to south. These exact distances, if not accurate, is still justifiable for its description of the vastness of the sea area as being long from north to south and narrow from east to west. "*Zhu*" means an islet; while "no water or spring" means that there is no well water or spring water on the islet, with "giant trees" referring to coconut trees. There could not have been any accurate portrait of South China Sea Islands like this as early as more than 1,600 years ago if the describer had not been an immersive investigator.

This, again, serves as the most convincing evidence that the Chinese were the first to discover and develop the South China Sea and South China Sea Islands.

During the Three Kingdoms period, Sun Quan of Wu controlled all parts of Lingnan and divided Jiaozhou into two parts: Jiaozhou and Guangzhou in the fifth year of *huangwu* (AD 226).At that time, the Sun Wu regime attached great importance to maritime transportation and foreign trade, continuously dispatching personnel to sea. Especially from AD 226-231, Sun Quan sent Zhu Ying, Kang Tai and others as envoys for religious propaganda to countries including Fu'nan in the South China Sea. The envoys stayed in Fu'nan for a long time and traveled to many islands in the South Seas. After returning, they wrote *Fu Nan Zhuan (A Memoir of Fu'nan)*, which describes, "In Zhanghai to the coral continent, there are rocks at the bottom of the continent with coral born on it." Obviously, this is the scene they experienced in South China Sea Islands during their travel to and from Fu'nan. *Fu Nan Zhuan (A Memoir of Fu'nan)* is also the first masterpiece in the world that includes scientific explanation of the formation of South China Sea Islands.

During the Jin dynasties and Southern and Northern dynasties, when the north was plagued by years of warfare while the situation in the south was relatively stable, a large number of refugees from the Yellow River basin fled south to Lingnan, leading to rapid economic development in southern China. Notably, shipbuilding technology saw significant advancements, empowering the construction of ocean-going ships that could withstand strong winds and waves, gradually freeing the country from the previous constraint of navigation along the coastline. During this period, in addition to the development of maritime transportation and trade, maritime activities such as fishing, sea turtle hunting and coral harvesting in the South China Sea also experienced considerable development.

Relevant accounts are as follows: Zhang Bo in the Jin Dynasty said in *Wu Lu* (*the Record of Wu*) that "there are corals in Zhanghai near Jiaozhou, which can be taken with iron nets" and "there are hawksbills turtles as large as ordinary turtles in Zhanghai of Lurong County, Lingnan". Besides, Pei Yuan of the Jin Dynasty mentioned in *Guang Zhou Ji* (*The Story of Guangzhou*) that "some people used to fish in the sea and get coral". Guo Pu from the same dynasty wrote in his book annotating the masterwork *Erya* (*The Literary Expositor*) that "snails found in Zhanghai near Ri'nan are as large as buckets that can be used as goblets".

Due to the large amount of fishing and coral harvesting in the South China Sea, a coral market began to take shape in Yulin County at that time. As Renyun in the Liang Dynasty of the Southern dynasties described in *Shu Yi Ji* (*A Record of Anecdotes*): "There is a coral market in Yulin County where overseas customers can purchase corals." Also, Xu Zhong described in *Nan Fang Cao Wu Zhuang* (*Descriptions of Botany in Southern China*) the custom of Chinese fishermen collecting pearls in Zhanghai: "Whenever pearls are harvested in March, it is customary to offer five types of livestock as offerings.

If the sacrifice goes wrong, the wind will stir the sea water, or there will be big fish around the clam. The white clam pearls measure three and a half inches long and are found in Zhanghai. One of them measuring one and a half inches is regarded as the best since it is luminous with one side of it slightly flat, resembling an inverted pot...”

During the Jin, Southern and Northern dynasties (AD 265-589), Chinese fishermen working in the South China Sea were already aware of the importance of using seagulls for navigation. As Shen Huaiyuan of the Southern Dynasty described in his *Nan Yue Zhi* (*Treatise on Nanyue*): “The river gull, also known as the seagull, rises and falls with the surging tide. It usually returns to the islands when the March winds arrive, showing a keen awareness of the changing weather. When a flock of gulls flies to the shore, it surely indicates an imminent storm, serving as a sign for those who travel across the sea.” The river gull or seagull mentioned here may well be the boobies that still inhabit in Xisha Qundao and Nansha Qundao. Notably, China has designated Dong Dao of Xisha Qundao as a natural reserve of boobies. These birds, persisting their habit above, are still leveraged as a traditional navigation approach by Chinese fishermen.

Section 2 Development and management of the South China Sea and its affiliated islands and reefs during the Sui, Tang and Five dynasties

During the Sui and Tang dynasties (AD 581-907), ending the turmoil plaguing the Two Jin, Southern and Northern dynasties for more than 300 years, China entered a period of great reunification. With further development of transportation and trade in the South China Sea, along with favorable relations with coastal countries, China witnessed increased maritime activity in the sea region, encouraging some people to live and work in South China Sea Islands.

In 1974 and 1975, archaeologists from Guangdong Provincial Museum and Hainan Bureau of Culture Relics went to Xisha Qundao twice for cultural relic investigation, whose archaeological excavations on some cultural relic sites unveiled a considerable amount of materials about cultural relics. The briefings of these two investigations were published in *Cultural Relics*, No.10 (1974) and *Archaeology,* No.9 (1976) respectively. More than 2,000 samples of various kinds were collected in the two investigations, among which the most numerous was porcelain dating from the Sui and Tang dynasties to the Ming and Qing dynasties. This indicates that China's maritime trade shifted from being primarily silk-based to porcelain-based. This is why the route is also referred to as the "Porcelain Road". Most significantly, the investigation team discovered the residential sites of Tang and Song dynasties on Ganquan Dao, and unearthed some artifacts including ceramics, iron tools, copper ornaments, bird bones, snail shells, etc. Through investigation and analysis, the ceramics unearthed here are similar in characteristics to those in some kilns in Guangdong. In addition to a variety of artifacts, during the excavation of the residential site, the team also collected boobies and snail shells tucked in the stratum. Among them, the longest bone fragments of booby bones were

18 cm.

To promote maritime trade in the South China Sea during the Sui Dynasty, Emperor Yang of Sui sent Chang Jun and Wang Junzheng to the Kingdom of Chi Tu (now Malay Peninsula) in the third year of Daye (AD 607).The two set off by boat from Nanhai County (now Guangzhou) in October of the lunar calendar of that year, passed through Jiaoshi Mountain (now Champa Island, Vietnam) after 20 days and nights with favorable winds, and arrived at Lingga Boba Duozhou (now Guiren, Vietnam). After that, they sailed southward to Lion Stone (now an island near Kunlun Island) into the Gulf of Siam and arrived in the Kingdom of Chi Tu. Before the mission, Emperor Yang "bestowed one hundred bolts of fine silk and other silk textiles to Jun and others, along with one set of seasonal clothing and five thousand yards of satin, to be granted to the King of Chitu." (*The Book of Sui: the Biography of Chi Tu*). Chang and his team were grandly welcomed by the King of Chi Tu, who sent his prince to China with Chang as a return. Since then, according to *Sui Shu* (*the Book of Sui*), there have been more than ten countries from Nanyang that have come to Guangzhou for trade, such as Chenla (Cambodia), Poli (Bali, Indonesia), Pan Pan (northern Malay Peninsula), Tendong (central Malay Peninsula) and so on.

Based on the unification of the north and south of China during the Sui Dynasty, the Tang Dynasty established a powerful feudal dynasty in history that witnessed both the rapid development of handicraft industries such as silk and ceramics, and the remarkable progress and expansion of the shipbuilding industry. It is recorded that during the reign of Emperor Daizong and Dezong of Tang (AD 762-805), China was already capable of building large ships that could carry cargo of 10,000 *dan* (one *dan* weighs 75 kilograms) and hold 600-700 people. The hull is so strong as to withstand the impact of strong winds and waves. As Ibn Fadlan, an Arab, said in his book

Dong You Ji (*Journey to the East*), "During the Tang Dynasty when Chinese ships were extremely colossal, only Chinese ships could sail unimpeded through the perilous wind and waves in the Persian Gulf. Goods from the Arab world were all loaded on Chinese ships for export." This remark evidently reveals the significance of Chinese ships among the ocean-going fleet along the South China Sea and even the Indian Sea coast at that time.

Against this backdrop, during the Zhenyuan period of Emperor Dezong of Tang (AD 785-805), Jia Dan, the prime minister and famous geographer of the country, wrote *Huang Hua Si Da Ji* (*Chronicle of the Imperial Splendor Reaching the Four Directions)*, in which the article "*Guangzhou Tonghai Yidao* (*The Maritime Routes to Guangzhou*)" was included to the *New Book of Tang: Treatise on Geography*. This article describes two maritime routes, one leading to Korea, and the other from Guangzhou to the Persian Gulf and North Africa via the South China Sea. The latter proves that China has been continuously leveraging the South China Sea and South China Sea Islands in history. The said text and relevant evidences are as follows:

From Guangzhou, sailing southeast over the sea for two hundred *li*, one arrives at Tunmen Mountain, and sails west for two days to reach Jiuzhoushi with the wind at his back. Continuing south for another two days, he arrives at Xiangshi. After that, sailing southwest for three days, he could reach the mountain of Culao Cham, which is located two hundred *li* east of the Kingdom of Huanwang in the sea.

Guangzhou has long been the political, economic and cultural center of South China since Qin and Han dynasties. During the Tang Dynasty, Guangzhou became not only the largest port on the southern coast of China, but also one of the most famous ports in the world at that time. Han Yu, a literary giant in the Tang Dynasty, once described Guangzhou in his poem "Farewell to Zheng Quan on His Journey to Nanhai", "Behold, the sea flags proudly wave, as towers rise where skies do pave... with trade flowing to the

Sinhalese land, and music plays at King Wu's stand." This perfectly shows that Guangzhou boasted prosperous overseas exchange in the Tang Dynasty. At that time, Guangzhou Port abounded with not only Chinese ships but also foreign vessels. Among them, more than ten kinds of foreign ships can be found in historical records, such as "Kunlun Ship", "Persian Ship", "Sinhalese Ship" and "Brahmin Ship". The situation in Guangzhou was also depicted in *Tang Da He Shang Dong Zheng Zhuan* (*the Eastern Expeditions in the Great Harmony of the Tang Dynasty*) as follows: There are unknown numbers of foreign ships sent to the rivers in Guangzhou, with incense, medicine and treasures on board. At that time, Arabs had lived in Guangzhou for a long time, and resided with Chinese people. For the convenience of management and contact, local officials in Guangzhou also set up the post of "the Chief of the Foreigners". Since the Tang Dynasty, China has set up the official position of "Maritime Trade Commissioner" for the management of trade with foreign countries.

Tuen Mun Mountain, formerly called Beidu Mountain, was located in present-day Hong Kong. Facing the sea, it has been one of the key coastal defence sites of our nation in the South China Sea since ancient times.

On the other hand, Jiuzhoushi and Xiangshi are in the northeast of Hainan Island in China. In ancient times, due to the limited navigation conditions, ships could not sail directly across the sea. Therefore, to reach places like the Sinhala kingdom, Persia, one had to first arrive at the Teun Mun Mountain area, then change course and sail southwest for three days to reach the mountain of Culao Cham along the eastern coastline of present-day Vietnam. *The New Book of Tang: Treatise on Foreign Countries* stated that "The Kingdom of Huanwang, originally called Linyi, Culao Cham or Champa, lies direct to the south of Jiaozhou, approximately 3,000 *li* by sea. The land extends 300 *li* east to west and 1,000 *li* north to south." Apparently, the Kingdom of Huanwang is located in the south-central area of present-day

Vietnam. According to the *History of Ming: Treatise on Foreign Countries*, "The Cham City... was referred to as Culao Cham or Champa during Tang Dynasty, with its capital called the Cham City." The mountain of Culao Cham refers to the area of Champa to the east of Da Nang in the South China sea. The text above describes the maritime route from Guangzhou to Champa Island along the central coast of Vietnam in the South China Sea during Tang Dynasty. This route normally took a seven-day voyage.

One will reach Lingshan after another two-day voyage; the Kingdom of Mendu after one more day; the Kingdom of Ancient Qie for another day; Panduranga for half a day, and Mount Juntunong for two days more.

Lingsha and the kingdoms of Mendu and Ancient Qie mentioned here are all located along the coast of Vietnam from the City of Cham to Fanlang; while Panduranga refers to Phan Rang in southeastern Vietnam. Mount Juntunong, a two-day voyage from Panduranga, could be the Côn Đảo Island outside the estuary of the Mekong River in southern Vietnam today. The next course of the voyage in the text is:

Another five-day sail will lead to a strait - known to the foreign residents as "*zhi*" - that is a hundred *li* from north to south. On the north bank of the strait is the Kingdom of Orang Laut, and on the south bank the Kingdom of Sri Vijaya.

The above-mentioned "strait" refers to the Strait of Malacca. And as is recorded in *The New Book of Tang: Treatise on Foreign Countries*, "Sri Vijaya is two thousand *li* away from Mount Juntunong covering an area of a thousand *li* from east to west and four thousand *li* from south to north." As Sri Vijaya is to the south of the said strait, extending a thousand *li* from east to west and four thousand *li* from north to south, it is none other than the Sumatra Island in Indonesia today. And accordingly, the "Kingdom of Orang Laut" on the north coast is situated in the southern part of today's Malay

Peninsula. Then the text continues:

After a four- or five-day travel by sea from east of the Sri Vijaya, one could arrive at the Kingdom of Kalingga, the largest land in the southern (sea).

This paragraph says to the effect that after reaching Sri Vijaya, it will take a voyage of about four or five days to reach the Kingdom of Kalingga. Yet the phrase "the largest land in the southern sea" in the article is indeed impalpable, which probably refers to the largest of all lands in the southern sea. This "land" here could refer to Borneo, namely present-day Kalimantan. Again, it is mentioned in *the New Book of Tang: Treatise on Foreign Countries* that "Kalingga, also known as She-po or She-bo, is in the middle of South China Sea, with Poli to its east, Duopodeng to its west, the sea to its south, and Chenla to its north.... The king lives in the City of She-bo." From this we know that the Kingdom of Kalingga corresponds to Borneo, with Chenla referring to Cambodia today. The same book also contains record that "Poli, southeast to the Kingdom of Huanwang, can only be reached via a sail from Jiaozhou after passing through kingdoms like Chi Tu and Tendong. This massive land...is thousands of *li* in length." The journey recorded by Jia Dan mentioned Kalingga (Borneo, now Kalimantan) only, whereas China, in fact, maintained contacts with many islands in the Nanyang during the Tang Dynasty. There are frequent archaeological discoveries of cultural relics of the Tang Dynasty in Kalimantan in recent years. Since the Tang Dynasty, people from Fujian and Guangdong in China have been moving to Nanyang continuously, which is still the place with the largest number of overseas Chinese in the world up to now. Back to the said article, it goes on like this:

Then, sailing westward out of the gorge for three days, one will reach the Kingdom of Kakap Jenggi, another island in the northwest corner of Sri Vijaya. Many people in Kakap Jenggi engage in plunder, stirring fear among those who travel by ship. To the north shore of Kakap Jengi is the Kingdom of Kalah, which is to the east of the Kingdom of Geguluo. After sailing four to five days from Kakap Jengi, one will arrive at Shengdeng Zhou, and then get to the Kingdom of Polu after five days westward. Another six-day voyage leads to Jialan Island in the Kingdom of Po. After a four-day sail northward, one will arrive at Sinhala, with its north coast a hundred *li* away from the bank of southern Tianzhu.

The kingdons of Kakap Jengi, Kalah and Geguluo are roughly located in the Greater and Lesser Nicobar Islands northwest of Malacca. One can reach the Sinhala kingdom directly via the said Isalnds instead of circling the coast of the Bengal Sea. The so-called Shengdenzhou, the Kingdom of Polu, Jialan Island of the Kingdom of Po and other places seem to be on the nearby islands.

The Sinhala kingdom, now the Republic of Sri Lanka, used to be called the "Kingdom of Ceylon" in the past. It is referred to as the Kingdom of Sengjialuo in Chinese historical books such as *Fo Guo Ji* (*A Record of Buddhist Countries*) by Faxian in the Eastern Jin Dynasty and *The Records of the Western Regions* by Xuanzang in the Tang Dynasty. While *Liang Shu* (*The Book of Liang*) and *Tang Shu* (*The Book of Tang*) both named the kingdom as Sinhala, only *Yuan Shi* (*the History of Yuan*) called it Sengjiaye. Sinhala, rich in products, humid in climate and developed in pearl-picking, has been communicating with China since the Eastern Jin Dynasty. In the records of the Indian Ocean throughout history, there is no lack of mention about Sri Lanka. And even *Ma Ke Bo Luo You J*i (*The Travels of Marco Polo*) includes records of pearl-fishery in Ceylon Island.Again, the ship mentioned earlier continues to move forward in the following route:

A four-day sail westward leads to the kingdom of Malé, the southernmost part of southern Tianzhu. Passing through more than ten small countries in the northwest, one will arrive at the western border of Poluomen. Traveling northwest for two days and you will reach the Kingdom of Bayu

(拔颶). Another ten-day travel through five small countries in the western border of Tianzhu leas to the Kingdom of Debal, where there is the Milan River, also known as Sindhu River, originating from the northern Bakkar, flowing westward to the northwest Debal where it enters the sea.

This passage describes the southbound maritime route to the Western Seas. After passing through the Sinhala, one reaches the southern waters of today's India. Sailing along the west coast of India from the southernmost Malé (now Comorin Cape, the southern tip of India), one will pass through "more than ten small countries". The "Kingdom of Tiyu"(verified as Koyampadi) mentioned in the text has been verified to be the Kingdom of Koyampadi as mentioned in Ma Ke Bo Luo You Ji (*The Travels of Marco Polo*), and is located in or near Mumbai on the west coast of India today. The Sindhu is now known as Indus River, with the Tiyu at its estuary. Therefore, it can be judged that the Tiyu in the Tang Dynasty refers to Karachi, Pakistan or its vicinity. The following voyage goes like this:

A 20-day travel passing over 20 small countries from the west of Tiyu leads to the Kingdom of Shiraf Lar, also known as Larwi. People in Shiraf Lar erected an ornamental column amid the sea, putting a torch on it at night to guide sailors during night navigation. Another day of westward sail leads to Obolla near the Furat River of the Kingdom of Tay, which flows southward into the sea. A sail against the current for two days leads to Malla, a place of military importance in Tay. Then, traveling thousand *li* northwest, one could arrive in Fuda City (now known as Baghdad), the capital of of the realm ruled by the Maomen King (also referred to as Amīr al-mu' minīn).

As is mentioned in the text, it takes only a day's voyage westward from Shiraf Larthe, which had erected an ornamental column in the sea, to the mouth of the Furat River of Tay. Specifically, the Furat River is dubbed the Euphrates River today; while Shiraf Lar should be located on the coast of the

Persian Gulf in Iran, whose "torch" functioned as lighthouse today. From this place, ships would enter the Persian Empire after leaving India. At that time, the Persian Empire not only dominated the most vital overland arteries (the Silk Road) between the east and the west, but also had those busy maritime arteries under its control. The establishment of ancient lighthouse was the proof of the Persian Empire's control over the Maritime Silk Road.

Generally, ships entered Tay from Obolla. Tay, namely the Arabia, Tay started its prosperity during the Daye years of Sui Dynasty (AD 605-617), with its territory surpassing Persia at its peak. Apart from western Asia and northern Africa, Spain in today's Europe is also within its territory. The sentence "then, traveling thousand *li* northwest, one will arrive in Fuda City, the capital of Maomen" might refer to Baghdad, the capital of Iraq today. Fuda played an important role in the ancient communication between China and the West. During the Tianbao period of the Tang Dynasty, Du Huan, a Chinese traveler, went to Fuda City, and wrote the *Jing Xing Ji* (*Record of Travels*) after returning home, which described the grandeur of the city that year. At that time, there were already a considerable number of Chinese people in Fuda. Then the voyage continued:

From Malé, south of Poluomen to Obolla, ships all sailed on the east coast of the sea. Area in the west of its west bank all belong to the Kingdom of Tay, of which the southernmost of its west coast is called the Kingdom of Samran. Sailing from the north of Samran for 20 days and passing more than ten small countries, one would reach the Kingdom of Sihar. Another ten-day travel through six or seven small countries will lead to the Kingdom of Sayi Quhejie, facing the west bank of the sea. Then a westward sail for six or seven days will lead to the Kingdom of Mezoen. Again, heading northwest for ten days and passing more than ten small countries, one would reach Bahrain Manama, and Obolla after another day, where the route of eastern coast joins.

The regions mentioned in the previous text roughly correspond to the eastern and western shores of the present-day Arabian Sea. However, due to significant changes in place names over time, it is now quite difficult to pinpoint their exact locations. However, according to the given orientation and the description of other documents, Samran may refer to "the Kingdom of Barbary" in *You Yang Za Zu (The Miscellaneous Morsels from Youyang)* by Duan Chengshi - that is, Somalia as is now called. While Samran might lie somewhere in the southwest of Arabian Peninsula today, Sayi Quhejie is thought to be in the southeast of the Peninsula, with Mezoen referring to the city of Sohar in Oman. Sohar used to be a junction for the distribution of goods from various countries. As Idrisi, an Arab, once described Sohar in his book at the beginning of the 12th century, "In the past, merchants from all over the world gathered here, which is also the origin of their voyages to China." Similarly, *Hui Jiao Bai Ke Ci Dian* (the *Encyclopedic Dictionary of the Islamic*) mentioned that "during the tenth century, Mezoen, in its utmost abundance and prosperity, was the warehouse of Chinese goods. Witnessing endless trades with China, it is also the place where the travelers to China packed up" (cited from *History of Sui and Tang Dynasties* by Cen Zhongmian). Besides, Bahrain Manama could be the place named as "Abraham" in the *History of Ming: Treatise on Foreign Countries* (also known as Bahrain), which is located in present-day Bahrain Island.

From the quotation, it can be seen that the time taken from Guangzhou to the Persian Gulf is 85 days, adding up to about 90 days including those are missed in the note. The considerable scale of China's fleet and the complexity of its navigation technology in Tang Dynasty were supposed to land the country at the top of the navigation industry in the world.

Through the analysis of routes in the Tang Dynasty, we can see that the traveling distance of the Tang fleet far exceeded that of the Han Dynasty which sailed only to Huangzhi and Yichengbu. Furthermore, the Tang fleet sailed to Obolla at the end of the Persian Gulf and the mouth of the Euphrates River, whence the crew traveled a thousand *li* overland to Fuda City and the coastal area of Africa.

During the Sui and Tang dynasties, the land of Annan was a part of the territory of the Sui and Tang courts, which is why local governmental agencies were set up here. In the fourth year of Wude (AD 621) in Tang Dynasty, the Area Command of Jiaozhou was set up, and was soon changed to Jiaozhou Dudu Fu. In the first year of Tiaolu (AD 679), this institution was changed to the Protectorate of Annan, with its administrative centre in Jiaozhou, hence the name Annan. Under the Protectorate, there were various levels of government such as prefectures and counties. In areas populated by ethnic minorities farther away from Jiaozhou, dozens of Jimi (loose-control) prefectures were established, all governed by the Annan Protectorate. In the tenth year of Tianbao (AD 751), the Tang government also appointed *military commissioner* (Commissioner for Pacification) in Annan , which in the first year of Qianyuan (AD 758), was promoted to *jiedushi* (military commissioner), etc. The Sui and Tang dynasties always directly ruled the Annan area through these local administrative agencies at all levels, such as the Area Command, protectorate, *military commissioner*, prefecture and county. At that time, Annan was still a native land of China.

But as the national power waned, the Tang Dynasty's control over Annan area was constantly undermined. Seizing this opportunity, the local forces in Annan began to rampage. At the beginning of the 10th century, Qu Chengyu, a local tyrant, separated Jiaozhou and claimed himself to be *jiedushi* of the local area, which was recognized by the Tang court. After the doom of the Tang Dynasty, China entered the period of Five Dynasties and Ten Kingdoms, when Annan belonged to the Southern Han Dynasty. In AD 939 (the 12th year of the Southern Han Dynasty), Wu Quan, the warlord of the Qu family tribe uprised in Aizhou (now Thanh Hóa, Vietnam), defeated the Southern Han army and established himself as king. This is the origin of the establishment of an independent regime in northern Vietnam in recorded history. From Qin Shi Huang's pacification of Annan in 214 BC to Wu Quan's establishment of his own state in AD 939, northern Vietnam was under the rule of China for a total of 1,153 years.

Section 3 Development and management of the South China Sea and its affiliated islands and reefs during the Song and Yuan dynasties

Song and Yuan dynasties were known to be the heyday of maritime transportation and trade in China's history. Compared with the previous generations, Song Dynasty had witnessed greater progress in its maritime routes as well as more frequent exchanges at home and abroad.

During the same time, the Chinese established a clear concept of territorial boundaries, and documented South China Sea Islands, historically referred to as "Qianli Changsha" and "Wanli Shitang," as part of China's territorial domain in various records concerning the South China Sea.

Zhu Fan Zhi (*A Description of Barbarian Nations, Records of Foreign People*), a work by Zhao Rushi in Song Dynasty, recorded that in the fifth year of Zhenyuan in the Tang Dynasty (AD 789), "Qiongshan of Ya Prefecture was designated to be a commandery, while Wan'an was established as a county and later promoted to a prefecture now known as Wan'an Military Prefecture. And specifically, Dan and Zhen refer to today's Jiyang and Changhua military prefectures. In the fifth year of Zhenyuan, Qiong was designated as a commandery, which still exists today...Upon reaching Jiyang, the extremity of the sea without land or shore beyond, there are shoals called Wuli and Sujilang outside, facing Cham City in the south and Chenla in the west. To the east of it is the boundless expanse of Qianlichangsha and Wanlishitang, with the sea seeming to melt into the sky. The ships in the region, taking compass as their sole navigation guide, watch it with vigilance day and night lest the slightest error may incur lethal results. The total of eleven counties in the four commanderies mentioned above were under the jurisdiction of Guangnanxi Circuit". In the text, apparently,

Qianlichangsha and Wanlishitang are deemed parts of Guangnanxi Circuit.

The ancient Chinese geographical masterpiece *Yu Di Ji Sheng* (*Exhaustive Description of the Empire*) by Wang Xiangzhi in the Song Dynasty, quoting the record of *Qiong Guan Zhi* (*Treatise on the Administration of Qiong*) prefaced by Yi Taichu, recorded that "Jiyang, a land of towering mountains, stretches eastward to the distant Qianlichangsha and Wanlishitang, where the horizon fades into a serene expanse of blue. Vessels come and go amidst this vastness while birds perch on board, undisturbed by the turbulence." The author of the text held that Qianlichangsha and Wanlishitang belong to the territorial sea of Jiyang Military Prefecture in Qiongzhou.

In addition, Cai Wei's *Qiong Hai Fang Yu Zhi (Geographical Record of Qionghai)*, Tang Zhou's *Qiong Tai Zhi (Chronicles of Qiongtai)*, Jin Guangzu's *Guang Dong Tong Zhi (Comprehensive Records about Canton)* (including its Yongzheng version), the Daoguang Version of *Qiong Zhou Fu Zhi (Treatise on the Prefecture of Qiongzhou)* and other editions of chronicles all quote *Qiong Guan Zhi (Chronicles of the Administration of Qiong)*, which was prefaced by Yi Taichu in jiatai period of the Southern Song Dynasty (AD 1201-1204), describing the territory of Qiongzhou territory in an item called "Territory" as follows: "(Qiongzhou) is surrounded by the sea, bordering the islands of Wuli, Sumi, and Jilang to the west, with Champa to the south, Chenla and Jiaozhi to the west, and Qianlichangsha and Wanlishitang to the east, reaching up to Xuwen County in Leizhou to the north." Here, by placing Qianlichangsha and Wanlishitang in the "territory" equivalent to Leizhou Prefecture and Xuwen County, the author undoubtedly deemed Qiongzhou within the said territory.

In the Song Dynasty, *Wu Jing Zong Yao* (the *Complete Essentials for the Military Classics*) and *Zhu Fan Zhi* (*A Description of Barbarian Nations, Records of Foreign People)* clearly pointed out that Culao Cham, Jiaoyang and Zhuyu were the maritime boundaries between China and foreign countries. As is recorded in Zeng Gongliang's *Wu Jing Zong Yao* (the *Complete Essentials for the Military Classics*), "Traveling southwest from Tuen Mun Mountain with the east (north) wind for seven days, a ship will reach Jiuruluozhou, for another three days to Culao (Cham) Mountain (original note: at the border of Huanzhou), and again three days southward to Lingshan." Here, Zeng Gongliang clearly pointed out that the mountain of Culao Cham (now Champa Island in central Vietnam) is the national boundary of Huanzhou (寰州) (probably present-day Huanzhou 环洲).

Similarly, Zhao Rushi recorded in the preface of his *Zhu Fan Zhi* that "I have been summoned to this place (referring to Quanzhou) and, in my leisure, perused the '*Illustrated Treatise on Various Barbarians*,' where I observe the ruggedness of Shitang and Changsha, as well as the limits of Jiaoyang and Zhuyu." Zhao's description of Shitang and Changsha as "ruggedness" and Jiaoyang (Champa) and Zhuyu (now Or Island on the Malay Peninsula) as "limits" (i.e. boundaries), can be deemed as an unequivocal and explicit illustration that Champa and Zhuyu were the maritime boundaries between China and Huanzhou in Song Dynasty.

That was a time when China's shipbuilding industry was not only highly developed, but also significantly advanced in sailing distance compared to the Tang Dynasty. Also, the China-built ships at that time could carry five or six hundred - or even as many as a thousand passengers thanks to the large hull and deep draft. However, large ships were not allowed to enter the port of Basra in the Persian Gulf. Therefore, as is marked in *Ling Wai Dai Da* (*Representative Answers from the Region beyond the Mountains*), "It is necessary for Chinese shippers aiming for Tay to change for small boats in Kollam... Whereas the people of Tay traveling to China will sail southward by small boats and change for big ones eastward after reaching Kollam." The Arab traveler Sulaiman, who had visited China before AD 851, wrote in his travelogue that "as for the ports where sea ships are berthed, it is said that most Chinese ships loaded their goods and set off in Siraf." The reason for this, according to Sulaiman, is that some ports have narrow routes and are not suitable for Chinese ships to pass through. He also mentioned that in the port of Kollam, Chinese ships had to pay an import tax of 1,000 dirham (silver coins) due to their large size and huge amount of cargo; whereas ships from other countries only paid one to ten dinars (gold coins) for passage. The exchange rate of the local currency is 12 dirham silver coins for one dinar gold coin, with an 8.3 to 83 times difference between the two. The Arabs from the east often took Chinese ships to Guangzhou directly. In Song Dynasty, the number of passengers in this route showed an ever-increasing trend, with Chinese ships dominating almost all of those sailing to and from the West.

The development of navigation technology has promoted the study of tides. In *Hai Tao Zhi* (*Treatise on Tides*), Dou Shumeng clearly expounded the relationship between the moon and causes of ocean tides, saying that "the moon and the sea beckon to each other, awaiting their destined moment. If it is not the right time, one cannot force it to be; when the time comes, it will arrive of its own accord, and cannot be held back". Later, Yu Jing wrote *Preface to the Illustrated Treatise of Tides*. Moreover, geographer Zhang Zai explained the causes of tides in a principle similar to universal gravitation, and applied tidal theory to navigational practice, based on which he came up with the "conventional time difference of ports" to ensure the safety of ships entering and leaving the port. During the same period, another significant maritime contribution was the creation of nautical charts. The Tang Dynasty began to attach importance to rendering maps of "waterways and roads". Later in the Song Dynasty, Xu Jing, in his work *the Illustrated Journal of the Envoy to Goryeo during the Xuanhe Era*, already showed "a map depicting the islands, islets, reefs, and shoals that the divine vessel had visited", not to mention *the Geographical Maps of Various Foreign Lands* and *Zhu Fan Tu*.

A particularly monumental event was the use of the compass in navigation, transforming the oceans of the world into thoroughfares. This innovation stands as a remarkable contribution of ancient Chinese civilization to the tapestry of global culture. This remarkable event was accurately described by Shen Kuo, a great scientist in the Northern Song Dynasty, in his masterpiece *The Dream Pool Essays*. Around AD 1180, magnetic needles spread to Europe through the Arabs, since which the global navigation industry has entered a new era.

There are two historical facts of exceeding significance in the Yuan Dynasty about the South China Sea - to be more specific, about South China Sea Islands: first, in the early Yuan Dynasty, Shi Bi led his army to attack Java; second, the navigator Wang Dayuan wrote *Dao Yi Zhi Lüe* (*A Brief Account of the Islands*) based on his two experiences of "sailing to the eastern and western oceans". The former still unmistakably defined South China Sea Islands within China's sea borders, while the latter believed that South China Sea Islands was a natural extension of the geomantic veins of Chinese mainland according to the relevant theory of Zhu Xi, a great scholar and philosopher in the Song Dynasty.

It was mentioned in *the History of Yuan: Biography of Shi Bi* that "in December of the 29th year of zhiyuan period, Shi Bi gathered an army of five thousand men before they set sail from Quanzhou. Their ships tossed by the roaring wind and the rushing waves, the soldiers could not eat for a few days when crossing Qizhouyang, Wanlishitang and passing the boundary between Jiaozhi and Cham City." And there were similar accounts in Ke Shaomin's *the New History of Yuan*: "... The army gathered in Quanzhou and set sail from Houzhu. Their ships tossed by the roaring wind and the rushing waves, the soldiers could not eat for a few days when crossing Qizhouyang, Wanlishitang and passing the boundary between Jiaozhi and Cham City."

Both authors mentioned "crossing Qizhouyang and Wanlishitang" before "the boundary between Jiaozhi and Cham City", making it clear that the "the boundary between Jiaozhi and Cham City" was definitive in Song and Yuan dynasties.

Wang Dayuan gave an explicit and vivid explanation about the item "Wanlishitang" in his work *Dao Yi Zhi Lüe* that "the skeleton of Wanlishitang has its root in Chaozhou, winding like a long snake across the sea through various coastal countries, thus commonly known as Wanlishitang (ten thousand-*li* sand cays). But If I were to speculate, would it be stretching only ten thousand *li*? A ship sailing from Daiyumen tends to hoist four sails, riding the wind and breaking the waves as if flying across the sea. It sometimes took over a hundred days to reach the western seas. In this light, Wanlishitang is no less than ten thousand *li* if the ship is traveling at a speed of a hundred *li* a day. Therefore, the geomantic veins of this place can be clearly examined. One vein extends to Java, one to Brunei and Timor, and yet another reaching the land of Kunlun in the distant Western Ocean. Indeed, as Master Zhu of the Ziyang School pointed out, the lands overseas are connected to the geomantic veins of Zhongyuan (the central region); is this not the case? With the vast ocean stretching with its boundless shores hidden by reefs, who can fully understand it? So, it is just wise to avoid them and dangerous to encounter them." Here, Wang believed that the sea "stretching with its boundless shores hidden by reefs" was a proof of Zhu Xi's theory of geomantic veins, holding that the coral islands and reefs in the South China Sea are composed of three veins that start from Chaozhou and lead to Java, Brunei, Timor and Kunlun. Consequently, these "skeletons of Wanlishitang" are undoubtedly regarded by Wang as the territory of China, which are exactly the alleged "the lands overseas are connected to the geomantic veins of Zhongyuan" in Zhu Xi's remarks.

In the Yuan Dynasty, Kublai Khan, the Emperor Shizu of the Yuan

Dynasty, attached great importance to overseas trade. As early as the 13th year of Zhiyuan era (AD 1276), during the conflict between the Song and Yuan dynasties, Kublai Khan tried his best to persuade Pu Shougeng, the envoy of Quanzhou in Song Dynasty, to submit to the Yuan. Pu, originally a descendant of Arabs, owned a large number of ships and engaged in foreign trade, which made him a powerful figure in Fujian. In the following year, Kublai Khan "established shibosi (Department of Maritime Trade) in Quanzhou". In the 15th year of zhiyuan era (AD 1278), Kublai Khan issued a decree to chancellors Suo Du and Pu Shougeng of the Executive Secretariat, saying that "since all the foreign countries in the southeastern islands entertain admiration for righteousness, you are of course allowed to announce my intentions in front of those foreign seafarers. If they are indeed able to come to court, I will bestow them with favor and courteous reception. Their exchanges and trades can proceed according to their respective desires." Receiving this decree, chancellors including Pu Shougeng sent an envoy to "send ten imperial edicts bearing the royal seal to issue orders and convey messages to the various tributary states". In the Yuan Dynasty, foreign trade in the country "involved more than 220 countries and regions", with maritime routes opened from coastal areas in China to Asia, Europe and Africa. Accordingly, Quanzhou became the largest port in China that even in the world at that time. Marco Polo once portrayed the scene of Quanzhou he saw in his travelogue, "Citong (i.e. Quanzhou) is one of the largest ports in the world where myriads of businessmen gathered and heaps of goods piled up in an unimaginable way." Similarly, Moroccan traveler Ibn Battuta mentioned in his travelogue that "Quanzhou has become one of the largest ports or, suffice to say, the one true largest port in the world. I had witnessed hundreds of big sailing vessels converging around the land, with other small boats even more innumerable."

Compared with the Song Dynasty, the categories and quantities of imported goods in the Yuan Dynasty saw a dramatic increase. Statistics show that there were as many as 250 kinds of imports in the Yuan Dynasty, which were dominated by treasures, incense and sundries. Those goods can be divided into 11 categories as listed below:

(1) Luxury goods, such as ivory, rhinoceros horns, etc.;

(2) Luxury and practical products, such as spices like borneol, frankincense, sandalwood and other spices;

(3) Metals, such as tin, Military-grade cast iron, etc;

(4) Fine decorations, such as tortoiseshell, betel nut trays, swords adorned with rhinoceros-horn, blue-and-white porcelain, etc;

(5) Practical handicrafts, such as bamboo mats, glass bottles, peacock umbrellas, etc.;

(6) Cotton, woolen and silk fabrics, such as jibei (cotton cloth), blankets, embroidered silk twists, etc.;

(7) Ornamental animals including elephants and peacocks;

(8) Industrial and daily necessities, such as hematoxylin, yellow wax, fire oil, etc.;

(9) Food including pepper and sweet jujube;

(10) Medicinal materials, such as Neopicrorhiza, Areca triandra, etc.;

(11) Religious articles, such as crystal Buddha statues, fire prayer beads, etc.

Among these, while a portion consists of high-end luxury goods, ornamental animals, and spices catering to the extravagant needs of the feudal court, the vast majority are for practical use. Specifically, traditional spices in China were imported mainly from Southeast Asia.

At that time, China's exports could be divided into 12 categories:

(1) Silk fabrics, such as green satin, brocade silk, valerian silk, etc.;

(2) Porcelain including blue and white porcelain, celadon porcelain and those made in Zhaozhou ware;

(3) Metals, such as gold, silver, lead, etc.;

(4) High-grade supplies, such as gold and silver ware, lacquerware, etc.;

(5) Coins, such as rouleau coins, utensil coins, etc.;

(6) Chemical and medical supplies, such as mercury, tung oil, camphor, etc.;

(7) Decorations, such as silver beads, five-color burned beads, etc.;

(8) Practical products, such as fine horses, weapons, iron tripods, etc.;

(9) Daily necessities, such as paper, mat, iron pot, etc.;

(10) Animals and other products, such as fine horses, tails white yaks, etc.;

(11) Food, such as rice, wine, etc.;

(12) Weapons.

The list above indicates that industrial and practical products account for the majority of the 12 categories of exports, of which the bulk were silk fabrics and porcelain.

Since the Tang and Song dynasties, the export volume of porcelain has gradually surpassed that of silk, becoming the largest export in China. That is why some dubbed the Silk Road as "the Porcelain Road" or "the Ceramic Road". It was recorded in the second volume of *Ping Zhou Ke Tan* (*Matters Worth Discussing from Pingzhou*) that "the ships are dozens of *zhang* (Chinese yard) deep and wide, of which the storage spaces are divided and occupied by merchants. Each person has a space of several *chi* (Chinese foot) to store their belongings, resting on top of them at night. Most of their goods are porcelain nesting one in another, with no gaps in between," showing the immense amount of porcelain in the ship. Archaeological discoveries of Chinese porcelain in Southeast Asia are also a testament to the considerable volume of porcelain exported in ancient China. Japanese scholar Mikami Tsugio, the author of *the Ceramic Road*, spent more than 30 years traveling from distant Egypt and East Africa to the South China Sea since the mid-1950s. He saw Chinese porcelain everywhere during his journey through the Arabian Peninsula, Istanbul, the Eastern Mediterranean, Mesopotamia, Persia, Afghanistan, Pakistan, India, Sri Lanka, Southeast Asia. He believed that the Ceramic Road was a symbol of trade between East and West in the medieval era.

Among the sites Mikami investigated, such as Fustat, a famous ancient city site in Egypt, there were as many as 600,000 to 700,000 pottery pieces found. Among them, despite the ceramic fragments produced in other countries or regions, Chinese ceramic fragments are not only diverse in variety, but also of excellent quality. The ancient Chinese ceramics discovered in Fustat include *sancai* ceramics, white ceramics from the Xing kilns, Yue ware, yellow-brown glazed porcelain and those from the Changsha Kiln, among which Yue ware outnumbered the others. Even 70%-80% of the pottery produced in Egypt was a mere duplicate of Chinese ceramics. In examining the pottery pieces at the site of Fustat, Mikami figured out the origin of them, which was a port called Aydhab on the coast of Red Sea in present-day Sudan. He discovered during his investigation of the port site that "everywhere we go, there were scattered fragments of Chinese ceramics scattered," including those of Yue ware, Longquan celadon, white porcelain, bluish white porcelain, blue-and-white porcelain (celadon glazed porcelain) and black-and-brown-glazed porcelain. In Cairo, there are still more places where fragments of ancient Chinese ceramics were found. During the excavation of rubble in the streets of Cairo, a large number of ancient Chinese ceramic fragments were discovered. These fragments are remnants of a luxury residential area that was destroyed, seemingly indicating that every household at that time used Chinese ceramic wares.

Also, Chinese ceramic fragments from the Tang and Song dynasties can be found at the site of Kosseir City, 50 km south of Suez in the Red Sea. And there is no lack of their Chinese counterparts in the proximity of Alexandria, the home of the Cairo rich Sehnu, and the Aswan Waterfall.

In Ethiopia and along the coastal port cities of East Africa, moving south along the coastline along the Indian Ocean, one reaches places like Somalia, Kenya, and Tanzania. Along the coasts and islands in this region, there are a staggering number of Chinese ceramic sites scattered throughout, which can also be found on the islands of Zanzibar and Madagascar. As is reported by the British Freeman Greenwell, "during the three years in the mid-(19)50s, 46 sites with Chinese ceramics unearthed were found on the coast of Tanzania alone." Thus the abundance of these relics speaks for itself.

Other than being daily necessities, precious Chinese ceramics, a symbol of elegance and prosperity, also serve as interior decorations. They are also employed for the ornament of the interior of mosques and pillar tombs in many places. In the ruins of mosques in the 15th-16th centuries in Gedi and Kilifi, there are Chinese ceramic bowls or plates embedded in the walls as decoration; Besides, the pillars of large tombs are also decorated with Chinese ceramic bowls and plates. A good case in point is the nine-meter-high pillars of the pillar tomb in Malindi, which are all adorned with Chinese ceramic bowls and plates. This ornamental custom is not restricted to East Africa, but has gone so far as to permeating places like Thailand, Kuching of Sarawak, etc. This custom stands a chance of being related to the indigenous consciousness of Islamists.

The Arabian Peninsula, lying between the area from Indian subcontinent to Egypt and East Africa, is located at the hub of maritime and overland transportation, thus being a vital stop on the Porcelain Road. Chinese ceramics have been found in many ports including ruins in Aden and its nearby Kut Amsela, Ardabil and Abu Yan, a seaport 56 kilometers northeast of Aden. Apart from that, places in the Arabian Peninsula where a large number of Chinese ceramics have been found include Basra (the connecting point between Mesopotamia and the Persian Gulf), Mecca (where the holy Islamic shrine of Kaaba is located), Jeddah (the port city near Mecca), and Sohar (the only entrance to the Persian Gulf from the southern coast of the Arabian Peninsula). Additionally, Bahrain (an oil-rich emirate in the southern coast of the Persian Gulf) witnessed the discovery of both Chinese ceramics and the currency of the Northern Song Dynasty, indicating that China had traded with residents of the Arabian Peninsula as early as the 10th century.

Another exciting place on the Maritime Silk (or Porcelain) Road from China to the Middle East, Africa and Europe is Istanbul, an ancient Turkish capital. At the junction of the Bosphorus Strait and the Sea of Marmara, Istanbul is home to a large museum built on the basis of an Ottoman palace, namely the Topkapı Sarayı Museum. Suffice to say, there is none among the countless museums in the world displaying as dazzling medieval Chinese ceramics as those in the Topkapı Sarayı Museum.

Upon your entrance to the exhibition hall, what greets the eye will be all kinds of colorful celadon, blue and white porcelain plates and bowls from the late 13th century (the late Southern Song Dynasty) to the Yuan and Ming dynasties, whose colors and styles are so stunning that some of them have been honored as peerless treasures in the modern world.

The eastern Mediterranean coast was not only the terminal of the ancient Silk Road, but also the starting point of trade from the European Mediterranean region to China, South Asia and India. Being the intersection of ancient East-West trade, the coast is home to a bulk of ports such as Seleucia, Latakia, Tartus, Tripoli, Byblos, Beirut, Sidon, Tyre, etc. As the silk and porcelain from the East gathered in this place, a multitude of westerners were also attracted here.

In Iraq, Chinese ceramics were not only found in the above-mentioned major cities, but also in some smaller cities such as Wājit, Ctesiphon and Erbil.

So, again, Mr. Mikami said, "From the 9th to the 10th centuries, Chinese porcelain permeate the cities of Mesopotamia like a stream."

Persia, as the center of Central Asian culture and the only place where the route ancient east-west trade passed, retains many ancient and medieval relics - including Chinese pottery - both in the ancient cities in overland oasis and the ports along the Persian Gulf.

In Persia, ceramics are mainly found along along two routes, one by sea and the other by land.

The maritime route contains two lines: one leading across the Indian Ocean starts from the Malabar Coast of South India, crosses the Arabian Sea and arrives around Aden where it turns northeast along the south coast and enters the Persian Gulf via Oman; the other begins at the same coast as the previous one. medieval Chinese ceramics are found everywhere when the latter route heads north along the west coast of India to the coastal area along the border between India and Pakistan.

Needless to say, in addition to coastal port cities, the Iranian plateau is also a critical passage along the overland Silk Road, where a wealth of high-quality Chinese porcelain was found.

Another important site on the Maritime Porcelain Road is the site of Panjpir, which is located in southern Pakistan, 64 km east of Karachi, a big city that only prospered in modern times. From ancient times to the Middle Ages, it used to be a prosperous city and an important section on trade route between the East and the West, but went downhill rapidly after the 13th century. After the independence of Pakistan, archaeological excavations of the site of Panjpir were initiated in 1958, during which a number of Chinese ceramics were found, including Yue wares in the late Tang Dynasty, and even fragments of large bowls fired in Hu'nan. The constant overseas discovery of this particular kind of Chinese porcelain, which is under-appreciated at home, indicates that from the ninth century to the 13th century, Chinese porcelain was imported here and also exported to places like inland Bramanabad, Punjab, Makran.

In India, whether in inland cities like Mysore or coastal ports, Chinese porcelain can be found everywhere. For instance, in Madras on the Coromandel Coast along the eastern shore, complete Longquan celadon bowls from the Song Dynasty have been unearthed. Additionally, "Xuanhe Tongbao" coins minted during the Xuanhe period of the Northern Song Dynasty (AD 1119–1125) have also been discovered in the same place.

Another important place on the ceramic road is Sri Lanka (Ceylon), a country dubbed as Sinhalese by the ancient Chinese. As the hub connecting the Bay of Bengal and the Arabian Sea, this country is arguably a necessary berth for ships shuttling between the East and the West. Colombo, the capital of the Sri Lanka, is home to a clossal museum housing Chinese ceramics and various cultural relics, with a monument to Zheng He standing therein. In an ancient village called Dadigama, located over a hundred kilometers from the capital Colombo in the central highlands of Sri Lanka, there stands a brick-stupied Buddhist stupa. Surrounding the stupa, many fragments of Chinese porcelain from the Song Dynasty have been discovered, including pieces from large bowls of the Yue kiln, shards of celadon from the Longquan kiln, small pots of blue-and-white porcelain, small incense burners, and fragments of four-eared jars with glaze. In addition to exquisite ceramics from the Song and Yuan dynasties in China, 1,364 Chinese copper coins were also found in Yapahuwa. There has been no precedent for discovering such a large number of Chinese coins in a location outside of China, which serves as strong evidence of Sri Lanka's significant position in East-West trade.

Now, let's shift our focus back to the South China Sea, the departure place of everything we saw above along the Maritime Silk (or Porcelain) Road. There are remains of Chinese ceramics everywhere in the countries around the South China Sea. As Vietnam has never studied those relics, the overall situation of ceramic research in the country is still unclear; yet the Philippines has become the center of ceramic culture research in Southeast Asia.

Traces of Chinese ceramics are found on many major islands in the Philippines, such as Luzon, Sulu Islands, Cebu Island and Mindanao. Many of these ceramics are preserved as exhibits in the Museum of Anthropology at the University of Michigan. As early as the 1920s, the University of Michigan embarked on archaeological surveys and ceramic collections in the Philippine Islands. In the exhibition room and research room of the museum, what come into sight are glazed celadon, celadon, white porcelain, black porcelain and those with red underglaze painting from Yuan, Ming and Qing dynasties in China. In March, 1968, during the conference in Manila on oriental ceramics, Mr. Mikami Tsugio ventured to the vicinity of Santa Cruz, Luzon Island, Philippines, and conducted archaeological excavations at a medieval grave site. Interestingly, he noticed that local farmers were also digging in their own backyards which were then riddled with gaping holes. In such a small area, there exist over a hundred medieval tombs, with a wealth of Chinese ceramics from the 11th to the mid-14th century unearthed, including those from the Song, Yuan, and early Ming dynasties. Alongside these treasures, one can also find ceramics crafted in Thailand and Annan.

Cemeteries containing sacrificial Chinese ceramics can be found everywhere, with over a hundred such sites discovered along the coastal areas of various islands in the Philippines alone. During the construction of Santa Ana Church in Manila, 1,513 pieces of Chinese ceramics from the 10th to the mid-14th centuries were unearthed from 202 cemeteries. In the Philippines, Chinese porcelain also prevails in private collections, which might well add up to an estimated 50,000 pieces or more.

Borneo and even Indonesia are no exception. The Museum of Kuching, the capital of Sarawak, Borneo, embraces a large collection of porcelain of Yue kiln from the ninth to tenth centuries, as well as specimens of celadon, white porcelain, blue-and-white porcelain, black glazed porcelain, celadon-glazed porcelain from all over the world after the 11th century.

The National Museum in Jakarta, the capital of Indonesia, also houses thousands of Chinese ceramics - even those from the second to eighth centuries (that is, from the Eastern Han Dynasty to the Tang Dynasty) unearthed in Java and Sumatra. This serves as definitive proof that the exchanges between China and Southeast Asia did not begin after the Tang and Song dynasties, but in ancient times that was even earlier than the Qin and Han dynasties.

The formidable amount and massive distribution of Chinese ceramics along the Maritime Porcelain Road has proven the frequent maritime activities of China starting from the South China Sea since the Tang and Song dynasties. It was through such activities that China became the first country to discover, develop and exercise jurisdiction over the South China Sea.

Another major event in the discovery and management of South China Sea Islands in Chinese history is the astronomical measurement in this region in Yuan Dynasty. As early as the 13th year of Zhiyuan period in the Yuan Dynasty (AD 1276), Kublai Khan issued an edict to establish the Imperial

Astronomical Bureau, which was then presided by Xu Heng (the former Left Deputy Minister of the Central Secretariat), Wang Xun (the Crown Prince's advisor) and Guo Shoujing (the Deputy Director of the Waterworks), in order to reformed the calendar. To obtain the measured data, the presiders of the Bureau designated 14 supervising officers to many places across the country to carry out the "Measurement of the Four Seas", of which the southernmost spot selected was situated in South China Sea Islands. There, the given measurement was that "the shadow at the summer solstice, pointing south, is measured at one foot, one inch, and six tenths in length". Hence it can be inferred that this might refer to the particular spot at 15°12' N latitude, 116°07' E longitude. Yet the latitude should be 14°47' north due to the limitation of science and technology, and the difference of circumference between the Yuan Dynasty (365°25') and that in the modern time (360°), which leads to a discrepancy of about one degree in latitude compared to modern measurements. With a margin of error of about one degree, the measurement spot in the South China Sea might well situated in Xisha Qundao. This astronomical measurement was arguably an important activity of territorial management carried out by the central government in Yuan Dynasty within its own territory.

Section 4 Development and Management of the South China Sea and its Affiliated Islands and Reefs in the Ming Dynasty

Unlike the Yuan Dynasty, the Ming government implemented a maritime ban policy called "**intermittent forbidding and opening**". This was related to the growing plague of Japanese pirates along the southeast coast of China at that time. For this reason, "sea ban" policy was enforced in the Ming Dynasty for an extended period. However, due to the significant influence of "Zheng He's Seven Voyages to the West" in the early Ming Dynasty and the economic development in the Pearl River Delta, the Ming court designated Guangzhou as the only port for foreign trade in China, which greatly boosted China's trade and exchange with other countries in the world through the South China Sea. The specific indicators of advancement can be listed as follows: (1) Among the ancient historical records of China, there were a surge of descriptions of the South China Sea and South China Sea Islands during the Ming Dynasty; (2) The number cultural relics of the Ming Dynasty found in the South China Sea and South China Sea Islands has experienced a drastic growth.

Literature in the Ming Dynasty on the South China Sea and South China Sea Islands include: *Qiong Tai Wai Ji (Records of the Qiong Platform)* by Wang Zuo; *Zheng De Qiong Tai Zhi (Chronicles of the Qiong Platform from the Zhengde Era)* by Tang Zhou; the Jiajing version of *Guang Dong Tong Zhi (Comprehensive Treatises on Guangdong)*; *Yue Da Ji (Grand Record of Guangdong)* by Guo Fei; *Xing Cha Sheng Lan (Overall survey of the Star Raft)* by Fei Xin, an aide of Zheng He in his seven voyages; *Xi Yang Chao Gong Dian Lu (Book on the Tribute Missions of Western Countries)* by Huang Xingzeng; *Xi Yang Fan Guo Zhi (Chronicles of Foreign Countries in the West)* by Gong Zhen; *Hai Guo Guang Ji (Comprehensive Chronicles of Maritime*

Nations) by Shen Maoshang; *Shou Xi Chang Yu* (*Long Conversations by Shouxi* and *Zhen Ze Ji Wen* (*Chronicles of Zhenze*) by Wang Ao; *Hai Yu* (*Report on Southeast Asian Countries*) by Huang Zhong; *Shun Feng Xiang Song* (*Fair Winds for Escort*) by unknown author; Gu Jie's *Hai Cha Yu Lu* (*Records of Maritime Events*); *Dong Xi Yang Kao* (*Studies on the Oceans East and West*) by Zhang Xie; Zhang Huang's *Gu Jin Tu Shu Bian* (*A Compendium of Ancient and Modern Books*); *Xian Bin Lu* (*Record of All [Tribute-delivering] Guests*) by Luo Yuejiong, etc. In particular, *Zheng He Navigation Chart* (formerly known as "*The Maps for Direct Voyages to Foreign Lands from the Baochuanchang Shipyard (Departing from Longjiangguan Pass)*") preserved by Mao Yuanyi in *Wu Bei Zhi* (*On Military Preparedness*), etc., retained a large number of information on the development and management of the South China Sea and South China Sea Islands in the Ming Dynasty.

As is recorded by Wang Zuo in his *Qiong Tai Wai Ji* (*Records of the Qiong Platform*), "Changsha and Shitang in the east of the island (Wanzhou) are surrounded by the sea. Whenever formidable hurricane hits with strong tide, flooded houses and fields always take their toll on people living therein." That is to say, Changsha and Shitang (now the islands in the South China Sea of China) are surrounded by the sea in Wanzhou. When typhoons rage, the people living in these sea-surrounded places are afflicted with flooded houses and drowned fields. And this further shows that there were already houses and fields in the islands of the South China Sea in the Ming Dynasty.

Chances are that these places were plagued by pirates at that time, which accounts for the establishment of navy for sea patrol and guard against pirates during the Ming Dynasty. In *Guang Dong Tong Zhi* (*Comprehensive Treatises on Guangdong*), there is an article titled "sea pirates", stating that "there are three branches of sea pirates, for which the government established Naval Patrol Forces Against Japanese Pirates to guard against them. In late spring and early summer when the wind was strong, the supervisor sent troops to the sea for defence. The middle branch sails from Nantou City, Dongguan County, leaving Fotangmen, Shizimen, Lengshuijiao, and Zhuhai'ao (original nrote frrom*Hai Yu* (*Report on Southeast Asian Countries*): Setting sail from Nantingmen in Dongguan, one will proceed to the three seas of Wuzhu, Duzhu, and Qizhou, using the the Kunwei needle on the planispheric astrolabe. Upon reaching Wailuo and navigating towards the Kunshen direction, one will enter the territory of Cham City. Continuing to the Kunlun Sea, one sails directly towards the north-south line leads to Longyamen Port, from where he will arrive in Siam. Since there are likely to be thieves and pirates entering Shizimen for robbery, it will be necessary to guard against them)." This particular article shows the scope of the navy's patrol and coastal defence inherited from the Yuan Dynasty, covering the entire waters of the South China Sea bounded by Wailuo, Zhanpo, Zhuyu and Kunlun, with Changsha and Shitang (now South China Sea Islands) under protection.

In *Yue Da Ji* (*Grand record of Guangdong*), Guo Pei recorded the designation of branch commander in the 19th year of Jiajing (AD 1540), the first, third and fourth years of wanli (AD 1573,1575 and 1576), specifically mentioning that "the superintendent and minister Yin Zhengmao proposed the special designation of overland branch commander in Qiongya. In the third year of Wanli, he also suggested assuming his duty of maritime defence. In the fourth year of Wanli, Ling Yunyi, a governor-general and vice minister, commanded the local garrison and led the Baisha Water Fort to defend the coastal areas of Qiongzhou. Each year, during the summer and autumn, the forces were stationed in Yazhou, and in Qiongzhou During the spring and winter." This indicates that the military authorities of Hainan had then placed coastal defence as their top priority.

Another crucial work on the South China Sea and the proof of China's sovereignty therein is *Hai Yu (Report on Southeast Asian Countries)* written by Huang Zhong in the 15th year of Jiajing in the Ming Dynasty (AD 1536). In this book, the boundaries between China and foreign countries in the South China Sea are dubbed as "fenshui (water boundary)". Huang said, "Fenshui lies beyond Champa in the waters of Luohai, with sandy islets faintly visible like a threshold, stretching endlessly for hundreds of miles. Towering waves crash against the heavens, unlike those of ordinary seas. From Ma'anshan to the old port, the eastern route leads to various foreign lands, while the western route to Zhuya and Dan'er. The heavens and earth set formidable barriers, delineating the realm of Huayi." The Outer Luohai is named for its location in the central sea of Vietnam and the ocean outside Champa Island in Quang Nam. After examination, French scholar Pelliot proved that this particular spot is in CulaoRay (also known as Guangdong Islands, i.e. PalouCanton).

An even greater feat in the Ming Dynasty was Zheng He's seven voyages to the West during the 28 years from the third year of Yongle to the eighth year of Xuande (AD 1405-1433), which opened a new chapter in the history of world civilization.

In 1405, Zheng He made his maiden voyage to the Western Ocean, 87 years earlier than Columbus' arrival in America in AD 1492, 92 years earlier than Vasco da Gama's arrival in Guri (Kozekot), India, and 114 years earlier than Magellan's sail around the world in 1519. At that time, Zheng's navigation fleet had "27,670 officials, flag troops, warriors, general affairs, civilians, compradores and calligraphers, and 249 ships". In comparison, Columbus sailed to America with merely 3 ships and 88 sailors, and 4 ships and 160 sailors in da Gamma's case and 5 ships and 260 sailors on Magallan's side. These western navigators suffered from food shortage, water cut-off and diseases during their voyage. Among them, da Gamma's fleet was even landed in a dilemma at sea because of their inaccurate knowledge of the monsoon, delaying its trip for nearly two months. In this regard, Zheng was indeed the pioneer of the great geographical discovery and made outstanding contributions to the progress of human society and mutual understanding.

The three purposes of Zheng He's seven great voyages to the West were to "display military muscle in foreign places, flaunt the prosperity and strength of China", and promote maritime trade, which had arguably been achieved on the whole. Yet Zheng's feat still seemed inferior to later achievements (nearly a hundred years later) of Columbus' and da Gamma's, who discovered the New World and sailed around the world respectively. Compared to the latter two, the equipment, capabilities and navigational expertise of Zheng's fleet at that time were far above them. Nonetheless, bound by the mindset of feudal rulers, the lack of economic motivation and a narrow worldview, Zheng's voyage come to a halt ultimately. This is the lesson we Chinese people should learn in the present day. By upholding Zheng He's spirit and striving for higher aspirations in this brand-new era, we are bound to achieve new and greater accomplishments.

Section 5 China's exercise of sovereignty over South China Sea Islands in the Qing Dynasty

The Qing Dynasty had long implemented the seclusion policy during its early reign, commanding that "no single inch of board is allowed to go into the sea and no single piece of sail is allowed to enter". That said, due to the time-honored trading between China and the coastal countries along the South China Sea, the seclusion policy affected the trade and exchange of the South China Sea only in the early Qing Dynasty from the first year of Shunzhi to the 22nd year of Kangxi (AD 1644-1683). In the 24th year of Kangxi (AD 1685), in the wake of the pacification of Taiwan, the Qing government announced the abolition of the sea ban since its early reign. This led to the establishment of trade ports, and the revival of maritime exchanges in China. In the 22nd year of Qianlong (AD 1757), three customs offices in Fujian, Zhejiang and Jiangsu were closed, leaving only the Guangdong customs. Therefore, during the Qing Dynasty, maritime traffic in the South China Sea and exchanges with neighboring countries were not only unaffected but also became more active. Trade taxes in the South China Sea accounted for a large proportion of tax revenue in Qing Dynasty. And Britain was a major trading partner of China at the time. From the 25th to 29th year of Qianlong (AD 1760-1764), the total import and export trade volume of Guangzhou Port was 1,449,872 taels of silver on average per year, of which the import value was 470,286 taels, and the export value was 979,586 taels - more than double of the imports. From the 35th to 39th years of Qianlong's reign (AD 1770-1774), the average annual import and export trade volume stood at 3,585,524 taels, of which the import value was 1,466,466 taels and the export value was 2,119,058 taels, both increasing exponentially. So, it is demonstrated that the Qing Dynasty had always attaching great importance to and safeguarding in various ways its maritime rights and interests in the South China Sea and

South China Sea Islands.

The maritime boundaries of China in the South China Sea were explicitly described in the documents in the Qing Dynasty.

According to Yan Sizong's *Nanyang Lice* (*Speculation about Nanyang*), "Between Nanyang (Southern Ocean), there are ten thousand *li* of rocky reefs, commonly known as Wanlichangsha (ten thousand-*li* sand cays), which have long been uninhabited. To the south of the reefs lies the Outer Ocean, and to the east lies the Fujian Ocean. Foreign ships sail east from the Outer Ocean, turning north into the Guangdong Ocean when Taiwan Mountain is in sight, and entering Humen from Macao after passing through Laowanshan. It is these rocky reefs that they deemed the boundary between China and foreign countries...Situating to the north of the reefs, the Qizhou Ocean is known to the foreigners for the bulk of submerged rocks therein, thus being the last route for even small boats. Near Baishikou, the west of the reefs, there is a port... which was occupied by the English and named Xingjilipo more than ten years ago... Starting from this island, it takes only more than ten days to Canton via the route in the Outer Ocean, and only seven or eight days via that in Qiyang Ocean."

"Xingjilipo" in the text above refers to Singapore, which was occupied by British colonists in 1819. Therefore, it can be inferred that it was written by Yan Sizong in the 1830s. In this article, Wanlishitang refers to the present Nansha Islands. Additionally, it defines the region to the south of Wanlishitang as the Outer Ocean, to its east as Fujian Ocean, and to its north as the Qizhou Ocean, calling it "the boundary between China and foreign countries", which clearly determines China's territory in the South China Sea.

This view was accepted by Wei Yuan, a modern thinker and reformer in China. Not only did quote the said passage in his book *Hai Guo Tu Zhi* (*Atlas and Description of the Countries Beyond the Seas*), but he also made further supplements, pinpointing that "Wanlishitang is the boundary between China and foreign countries".

Thanks to the clear definition of the territory of the South China Sea in the Qing Dynasty, there were no lack of clear records about South China Sea Islands in provincial, prefectural, county and other chronicles compiled by governments at all levels during the Qing Dynasty.

It is recorded in *Guang Dong Tong Zhi* (*Comprehensive Treatises on Guangdong*), a work supervised by Hao Yulin, that "Qiong is bounded by the sea...Wanzhou is surrounded by the winding waters of Sanqu, with the mountainous terrain of Liulian shielding its administration center, and with Qianlichangsha and Wanlishitang drifting in and out of the mist and waves." The record in the territorial chronicles of Guangdong Province about "Qianlichangsha and Wanlishitang", which are "drifting in and out of the mist and waves", is a clear indication that the Cantonese officials at that time had a clear idea that Qianlishitang and Wanlichangsha were within their jurisdiction.

Ming Yi and Zhang Yuesong, the compilers of *Qiong Zhou Fu Zhi* (*Treatise on the Prefecture of Qiongzhou*), quoted in a chapter entitled "Treatise on Haili: the Coast Defence of Wanzhou" the record of *Shui Shi Ying Ce* (*A Book for Navy*) that "220 *li* north of the Jiuling Port in Lingshui County lies Dazhou Bay, which is affiliated with Wanzhou and also known as Dazhou Port...It was said that Wanzhou, with Qianlishitang and Wanlichangsha within its jurisdiction, was known as the most perilous place in the waters around Qiongzhou." In this book, the authors had deemed Qianlishitang and Wanlichangsha as vital spots of maritime defence in Wanzhou, both through the statement of these two places in its chapter about coast defence, and the quotation of *Shui Shi Ying Ce* (*A Book for Navy*) about maritime defence. The responsibility of the naval forces in patrol and defence must encompass the vast regions of Qianlishitang and Wanlichangsha.

Therefore, the author had aptly cited *Shui Shi Ying Ce* (*A Book for Navy*).

In Volume Twelve of Zhong Yuandi's *Ya Zhou Zhi* (*Chronicles of Yazhou*) under the section on "Coastal Defence," there are records regarding the maritime waterways, "…Heading northward from Ganzhezhou for six *li*, one reaches Dazhou Bay, and can sail both from the inside and outside of the Bay…The east of Ganzhezhou is connected to the Dazhou Ocean, which is home to the most dangerous places in the Ocean near Qiong - Qianlishitang and Wanlichangsha." Here, Qianlishitang and Wanlichang are regarded as both the most risky spots in maritime waterways and the most important part of the coast defence of Yazhou.

Gan En Xian Zhi (*The Chronicles of Gan'en County*), which was first compiled in the 11th year of Kangxi, recompiled in the 44th year of the same reign and the 18th year of the Republic of China, also recorded in the chapter "Coastal Defence Record" of its 12th volume that "Dazhou Bay, … the east of the sand cay, is bordered by Dazhou Ocean, home to Qianlishitang and Wanlichangsha, the most dangerous places in Qiongyang."

Therefore, the Qing Dynasty has, through its defensive implementation, clarified the significance of South China Sea Islands (the Nanhai Islands) for the maintenance of China's sovereignty in the waters of the South China Sea. As *Guang Dong Tu Zhi* (*the Illustrated Treatise on Guangdong*), compiled by Mao Hongbin, puts forward, "Qiong Commandery is isolated in the ocean…with an array of diverse ports, bays and islands emerging in disarray, and hidden sands and reefs lurking here and there. Among them, the most dangerous is Wanlichangsha. From the east of Wanzhou to Nan'ao, lies the natural moat of the Canton Sea."

Xu Jiagan said in the section about Cantonese waterways in *Yang Fang Shuo Lue* (*A Brief Introduction to Maritime Defence*) that "Qiongzhou stands alone in the ocean…with Wanlichangsha therein stretching from Wanzhou to

Nan'ao. Also, Qianlishitang, extending from the south of Wanzhou to Qizhou Ocean, encompasses the most dangerous natural moat of the Cantonese Sea. And these are all considerations that those discussing coastal defense should take heed of."

Therefore, Wu Bi, deputy general of the Cantonese Navy, patrolled South China Sea Islands as early as the Kangxi period.

Both *Quan Zhou Fu Zhi* (*Treatise on Qaunzhou Prefecture*) and Tong An Xian Zhi (Treatise on Tong'an County) during the Jiaqing period have similar records that"Wu Bi, courtesy name Yuanze, originally surnamed Huang, served as a squad leader. He fought against bandits at Guotang and was appointed as a company commander at the lowest level. After joining the battles in Jinmen, Amoy, Penghu and Taiwan, he was appointed the Brigade Commander of Shaanxi, and later promoted Regional Vice Commander of Canton before being transferred to Qiongzhou. From Qiongyai, he traveled across Tonggu, passing through Qizhou Ocean and Sigengsha, covering an area of three thousand *li*, and embarking on personal patrol of the serene region of his duty." Wu Bi's "personal patrol" of Nansha proves that China has exercised sustained and effective sovereign jurisdiction over the South China Sea and South China Sea Islands through maritime patrol defence.

Ming Yi, Magistrate of Qiongzhou, asked Zhang Yuesong to preside the recompilation of *Qiong Zhou Fu Zhi* (*Treatise on the Prefecture of Qiongzhou*) (Daoguang Edition), which described the scope of the navy patrol, "The Associated Navy Battalion of Yazhou was responsible for the ocean surface from Dongao Port in the east of Wanzhou to Sigengsha in Changhua County in the west, covering a total of a patrol sea area of a thousand *li*. This area lies directly to the north of Siam and the outer sea of Champa." In the Qing Dynasty, the Associated Navy Battalion of Yazhou was set up in the south of Hainan Island, with a patrol range from Dong'ao Port in Wanzhou in the north, to Sigengsha in Changhua County in the west, and to Siam and Zhancheng oceans in the south. It can be seen that this patrol area encompasses the entire range of South China Sea Islands, which is generally consistent with China's traditional sea borders.

There is also description in the Treatise that "The Navy Battalion of Danzhou is in charge of patrolling the ocean...which is connected to the waters around Vietnam and can be reached after a three-day downwind sail," stating to the effect that the Navy Battalion of Danzhou patrols the ocean and extends far to the outer seas of Vietnam.

Ya Zhou Zhi (*Chronicles of Yazhou*) (Guangxu Edition) also mentioned that "the Associated Navy Battalion of Yazhou patrol the ocean area starting from Dongao Port in Wanzhou in the east, and ending at Sigengsha of Changhua Cocunty in the west, covering a total of a thousand *li* of the ocean surface. This ocean area is directly connected to Siam and the outer seas of Champa in the south, the maritime boundary of the Navy Battalion of Danzhou in the west and that of the Navy Battalion of Haikou in the east." The author also added that "in the ninth year of Shunzhi period (AD 1652), a brigade commander was appointed, who was transferred to a branch commander in the eighth year of Yongzheng (AD 1730), and a regional vice commander in the 12th year of Daoguang (AD 1832), in charge of overland and maritime officers and soldiers that patrol the ocean, and in control of Lijiang." It can be seen that since the beginning of the Qing Dynasty, there has been a relatively complete system of maritime patrol of the South China Sea to defend China's sovereignty of the South China Sea and South China Sea Islands. And this system has met no interruption until the end of the Qing Dynasty.

The book *Gan En Xian Zhi* (*The Chronicles of Gan'en County*) in the Republic of China expounded the evolution of the patrol system of navy battalion in the Qing Dynasty, "In the 12th year of Daoguang period (AD 1832), it was approved that the Regional Vice Commander of Haikou be transferred to Yazhou, where he became the Associated Regional Vice Commander of Yazhou and designated as a member of the outer sea navy. The personnel shortages at the frontier defense due to disease would be supplemented from outer sea navy. One officer was kept in charge in the originally established naval battalion, still responsible for the naval operations of the battalion, and would go on alternative patrol at sea with the regional vice commander. There were four naval ships, which, aside from guarding various stations, actually consisted of 146 sailors assigned to patrol the outer seas. The ocean area in their charge starts from Dongao Port in Wanzhou in the east and ends at Sigengsha in Changhua County in the west (cf. *Treatise on the Prefecture of Qiongzhou*)". Also, it mentioned that "the Associated Navy Battalion of Yazhou sent regional vice commander to patrol the outer seas during working hours, and the assistant brigade commander during off hours. They went on special patrol in the waters of their own battalion, without any established regulations for meetings or inspections. In the 17th year of Daoguang's reign (AD 1837), Zhang Yuchun, a head of circuit, petitioned to meet regularly with the Navy Battalion of Danzhou on the 10th of October every year in the ocean near Sigengsha, Changhua County and have a sentry meeting with civilian and military officials. With his petition approved, Zhang embarked on his journey (cf. *Treatise on the Prefecture of Qiongzhou*)". Starting the 17th year of Daoguang (AD 1837), the navy battalions of Yazhou and Danzhou began to carry out their assembly system of patrol in the South China Sea on the 10th day of October every year.

Guang Dong Yu Di Tu Shuo (*Books on Geography of Canton*), compiled by Li Hanzhang and others, also described that "because the islands in Canton are mostly dangerous, the navy patrols the ocean every year from Nanpeng Island in the southeast of Nan'ao, and to the big and small sand cays, Laoshu Moutain and Jiutoushan Mountain in the west... all with the boundary of Canton. The maritime boundary today is divided by Qiongnan. Beyond this boundary is Qizhou Ocean, from which the patrolling navy of Canton returned home". At the end of the Qing Dynasty, due to China's waning national strength, the boundary of maritime patrol on the waters of Siam and Champa had retreated to the ocean area of Xisha Qundao, from which the patrolling navy returned.

The Qing government and Canton were clear about the scope of the South China Sea. Therefore, when Germany sent ships to Xisha Qundao and Nansha Qundao in South China Sea Islands in 1883 for investigation, they had to call it an end when confronted with the immediate protest from Canton.

References

1.**SIMA Qian.** *Records of the Grand Historian* [M]. Beijing: Zhonghua Book Company, 1959.

2.**SIMA Guang.** *Comprehensive Mirror for Aid in Governance* [M]. Beijing: Guji Press, 1956.

3.**BAN Gu.** *Book of Han* [M]. Beijing: Zhonghua Book Company, 1959.

4.**CHEN Shou.** *Records of the Three Kingdoms* [M]. Beijing: Zhonghua Book Company, 1959.

5.**SHEN Fuwei.** *History of Cultural Exchange Between China and the West* [M]. Shanghai: Shanghai People's Publishing House, 1985.

6.**GU Zuyu.** *Essentials of Geography for Reading History* [M]. Beijing: Zhonghua Book Company, 2005.

7.**FENG Chengjun.** *Annotation of Zhu Fan Zhi* [M]. Beijing: Zhonghua Book Company, 1956.

8.**MIKAMI Tsugio.** *Ceramic Road* [M]. HU Defen, trans. Tianjin: Tianjin People's Publishing House, 1983.

9.**CEN Zhongmian.** *History of Sui and Tang Dynasties* [M]. Shijiazhuang:

Hebei Education Press, 2000.

10.**WU Zimu.** *Record of Millet Dreams* [O]. *Series Integration First Edition.*

11.**XIA Xiurui.** Friendly Trade Relations Between China and Malay Archipelago States During Tang and Song Dynasties [J]. *Maritime History Studies*, 1988(2).

12.**WANG Dayuan.** *Annotation of Brief Records of Foreign Islands* [M]. SU Jiqing, annot. Beijing: Zhonghua Book Company, 1981.

13.**WU Bolun.** Overseas Trade from Guangzhou to the Persian Gulf in the Tang Dynasty [J]. *Cultural Relics*, 1972(6).

14.**QI Chen.** Guangzhou's Overseas Trade in Yuan and Ming Dynasties [M]. In: CHEN Baijian. *Two Thousand Years of Guangzhou's Foreign Trade.* Guangzhou: Guangzhou Culture Press, 1989.

15.**CHEN Hanqiang.** Guangzhou's Maritime Silk Road: Asleep for Two Thousand Years [M]. in CHEN Baijian. *Two Thousand Years of Guangzhou's Foreign Trade*. Guangzhou: Guangzhou Culture Press, 1989.

16.**ZHAO Shiyan.** *Records of Yuan Maritime Transport* [O]. HU Jing, coll. Qing Dynasty Manuscript.

17.**GONG Zhen.** *Records of Foreign Countries in the Western Oceans* [M]. XIANG Da, annot. Beijing: Zhonghua Book Company, 1982.

18.**YAN Congjian.** *Record of Foreign Lands* [M]. YU Sili, annot. Beijing: Zhonghua Book Company, 1993.

19.**Anonymous.** *Fair Winds for Escort* [M]. XIANG Da, annot. *Two Navigational Guides*. Beijing: Zhonghua Book Company, 1961.

20.**ZHENG Ruozeng.** *Illustrated Compendium on Maritime Security* [O]. Jiajing Block-Printed Edition.

21.**WEI Yuan.** *Complete Works of Wei Yuan: Sacred Military Records* [M]. Changsha: Yuelu Press, 2005.

22.**China Institute of Navigation.** *History of Chinese Navigation · Ancient Navigation History* [M]. Beijing: People's Communications Press, 1989.

1.司马迁.史记[M].北京：中华书局，1959.

2.司马光.资治通鉴[M].北京：古籍出版社，1956.

3.班固.汉书[M].北京：中华书局，1959.

4.陈寿.三国志[M].北京：中华书局，1959.

5.沈福伟.中西文化交流史[M].上海：上海人民出版社，1985.

6.顾祖禹.读史方舆纪要[M].北京：中华书局，2005.

7.冯承钧.诸蕃志校注[M].北京：中华书局，1956.

9.三上次男.陶瓷之路[M].胡德芬，译.天津：天津人民出版社，1983.

9.岑仲勉.隋唐史[M].石家庄：河北教育出版社，2000.

10.吴自牧.梦粱录［O］.丛书集成初编本.

11.夏秀瑞.唐宋时期中国同马来群岛各国的友好贸易关系［J］.海交史研究，1988（2）.

12.汪大渊.岛夷志略校译[M].苏继顸，校译.北京：中华书局，1981.

13.武伯纶.唐代广州至波斯湾的海外贸易［J］.文物，1972（6）.

14.杞晨.元明时期广州的海外贸易[M]‖陈柏坚.广州外贸两千年.广州：广州文化出版社，1989.

15.陈翰强.沉睡了两千多年的广州海上丝绸之路［M］‖陈柏坚.广州外贸两千年.广州：广州文化出版社，1989.

16.赵世延.大元海运记［O］.胡敬，辑.清抄本.

17.巩珍.西洋番国志[M].向达，校注.北京：中华书局，1982.

18.严从简.殊域周知录[M].余思黎，校注.北京：中华书局，1993.

19.佚名.顺风相送［M］‖向达，校注.两种海道针经.北京：中华书局，1961.

20.郑若曾.筹海图编［O］.嘉靖刻本.

21.魏源.魏源全集：圣武记[M].长沙：岳麓书社，2005.

22.中国航海学会.中国航海史·古代航海史[M].北京：人民交通出版社，1989.

Chapter 4

The Chinese Government's Fight for its Sovereignty in South China Sea Islands

Section 1 A historical review on the foreign aggression in South China Sea Islands during the modern times

Throughout history, China has maintained an unassailable lead compared to other countries along the coast of the South China Sea - both in terms of national strength, productivity, and navigation equipment and technology. Countries and regions in the South China Sea, being included in the Chinese territory or affiliated to the country, had long maintained a peaceful tie with one another.

In the 16th century, some western countries embarked on their primitive accumulation of capital in succession, starting their plunder in overseas colonies. Since then, the geopolitical situation in the region around South China Sea has undergone drastic changes.

Early in 1511, the Portuguese invaders set foot in the Southeastern maritime territory of China,seizing the convenience to live and dry their goods in Macao in 1533 through vicious approaches like fraud and bribery. In 1571, Luzon was seized by Spanish intruders. In 1624, the Dutch invaded Taiwan and stayed there until being expelled by Zheng Chenggong in 1662. Nonetheless, the Dutch invaders established the City of Batave in Java and subsequently occupied the entire archipelago in Nanyang. After China's defeat in the Opium War, Hong Kong Island was ceded to Britain under to the *Treaty of Nanking* signed in 1842.In 1885 and 1886, according to the Sino-French and Sino-British treaties, Vietnam and Myanmar were respectively reduced to colonies of France and Britain. These incidents marked a fundamental change in the political landscape of the coastal region in the South China Sea.   China, ceasing to be the suzerain of the countries in the region and the most powerful country in the world, was then confronted with the imperial powers that sought to carve up the world and transform China into one of their colonies.

Since the First Opium War in 1840, the western imperial powers stepped up their invasion into China, gradually landing the latter into a semi-colonial and semi-feudal society. The imperialist powers viewed China as a tempting morsel, all converging to seize their share, relentlessly devouring and partitioning the nation's territories. South China Sea Islands, part of China's territory, has long been coveted by the imperial powers as it is the hub of the waterways for the communication between the eastern and western world. Relevant records show that early in 1701, a British ship called Macclesfield conducted illegal measurement in China's Zhongsha Qundao; also, in 1800, another British ship intruded Pyramid Rock in Xisha Qundao; in 1807, the Portuguese ship Vulador intruded Yuzhuojiao (Vuladdore Reef) in Xisha Qundao; in 1808, two Englishmen named Ross and Maughan took the liberty to measure Xisha Qundao. *Hai Dao Tu Shuo (Treatise on Navigation)*, a book by the British author John William King in the 19th century, bore record that Dongsha Qundao had already undergone foreign measurement. In 1835, an American survey ship entered Aoyuan Ansha (Owen Shoal) in Nansha Qundao for investigation. Yet in 1883, a German vessel, after its unauthorized survey in South China Sea Islands, withdrew against the protest of the Qing government, which indicates that the Qing government exerted jurisdiction on South China Sea Islands, but also rejected any foreign vessels that sabotage China's sovereignty in the region.

Notably, France had long been harboring territorial ambition toward China's South China Sea Islands. From 1858 to 1884, France extended their influence to Xisha Qundao and Nansha Qundao of China after occupying and colonizing Vietnam. Emphasizing that Xisha Qundao and Nansha Qundao held "great strategic importance" for Vietnam, France claimed unjustifiably that "an adversary could find a formidable naval base there... From this base, a small fleet of submarines could blockade Annam's most vital port, Toulon, and could also isolate Tokyo (North Annam) by sea." In order to deny another powerful nation of its chance of development in the South China Sea, France bent over backwards in its seeking pretexts to occupy islands in the region. Nonetheless, not a single trace of evidence can be found in documents and materials within French records proving the affiliation of these islands to French Vietnam. Instead, we can easily locate records that "these islands are actually the natural extension of Hainan Island. The present-day Annam (Vietnam) seems to have nothing to do with the Xisha Qundao. These islands were unknown to any coastal fishermen and boatmen in Annam, let alone being entered by any single person in Annam." In this regard, the aggressive French authority initiated their military operation for the occupation of the said islands.

In 1927, the French warship "De Lanessan" was dispatched to Nansha Qundao for an "investigation" of dubious nature. On April 12th, 1930, a French gunboat "Malloisuss" and three small battleships called "Laperouse", "Astralabe" and "Octant" sneaked to Nanwei Dao (Spratly Island) in Nansha Qundao where they secretly raising the national flag of France, only to find three Chinese inhabitants from Hainan on the island. In April, 1933, Nansha Qundao was occupied by two French surveying vessels "Astralabe" and "De Lanessan", together with a gunboat "Alerte". On April 6th, French took possession of Nanwei Dao, Anbo Shazhou on 7th, Taiping Dao on 10th, and Zhongye Dao and Shuangzi Qunjiao on 16th. Notably, all of those islands were inhabited by Chinese, with seven in Nanzi Dao (Southwest Cay, including two children), five in Zhongye Dao, four in Nanwei Dao, and temples, thatches and wells built by Chinese on Nanyao Dao. Though no people were seen on Taiping Dao, some food were found left by the owner of a cabin, with a note reading, "Carrying food with me, I came here in March as the owner of a sailing boat, seeing not a single soul here. Now I am about to leave with the rice hidden under the stone here." Moreover, there were no people from any other country on these islands.

On July 25th, 1933, as a cohort of Chinese fishermen returning to Chinese mainland, French authority forcibly seized seven islands including Anbo Shazhou, Nanwei Dao, Nanyao Dao, Taiping Dao, Zhongye Dao, together with nine isles that had not actually been occupied (e.g. Hongxiu Dao and Yangxin Shazhou). After that, France blatantly professed that "the nine isles in the China sea are now subject to the sovereignty of France", and proclaimed subsequently that the nine small islands in Nansha Qundao were placed under the jurisdiction of Ba Ria Province in southern Vietnam.

These abhorrent conduct immediately ignited drastic protest of the Chinese government and unanimous opposition among the Chinese people. Shortly after the French occupation of the nine small islands in Nansha Qundao, the Chinese government immediately ordered the General Staff, the Navy, and the Guangdong provincial government to investigate and confirm that these reefs belonged to Chinese territory. On July 26th, 1933, the Ministry of Foreign Affairs of the Nationalist Government lodged a stern protest to the French government through a special dispatch, earnestly pointed out that "there are Chinese fishermen living in Nansha Qundao, which has been affirmed as part of China's territory by the international community." In August, 1933, The Southwest Political Conference adopted a resolution, "Please send back to the Chinese government a detailed telegraph about evidences like the location, landscape, latitude and longitude of the nine islands in the territory of Guangdong, and lodge stern protest to the French government on just ground so as to guarantee China's territorial integrity." In August, the Guangdong Provincial Government "lodged protest to French authorities under orders."

The French occupation of Nansha Qundao stirred up a towering rage nationwide in China. Labor unions, agricultural associations, seafarers, fishermen, Qiongya Association of Fellow Townspeople in Beijing and mass organizations alike sent telegraphs, urging the Chinese government to strive to remonstrate with the intrusive action of France.

Part of the documents are shown hereunder, containing the telegraphs from people from all walks of life nationwide calling for solemn protest against French authorities:

On August 2, 1933, the Labor Federation of Nanjing held a standing committee meeting, during which it was resolved to request the Party Committee of Nanjing to forward a formal protest to the central government regarding the incident involving the French occupation of the nine islands of China. We hereby call for a strong protest against France, and propose nationwide through this telegraph with unanimous support for this stance. (Central News Agency report, August 2nd)

To the Ministry of Foreign Affairs of the Nanjing National Government:

Newspaper reports came that on the 25th of last month, the French government audaciously occupied the nine small islands in southern Guangdong, provoking collective outrage. It has been verified by the Guangdong Province that these nine islands, located to the south of Qiongya, are indisputably part of our territory. They lie between the Philippines and Annam, boast abundant marine resources, and have long been inhabited by Chinese people. The significance of these islands is especially pronounced in matters of transportation and national defence. Now, with the French government seeking to lay claim to these islands, should we remain silent, refraining from protest, the imperialist powers will be left rampaging unchecked, gradually encroaching and devouring our rightful lands. There is a grave danger that we may irretrievably lose our precious territories, with consequences too dire to contemplate. Therefore, we urgently beseech you to promptly engage in serious negotiations with the French government to thwart their covetous designs and protect our territorial integrity. We earnestly await your swift action.

Shanghai General Labor Union August 18, 1933

To the Nationalist Government of Nanjing:

We have learned that the French government has occupied our nine small islands, and that Japan has seized the opportunity to assert its claims of established rights over them. This news has spread far and wide, causing profound alarm and outrage. It is imperative to note that these islands are indisputable part of our territory, and there are tens of thousands of fellow countrymen from Fujian and Guangdong engaged in production and livelihood in the surrounding areas who can attest to this fact... Our association hereby pledges the unwavering support of 200,000 farmers from the entire county, and earnestly urge swift and decisive action to safeguard our territory and strengthen our national defence.

Farmers' Association of Ninghai County, Zhejiang Province August 15, 1933

To the Nationalist Government:

On the 25th of the last month, the French government officially announced its occupation of the nine small islands in China's territory. In examining our territorial waters of the South China Sea, we find that they extend from the Taiwan Strait in the east, through the Philippines in the southeast, to the vicinity of the Malacca Peninsula and southward to Hainan Island and Xisha Qundao. There is no part of this expanse that does not belong to our national territory, with clear boundaries delineated in geographical records. It is inconceivable that such areas could be violated. The nine small islands occupied by the French government lie to the south of Qiongya, situated between the Philippines and Annam. That they are part of the Chinese territory is beyond question. Moreover, the surrounding waters are rich in marine resources, with tens of thousands of fishermen from Fujian and Guangdong relying on these waters for their livelihoods, further substantiating our claim to these lands. From a transportation perspective, these islands serve as crucial key navigation points between Hong Kong and Nanyang. From a national defence standpoint, they are critical passageways for vessels traveling between Europe and Asia, with significant implications for military, commercial, and colonial interests. Yet, the French government has audaciously taken possession of these islands, not only violating international law but also undermining the integrity of our nation. Should this precedent be established, it would spell the end of our sovereignty. Therefore, we urgently implore your esteemed government to enter into serious negotiations, vowing to protect our territory and secure our maritime borders.

Chamber of Commerce in Shaoxing County August 22, 1933

The aggressive movements of France had met formidable resistance from the Chinese fishermen on the said islands. While erecting national flags of France and signs on the islands, the French encountered sharp opposition from Chinese fishermen on the spot; in Nanwei Dao, Fu Hongguang, a fisherman from Wenchang County, tore a national flag of France to shreds; in Zhongye Dao, Wang Anrong, another fisherman from Wenchang County, dug out and smashed up an occupation sign erected by the French, with yet another fisherman Zheng Landing climbed a tree to drag down a French flag; in Nanzi Dao, Wenchang fishermen including Fu Guohe, Shi Yujiao, Lin Qing ripped down a French flag and cut off the flagpole. When French vessels attempted to crashed Chinese fishing ships in revenge of the defensive actions above, Chinese fishermen managed to damage those French vessels with traditional cannons in self-defence.

Japan was yet another imperial power proved to be the first to covet China's territory in the South China Sea. In 1917, Japanese businessman Hirata Sueji, while surveying Xisha Qundao, intruded into Taiping Dao in

Nansha Qundao on watch. In December 1918, the Japanese company RASA Phosphate Company sent Okazaki Munezo to Nansha Qundao for a so-called "expedition," only to find surprisingly that three Chinese fishermen had already been residing on the island. In 1920, the same company appointed Fukushima Murahachi as the leader of another "expedition" for the survey of resources on the islands in Nansha Qundao, and arbitrarily renamed Nansha Qundao as "Shinnan Archipelago". In 1921, RASA dispatched over 200 men for the construction of wharfs on Taiping Dao and Nanzi Dao in Nansha Qundao, building railways, barns, dormitaries and offices while also going on blatant exploitation of the guano and marine products here. It was not until 1929 that the company ceased operations because of the global economic crisis. Yet in 1938, Japan seized by force some more islands in Nansha Qundao. In 1939, the Japanese government placed the Nansha Islands under the jurisdiction of the Governor-General of Taiwan.

However, it was not long before the Japanese encroachment was withdrawn from Nansha Qundao. At the end of World War II in 1945, the Chinese government dispatched naval vessels and officially took possession of Nansha Qundao at the end of 1946, deploying troops to garrison the islands herein.

Section 2 Major operations for the defence of China's sovereignty in the South China Sea during the period of the Republic of China

I. The enforcement and defence of the sovereignty in the South China Sea by the Chinese government before the War of Resistance Against Japan

1. Lodging solemn protests

On July 25th, 1933, the French government forcibly seized the nine islands in Nansha Qundao including Anbo Shazhou, announced that "the French Indochina, together with the nine small islands in the China seas to the northwest Philippines, is now under the jurisdiction of France. The respective islands were sequentially occupied by French warships that raised the French flags in the first half of April this year." On July 26th, the Ministry of Foreign Affairs of the Nationalist Government staged protest in a special dispatch to the French government, solemnly pointed out that Nansha Qundao "was inhabited by Chinese fishermen and internationally recognized as part of the Chinese territory." In August, 1933, The Southwest Political Conference passed a resolution, "Please send back to the Chinese government a detailed telegraph about evidences like the location, landscape, latitude and longitude of the nine islands in the territory of Guangdong, and lodge stern protest to the French government on just ground so as to guarantee China's territorial integrity."In August, the Guangdong Provincial Government "lodged a protest with French authorities under orders."

2. Surveying the sovereignty of Nansha Qundao

Soon after the French occupation of the nine small islands in Nansha Qundao, the Chinese government immediately ordered the General Staff, the Navy, and the Guangdong provincial government to investigate and verify that these reefs belonged to Chinese territory. For example, in July, 1933, the Nationalist Government announced according to the telegraph from the Guangdong provincial government that "the nine small islands in discussion, located to the south of Qiongya, belong to the territorial sea of China as is verified. Fishermen from Guangdong and Fujian take turns going there each year, with several hundred people regarding the islands as bases for fishing.... There is no difference between the residents on these islands and the Qiong people in terms of language and customs. The fishermen from Qiongya make sure to sail on dozens of fishing boats to the islands every spring, departing from Qiongya and returning laden with catch by late autumn."

3. Examining and approving the names of the islands in the South China Sea and publishing detailed maps of the region

Another significant movement reflecting the sovereignty exercise of the Chinese government in Nansha Qundao is that in the 1930s, the Chinese government examined and approved the names of islands in the South China Sea (including Nansha Qundao), as well as compiling and publishing detailed maps of islands in China.

In June, 1933, the "National Committee for the Review of Maritime and Overland Maps", composed by official authorities like the Ministry of the Interior, the Ministry of Navy, the Ministry of Education and the Mongolian and Tibetan Affairs Commission of the Republic of China, was responsible for reviewing maritime and land maps published nationwide. The committee, at its 25th meeting held on December 21, 1934, specifically reviewed and approved the names of 132 islands, shoals, submerged rocks, reefs, and banks in the South China Sea, categorized into the Dongsha Islands, Xisha Islands, Zhongsha Islands, and Nansha Islands. These practices reiterated China's sovereignty over South China Sea Islands.

In January 1935, the first issue of the "Journal of the National Committee for the Review of Maritime and Overland Maps" published a comparative list of Chinese and English place names for the islands in the South China Sea, which included a total of 96 names for the islands, reefs, shoals, and banks of the Nansha Islands.

In April 1935, the Committee specifically drew the "Map of Islands in the South China Sea", which was later published in the second issue of the National Committee for the Review of Maritime and Overland Maps. It was the first official map published by the Nationalist Government during the period of the Republic of China, but also the first of its kind with detailed plotting of the names and locations of the islands, cays, reefs and shoals in South China Sea Islands. Later, the publication of this map became an essential evidence for China to issue maps relevant to South China Sea Islands.

II. The enforcement and defence of the sovereignty in the South China Sea by the Chinese government after the War of Resistance Against Japan

After its victory in the War of Resistance Against Japan, China adopted various methods to reclaim and assert its sovereignty over South China Sea Islands, which mainly includes:

1. Dispatching officials and naval personnel for the take-over of South China Sea Islands

In November 1943, the governments of China, the United States and the United Kingdom signed the *Cairo Declaration*, which clearly stipulated the deprivation of the territories unlawfully occupied by Japan it had unlawfully occupied since the outbreak of World War I in 1914. The *Potsdam Declaration* issued in July 1945 reiterated that the conditions of the *Cairo Declaration* be implemented. Hence, after the termination of World War II,

China was prepared to take over South China Sea Islands according to the spirit upheld by the *Cairo Declaration* and the *Potsdam Declaration*. At that time, the Ministry of the Interior suggested the Guangdong Provincial Government take over Dongsha Qundao, Xisha Qundao and Nansha Qundao. On August 1st, 1946, the Executive Yuan of the Republic of China issued Order No. 7391, instructing the Guangdong Provincial Government to "comply with the requirements and report accordingly". Before long, the Executive Yuan issued order via telegraph on the 31st as follows: It is reported that the Minister of Foreign Affairs of the Philippines purported to incorporate the so-called "Shinan Archipelago" (the name used during the Japanese occupation, referring to the Nansha Qundao) into Philippine territory. Hereby instruct the Ministries of the Interior and National Defence to address the issue appropriately and assist Guangdong Provincial Government in the reception process. On September 2, the Executive Yuan issued Order No. 10858, instructing the Ministries of the Interior, Foreign Affairs, and National Defence to consult and address the matter appropriately, and to assist the Guangdong Provincial Government in the reception of the Nansha Qundao. In accordance with this Order, the Ministry of Foreign Affairs held meetings with the ministries of the Interior, National Defence and the Navy Command Headquarters on September 13th. Attendees included Fu Jiaojin, representative of the Ministry of the Interior; Chen Shicai, Wang Sizeng, Shen Mo, Ling Nairui, Zhang Tingzheng, Li Wenxian, delegates of the Ministry of Foreign Affairs; Ma Dingbo, representative of the Ministry of National Defence, and Yao Ruyu, representative of the Navy Command Headquarters. The meeting was presided by Cheng Ximeng from the Ministry of Foreign Affairs, coming up with the resolution as follows:

(1) The Ministry of National Defense assists the Guangdong Provincial Government in swiftly receiving the Nansha Qundao, while the Ministry of the Interior will define the geographical scope of the reception;

(2) The location and names of islands in the Nansha Qundao shall be redrafted using the detailed maps drawn by the Ministry of the Interior, and ratified by the Executive Yuan;

(3) In the event of future disputes, the ministries of the Interior and National Defence, along with the Navy Command Headquarters, will transfer relevant materials to the Ministry of Foreign Affairs in case of further negotiation;

(4) The points above will be submitted to the Executive Yuan by the Ministry of Foreign Affairs, the Ministry of the Interior, and the Ministry of National Defence in collaboration.

The meeting minutes were submitted to the Executive Yuan by Zhang Lisheng, the Minister of the Interior, Wang Shijie, the Minister of Foreign Affairs, and Bai Chongxi, the Minister of National Defence in collaboration.

In October 1946, the Nationalist Government appointed Mai Yunyu and Xiao Ciyin as the commissioners for the reception of Nansha Qundao and Xisha Qundao respectively. The Deputy Commander-in-Chief of the Navy, Gui Yongqing, personally appointed Colonel Lin Zun, recently returned from the United States with eight naval vessels, as the commander of the fleet stationed in Xisha and Nansha Qundao, while overseeing the operations in Nansha Qundao.Colonel Yao Ruyu was appointed Lin's deputy, responsible for operations in Xisha Qundao.

It was said that Zhang Junran, the Chief of Staff of the Navy Command Headquarters who had participated in the administration of garrisons in Xisha and Nansha Qundao, recalled that the fleet stationed in Xisha and Nansha Qundao consisted of a destroyer "Tai Ping" (captained by Mai Shirao), a submarine chaser "Yong Xing" (captained by Liu Yimin), tank landing ships "Zhong Jian" (captained by Zhang Lianrui) and "Zhong Ye" (captained by Li Zhiqian).

With "Tai Ping" as its flagship, the fleet assembled in Shanghai on October 26th, 1946. A total of 59 men, including those from the National Defence, the Ministry of the Interior, the Air Force Command Headquarters, representatives of the Logistics Department, and soldiers from the independent platoon of the Chinese Marine Corps. On October 29th, the fleet began its voyage from Wusongkou and reached Hu'men on November 2nd.Zhang Rongsheng, the representative of the Guangzhou Executive Office, boarded the commissioner and personnel for surveying, agriculture, fisheries, meteorology, and medical services for Xisha and Nansha Qundao. Consuming its sailing from Hu'men on the 6th, the fleet arrived at Yulin on the 8th for replenishment and invited over ten Hainan fishermen as guides.On November 24, 1946, Yao Ruyu led the ships "Yong Xing" and "Zhong Jian" to complete the reception mission for Xisha Qundao. After that, the vessels for Nansha Qundao set sail from Yulin at 12:00 on December 9th, with Lin Zun leading the fleet on "Tai Ping" and "Zhong Ye" in the rear carrying personnel from the governments of Nanjing and Guangdong. They regarded the takeover of the main island of Nansha Qundao as the major goal of their mission, believing that this meant the reception of all islands therein.

At 5 a.m. on December 12th, the said vessels were one mile away from Nagashima Island (present-day Taiping Dao). In the book "South China Sea Islands After the Chinese Navy's Arrival," published in 1948, the situation at that time regarding the reception was recorded as follows: "It was not until the outposts on the advance boats landed and ascertained that there were no enemies on Taiping Dao that they transferred the materials aboard on to the island, sent garrisons therein, held a takeover ceremony, raised the national flags and thundered a salute with their cannons; at the same time, they renamed the islands and erected monuments and marks." "

After the outposts on the advance boats ascertained the situation on Taiping Dao, the troops and the reception personnel began to land on the island by boat. Encountering a low tide, they had to waded through water for over 200 meters across the surface of coral reefs due to the obstruction of atolls. Along the trek, they found sea cucumbers, fish and seashells lingering deep down the reefs, displaying marvelous spectacles. After a short break, they commenced their work on the islands as follows:

(1) Re-establishing monuments. Originally, there was an monument established by the Japanese at the end of the jetty on the south-eastern part of Taiping Dao, with the national emblem of Japan and five Chinese characters below reading "Da Ri Ben Di Guo (the Empire of Japan)". So, the first step after the landing was annihilating this specific remain of imperialist invasion and re-establish a Chinese concrete monument on the original site. In a square cone shape, the monument was inscribed with "Nan Sha Qun Dao Tai Ping Dao (the Taiping Island of the Nansha Islands)" on its front, "Re-established on December 12th of the 35th year of the Republic of China" on its back, "Visited by Vessel Tai Ping" on the left and "Visted by Vessel Zhong Ye" on its right. It was at both sides of the monument that all of the takeover personnel held the reception ceremony.

In memory of "Tai Ping's" participation in this reception, "Huang Shan Ma Zhi (Yellow Mountain Horse Undersea Mound)", the original name of the island known broadly by Chinese fishermen, was altered into "Taiping Dao".In addition, the "Tie Zhi (Iron Undersea Mound)" (folk name by Chinese fishermen) was changed to "Zhongye Dao" in memory of the vessel "Zhong Ye" in this reception.

(2) Measuring and mapping the island. Taiping Dao was densely forested of coconut trees, papaya trees, banana trees and other kinds of short trees in its middle, for which surveying panels were used. The measurement was mainly conducted through polygon traverse survey, encompassing the entire island with a scale of one to ten thousand. Moreover, the atolls around the island were surveyed via intersection, on which the wells, air-raid shelter

and buildings were surveyed by traverse cross the middle of the island. Hence the entire measurement was completed after ten hours of work.

(3) Exploring the circumstance on the island. The writings on the walls of the buildings on Taiping Dao were proved to be the last words left by the Japanese garrisons, on August 27th, 1945, who prepared to commit suicide after being informed that the Japanese imperialism had decided to make unconditional surrender.   Upon further inspection, the main and minor roads on the island were overgrown with vines and flowers. From this, we can infer that the time of the Japanese departure from the island was more than a year before China's reception. Also, examinations showed that the jetty of the construction on the island was built with concrete, with a 40-50-meter length and 2.8- meter height. 100 meters away from the west of the jetty, there was a ruin of a destroyed wharf lined with a light railway at a width of 60 centimeters. According to the picture of the French landing on Taiping Dao, this wharf was over 500 meters long, reaching the blink of the atolls. Therefore, it can be inferred that the phosphate could be transported from the mine to the ships via tip lorries without any transference. But it was impossible to determine when the trestle was destroyed. Still, there were constructions like radiophones, electric power plants, barns, wells, reservoirs, stone tablets, dorms, wall bases, roads, air-raid shelters, flake yards and tombs on the rest of the islands. Upon the completion of the new stone monument on Taiping Dao, a reception and flag-raising ceremony was held besides, when dozens of the reception personnel and naval garrison took commemorative photographs. Since then, Taiping Dao, the sacred Chinese island long drifting overseas for over 30 years, was again embraced by its motherland and served as an immortal outpost for the southern border of China.

2. Setting up administrative institutions in Nansha Qundao

In July, 1946, the Executive Yuan decided to place Nansha Qundao and

Xisha Qundao under the jurisdiction of Guangdong Provincial Government (which had been administered by Taiwan during the Japanese occupation). In January, the Ministry of the Interior and the Ministry of National Defence convened relevant personnel for the "conference for the construction of Xisha and Nansha Qundao". After discussing the jurisdiction of Xisha and Nansha Qundao, the conference made the following decisions, "Upon the establishment of the Special Administrative Region of Hainan Island under permission, Nansha Qundao, which is now under the administration of the Chinese Navy, will be placed immediately under the jurisdiction of the Region." Thus the Navy Command Headquarters set up "administrative offices" in Nansha Qundao, dispatching garrisons therein and in charge of the administrative and military affairs of the islands.

3. Reiterating that Zengmu Ansha is the southernmost territory of China

Prior to the Battle Against Japanese Aggression, Zengmu Ansha had already been the southernmost territory of China.In 1947, the Ministry of the Interior, Foreign Affairs, National Defence and the Navy Command Headquarters host meetings for "the establishment and announcement of the range and sovereignty of Xisha and Nansha Qundao", resolving that the territorial limit of the South China Sea will remain unchanged, with Zengmu Ansha being its southernmost section. Since "this territorial limit published by the Chinese government, institutions and publishing houses prior to the War of Resistance has been widely adhered to, a record was submitted to the Ministry of the Interior that it should remain unchanged according to the original proposal."In October 1947, the Chinese government established the geographical coordinates and boundaries of China, with the southernmost boundary defined as Zengmu Ansha in Nansha Qundao.

4. Drawing and publishing the maps of South China Sea Islands to clarify the dashed lines of the South China Sea

For a country, a map is not only an evidence to confirm its territory on an international basis, but also a symbol of its administration and territorial sovereignty. In September, 1946, the ministries of the Interior, Foreign Affairs and National Defence of the Republic of China, along with the Navy Command Headquarters, decided after negotiation that "with regard to the geographical location of Nansha Qundao and the names of the islands therein, the Ministry of the Interior would be responsible for drawing a detailed map and renamed the islands, which would then finally be checked and rectified (by the Executive Yuan)".In December, 1946, Fang Yusi from the Ministry of the Interior, after taking over South China Sea Islands with the technical personnel dispatched by the Geopolitic Bureau of Guangdong Province, drew the "Map of the Location of South China Sea Islands" (1:4,000,000), the "Map of Xisha Qundao" (1: 350,0000), the "Map pf Zhongsha Qundao" (1: 350,000), the "Map of Taiping Dao", the "Map of Nansha Qundao" (1:2,000,000) as well as the "Map of Yongxing Dao and Shi Dao". In December, 1947, Fang published the "Map of the Location of Nansha Qundao" along with some other maps, in which the names and landmarks of Donsha Qundao, Xisha Qundao, Zhongsha Qundao and Nansha Qundao, etc were all marked in the area of the South China Sea, demonstrating the territorial jurisdiction of these islands under China.

It is worth noting is that the maps above, a U-shaped line was marked in the waters between South China Sea Islands and neighboring countries like the Philippines, Malaysia and Vietnam, placing Zengmu Ansha (near 4° N) within the line. This U-shaped line, plotting the entire South China Sea Islands as part of the Chinese territory, first appeared in 1936 in *the New Map of the Construction of China (for Middle Schools)* (printed by Beiping Construction Library) by Bai Meichu. In the second map in this book, which is entitled "the Complete Map of China After the Southward Extension of its Maritime Border", there are marks of Tuansha Qundao (present-day Nansha

Qundao), Dongsha Qundao, Xisha Qundao and Nansha Qundao (present-day Zhongsha Qundao). Meanwhile, the map placed Zenmu Ansha, near 4° N, within the Chinese border line, thereby showcasing China's jurisdiction over it.

At the beginning of 1948, the Chinese government promulgated *the Map of the Location of South China Sea Islands*, which was drawn by Fang Yusi from the Ministry of the Interior, and printed by the Survey Bureau of the Ministry of National Defence. This was the first time that the specific dashed line in the map, which is still in use, was officially issued by Chinese government.

The backdrop against which the dashed line came into being was that on September 28th, 1945, Truman, the president of the United States, announced in a presidential proclamation that in hope of the maintenance and exploitation of the natural resources in the seabed and the subsoil of the continental shelf of 100 fathom (about 183 meters deep) near the American coast, waters of 70,0000 square nautical miles near the coast of American continent shall be placed under the jurisdiction of the United States.

This specific practice soon encouraged other coastal countries around the world to follow suit. For example, on October 25, 1945, Mexico claimed its right to develop the continental shelf up to a depth of 200 meters along its coast. Similarly, in 1947, Chile and Peru claimed their jurisdiction and control over the waters up to 200 nautical miles along their coasts, without affecting the rights for free navigation in relevant regions of the high seas. Since then, Latin American countries launched political proclamations through several international conference, claiming the establishment of their jurisdiction regions in and sovereignty over the 200-nautical-mile areas of their coastal line. In November, 1947, the Second General Assembly of United Nation approved the resolution to establish the International Legal Commission, prioritizing the law of the sea as a key agenda item.

Therefore, it was absolutely common and timely for the Chinese government to clarify its maritime jurisdiction range with the eleven-dashed line in December 1947, which was based on the effort made by the former National Committee for the Review of Maritime and Overland Maps. As a major victorious nation in World War II, China showed absolute conformity to the legal environment and actual circumstance at that time by establishing its maritime jurisdiction and control regions in the South China Sea according to its historical rights and the temporal reality of administration. Since then, China, along with many other countries, has described China's territory in the South China Sea with the same boundary line in their maps, which had never been opposed - and had even been acknowledged and approved by countries along the coast of this sea area. This indicates that this boundary line is supported by profound historical and legal basis.

5. Renaming the islands in South China Sea Islands

After the takeover of South China Sea Islands at the end of 1946, Fang Yusi from the Ministry of the Interior found that the majority of the place names in South China Sea Islands had been given by foreigners - even with some of which being "export names used domestically ". In this light, the Ministry of the Interior determined to review relevant place names therein and host meetings for discussion. Finally, 172 names in South China Sea Islands (12 collective names and 160 individual names) were confirmed, which was 40 more than the 132 names listed in *the Comparison Chart of the Chinese and English Names of Islands in the South China Sea* published by the Review Committee of Maritime and Overland Place Names in 1935. In December 1st, 1947, these names were officially announced by the Ministry of the Interior through the Central News Agency. Meanwhile, *the Comparison Chart of New and Old names of Islands in the South China Sea* (brochure) published by the Ministry of the Interior were printed and sent to relevant parties. The place names announced this time encompassed some commemorative ones, such as Zhenghe Qunjiao (Tizard Bank), Mahuan Dao (Nanshan Island), Feixin Dao (Flat Island), which are thus named to commemorate envoys like Zheng He, Ma Huan and Fei Xin traveling through places around Nanyang. Taiping Dao, Zhongjian Dao, Zhongye Dao and Yongxing Dao were thus named to commemorate warships responsible for the reception of South China Sea Islands in 1946, including vessels like "Tai Ping", "Zhong Jian", "Zhong Ye" and "Yong Xing", etc.

6. Setting up the Meteorological Observatory in Nansha Qundao

From May 21st to 24th, 1947, a meteorological team composed of 20 experts and scholars, including Ma Tingying, the head of the Department of Geology at National Taiwan University and director of the Taiwan Provincial Marine Research Institute, Guo Lingzhi, an associate professor at National Taiwan University, Xuan Guiqing, a teaching assistant, and Fan Chuanbo, a researcher at the Taiwan Provincial Marine Research Institute, conducted a scientific expedition to Nansha Qundao in coordination with personnel from the Central Meteorological Administration. On June 1st, the meteorological team of Nansha Qundao began its work and established a meteorological observatory on Taiping Dao, which located at 114°20' E longitude and 10°23' N latitude, with an elevation of 2.1 meters. The international meteorological station code for the observatory is 902 for the China region. Meteorological data is reported daily from 2:30 AM to 10:30 AM GMT, broadcasting at 13,000 kilocycles, including data of atmospheric pressure, wind direction, wind speed, cloud cover, and visibility.

7. Hosting the Exposition of Products in Xisha Qundao and Nansha Qundao

To raise awareness of the significance of the South China Sea among the Chinese, from June 11th to 15th, 1947, Guangdong Provincial Government held the Exposition of Products in Xisha Qundao and Nansha Qundao in the Provincial Archives of Guangdong. The Exposition, organized by the Guangdong Provincial Compilation Committee of the Treatises of Xisha Qundao and Nansha Qundao, was characterized by its academic features and focus on national defence. The Exposition was divided into five exhibition halls, housing over 1300 exhibits. Hall One displayed geographical documents and maps, showing South China Sea Islands as the long-established territory of China. Ancient coins, excavated during the years of Kaiyuan Hongwu, Yongle and so on in the Tang dynasty, were also exhibited in the same hall. Hall Two and Three were featured pictures, graphs and specimen of fishes, marine products in Xisha and Nansha Qundao. Hall Four and Five exhibited products like corals and seashells on the two archipelagos. Noticeably, this exposition stirred up widespread attention from people from all walks of life, attracting over three billion visitors. During the exposition, Xiao Ciyin, the commissioner of Guangdong Provincial Government chaired a press conference, introducing the reception of Xisha and Nansha Qundao as well as the historical evolution of the two archipelagos. Besides, Mai Yunyu, Xiong Daren, Guo Lingzhi and others, also introduced the resources of Xisha and Nansha Qundao to the audience, as well as scientific knowledge about the growth of pearls and the environmental conditions for coral growth.

8. The Declaration of Sovereignty over Taiping Dao issued by the Chinese Minister to the Philippines

In the spring of 1949, when the Filipino government attempted to encourage Filipino fishermen to migrate to Taiping Dao, Chen Zhiping, the Chinese minister to the Philippines, sent a letter to the Department of Foreign Affairs of the Philippines on April 13, 1949, declaring that Taiping Dao is part of China's territory. The full text is as follows,

Dear Sir,

On April 12, 1949, there was a report in a local newspaper in Baguio stating that the Philippine Cabinet had resolved to dispatch Rear Admiral Jose V. Andrada to inspect Taiping Dao (formerly known as Itu Aba) in China. I sincerely wish to draw your serious attention to this matter.

One morning newspaper in Manila even reported that "some Cabinet members suggested rewarding Filipino fishermen who frequently travel from Banaue to Itu Aba Island, in order to encourage the settlement of people in that area, so that claims could be raised for this part to be incorporated into the Philippines as a means of ensuring security."

In light of the above report, I must earnestly request your clarification on whether this newspaper account is accurate. On this point, I venture to take this opportunity to reiterate that Taiping Dao is the territory of the Republic of China.

Chen Zhiping, the Chinese Minister of the Republic of China, April 12th, 1929

After the dispatch of Minister Chen, **Neri**, the Secretary of the Department of Foreign Affairs replied in his letter on May 7th: The Cabinet has only discussed the need to provide greater protection for Filipino fishermen fishing in the waters near Taiping Dao. The reiteration of Ambassador Chen Zhiping about Taiping Dao's being the territory of China has been recorded for reference.

Overall, during the period of the Republic of China, the Chinese government had exerted tremendous effort to exercise and maintain China's sovereignty over South China Sea Islands, achieving many commendable results. This also demonstrates that China's historical facts and legal basis for sovereignty over South China Sea Islands are sufficient, conclusive, and indisputable.

Section 3 The Chinese Government's Fight for the Sovereignty Over South China Sea Islands After the Establishment of People's Republic of China

On October 1st, 1949, the People's Republic of China (PRC) was established. For decades since then, the Chinese government has been maintained the solemn position of viewing South China Sea Islands as our inherent territory, making long-term and unswerving efforts in diplomatic, military, economic and constructive development, in which we have made tremendous accomplishments.

I. China's solemn declarations about its sovereignty over Nansha Qundao

After the establishment of the PRC, the Chinese government, in order to preserve China's sovereignty over South China Sea Islands, issued solemn declarations and warnings against the foreign invasion into South China Sea Islands time and time again, affirming the indisputable objective fact that South China Sea Islands had been China's territory from time immemorial, and demonstrated the position and attitude of the Chinese government and the Chinese people that "the sacred territory of China is inviolable".

On December 4th, 1950, Zhou Enlai, the Premier of the Administration Council of China and Minister of Foreign Affairs, issued a declaration about the US and UK's treaty of peace with Japan, pointing out that "the preparation and drafting of the treaty of peace with Japan, without the participation of the People's Republic of China, are deemed by the Central People's Government to be illegal regardless of its content and outcome, thus being invalid as well."

On August 15th, 1951, Zhou issued a declaration about the draft of the US and UK's treaty of peace with Japan as well as the San Francisco Conference. Part of the declaration concerning China's sovereignty over

South China Sea Islands stated, "the draft deliberately stipulates that Japan shall give up all of its rights on Nanwei Dao and Xisha Qundao while mentioning nothing about the return of the sovereignty. As a matter of fact, Xisha Qundao and Nanwei Dao, like the entire Nansha Qundao, Zhongsha Qundao and Dongsha Qundao, have long been China's territory, and were occupied by Japanese imperialism who waged aggressive war against China. However, after the surrender of Japan, the said regions had all been taken over by the at the time Chinese government. Therefore, the Central People's Government of the People's Republic of China is hereby declaring that the inviolable sovereignty over Nanwei Dao and Xisha Qundao of the People's Republic of China will not be affected regardless of the stipulation (if any) in the draft of the US and the UK's treaty of peace with Japan."

The San Francisco Conference peace treaty with Japan was held from September 4th to 8th, 1951. Besides Japan, 51 countries and regions took part in this conference; whereas neither the PRC nor China's Taiwan authorities sent any delegate to attend this conference. On September 8th, an alleged signing ceremony of the treaty was held, which was attended by 51 countries, among which the Soviet Union, Poland and Czechoslovakia refused to sign. On the other hand, 49 countries including Japan signed on the treaty.

With regard to the terms concerning territorial issues in the treaty, it was stipulated in the San Francisco conference that: Japan shall renounce all of its rights, as well as basis and requirements of rights over Nanwei Dao and Xisha Qundao.

With regard to the signing of the treaty of peace with Japan by countries including the US, Zhou Enlai's declaration on September 18th, 1951 went as follows:

However, the US government, blatantly defying all of the international protocols to discriminate against the PRC, single-handedly held the San

Francisco Conference on September 4th, 1951, and signed its unilateral treaty with Japan on September 8th. All the people of our nation express their indignation and opposition to this...

Once again, the Central People's Government of the People's Republic of China hereby declares that the treaty with Japan in San Francisco was not prepared, drafted and signed with the participation of the People's Republic of China, the Central People's Government thus deemed it illegal, invalid and by no means warrantable.

In 1952, Xisha Qundao and Nansha Qundao, which Japan renounced under the San Francisco Peace Treaty, together with Dongsha Qundao and Zhongsha Qundao, were all marked as belonging to China on the 15th map, Southeast Asia, of the Standard World Atlas recommended by the then Japanese Foreign Minister Katsuo Okazaki with his signature.

In October, 1955, the International Civil Aviation Organization held a conference in Manila, attended by representatives from the United States, the United Kingdom, France, Japan, Canada, Australia, New Zealand, Thailand, the Philippines, the authorities from South Vietnam and China's Taiwan authorities. The Filipino and French representatives served as chair and vice chair respectively. Requested in Resolution No. 24 adopted at the conference that China's Taiwan authorities should enhance meteorological observation on Nansha Qundao, and no opposition or reservation raised.

From March 1st to May 27th, 1956, Tomas Cloma, the head of Philippine Maritime School, led 40 men on "Training Ship No.4" of the school towards Nansha Qundao for the alleged "expedition", carrying light equipment and seeds. They took possession of several spots on the islands, erected signs reading "occupied", and arbitrarily renamed the names of the islands. On May 15th, Cloma wrote to the Department of Foreign Affairs of the Philippines, claiming that "though these islands are not under jurisdiction of the Philippines, they are neither territories of any other countries." Based on the "principle of discovery and occupation", Cloma requested the Department of Foreign Affairs of the Philippines to "declare the intention to take possession of these islands". On May 19th, Garcia, the Vice President and Foreign Minister of the Philippines replied and declared that "these islands are adjacent to the Philippines, with neither subordination nor inhabitants therein. Hence the Philippines has the right to take possession of these islands following their discovery. In the future, other countries will also acknowledge the Filipino sovereignty for its occupation over these islands." But as a matter of fact, only two days later - that is, on May 21st, Wang Depu, the head of the internal affairs department of the Taiwan authorities, made a statement regarding the sovereignty of Nansha Qundao, pointing out that the Nansha Islands have always been an inherent part of China's territory, which is "indisputable in terms of history, geography, legal basis, and factual circumstances." On the next day (May 22nd), Chen Zhimai, the delegate of the Taiwanese Embassy in the Philippines, made another statement that Nansha Qundao in Cloma's words has always been within the territory of China, and "no one shall flock to occupy these islands for the simple reason that they are not inhabited".

On May 29th, 1956, the spokesperson of the Ministry of Foreign Affairs of the PRC issued a declaration on the Filipino encroachment on China's Nansha Qundao:

According to some recent reports from certain foreign news agencies, García, the Head of the Department of Foreign Affairs of the Philippines, purported in a press conference that the series of islands including Taiping Dao and Nanwei Dao in the southern China Sea "should" belong to the Philippines for the reason that it is the closest country to them. Moreover, foreign news agencies revealed that the Filipino government had been in contact with the group of Chiang Kai-shek in Taiwan, attempting to "resolve" the alleged issue about sovereignty over Nansha Qundao. With this regard, the government of the PRC deemed it necessary to launch a declaration as follows:

The above-mentioned Taiping Dao and Nanwei Dao in the South China Sea, as well as some islets nearby, are known as Nansha Qundao as a whole, which have always been part of Chinese territory. The People's Republic of China holds indisputable legal sovereignty over these islands. As early as August 15th, 1951, Zhou Enlai, the Minister of Foreign Affairs of the PRC solemnly pointed out in "the Declaration on the Draft of the US and UK's Peace Treaty with Japan and the San Francisco Conference" that "Just as the entire Nansha Qundao, Zhongsha Qundao and Dongsha Qundao, Xisha Qundao and Nanwei Dao, have always been the territory of China. Though having once fallen into enemy hands during the invasive wars waged by the Japanese imperialism, they were completely taken over by the then Chinese government after the surrender of Japan." The excuse lodged by the Philippines in the attempt to encroach on Chiina's Nansha Qundao was by no means tenable.

The government of the PRC earnestly declared that China brooks no violation - from any country under any pretext - of its legal sovereignty over Nansha Qundao.

However, the Philippines had not accepted its failure, still dispatching vessels in the waters around Nansha Qundao. Since September, 1956, Taiwan regularly delivered supplies to the garrisons on Nansha Qundao and patrolled the islands. On October 2nd, the Taiwanese naval garrison on Nansha Qundao intercepted and captured a training ship from a Filipino navigation school, seizing the weapons on board and releasing the crew afterward, warning them that they should not infringe on the Chinese territory again.

In 1957, the Taiwan authorities of China protested to the Filipino government, protesting about the Philippines' illegal infringement in Nansha Qundao. On June 3rd, 1957, Chen Maizhi, a representative of the Taiwanese Embassy in the Philippines wrote to the Department of Foreign Affairs of the Filipino government, protesting against the fact that Colonel Cloma led a mop of Philippines to land Nanzi Dao on May 13th in that year, attempting to migrate on the island. Chen urged the Filipino government to halt this attempt for its violation of the territorial integrity of China.

On June 17th, 1961, the Philippines approved Republic Act No. 3046, in which "the territory of the Philippines includes: all of the territory in the range stated in the third article of the Treaty of Paris, signed between the United States and Spain on December 10, 1898, which was ceded to the United States, along with the islands included in the treaty signed between the United States and Spain in Washington on November 7th, 1900, as well as all the territories over which the government of the Philippine Islands exercised jurisdiction at the time of the adoption of this constitution". Thus it is clearly illustrated that Nansha Qundao is not within the territory of the Philippines.

At the same time, the southern regime of Vietnam also began its invasion in South China Sea Islands.

On October 14th, 1950, France took it upon itself to transferring to Vietnam the jurisdiction and protection over Xisha and Nansha Qundao (referred to as Hoang Sa Islands and Truong Sa Islands by Vietnam).On September 7th, 1951, Prime Minister Chen Van Hieu of the Bao Dai government led a delegation to make a statement at the seventh plenary session of the San Francisco Peace Conference with Japan, declaring that "we confirm the rights and interests that have always been held by Vietnam in Hoang Sa Islands and Trường Sa Islands."

On June 15th, 1956, Nguyen Van Quyen, Deputy Minister of Foreign

Affairs of the Democratic Republic of Vietnam, met with Charge d'Affaires Li Zhimin of the Chinese Embassy in Vietnam, and solemnly stated: "According to the materials from Vietnam, Xisha Qundao and Nansha Qundao are supposed to be the territory of China from an historical standpoint." At that time, Le Lu, Deputy Director of the Asian Department of the Vietnamese Ministry of Foreign Affairs, further elaborated on the materials from the Vietnamese side, pointing out that "historically, Xisha and Nansha Qundao have belonged to China since the Song Dynasty."

In 1956, while the French army retreated from Indochina, the naval landing force of the Ngô Đình Diệm regime in Saigon, southern Vietnam had sneaked onto Nansha Qundao of China, erecting not only flags of their regime but also some landmarks. The newspaper *The Bell* in Saigon, southern Vietnam even went so far as to publishing two pictures of their naval personnel landing in Nansha Qundao.

For that, *China Daily* published an editorial entitled "To Warn the Bloc of Ngô Đình Diệm", pointing out that the above-mentioned behaviors of the bloc of Ngô Đình Diệm in Saigon, southern Vietnam was "both an action of violation of the sacred territorial sovereignty of China, and a grave provocation to the peace in Asia". Moreover, *China Daily* reiterated that "Nansha Qundao, just like Xisha Qundao, Zhongsha Qundao and Dongsha Qundao, has always been and will always be part of China's territory, which is a fact that no one can deny."

On October 22nd, 1956, Ngô Đình Diệm, the President of Saigon, Southern Vietnam, signed Act No. 143-NV, confirming the validity of Act No. 4762-CP by which the French Governor-general of Indochina transferred Nansha Qundao to Ba Ria, Cochinchina in 1933.

On February, 1957, the Taiwan authorities of China claimed their sovereignty over Nansha Qundao.

On September 4th, 1958, the Chinese government published a statement on its territorial waters, which explicitly stipulated in the section about South China Sea Islands, "The People's Republic of China hereby announces: I. The width of the territorial sea of the PRC is 12 nautical miles. This provision applies to all territories of the People's Republic of China, including the mainland and its coastal islands, as well as Taiwan and its surrounding islands, the Penghu, Dongsha Islands, Xisha Qundao, Zhongsha Qundao, Nansha Qundao, and other islands belonging to China, which are separated from the mainland and its coastal islands by international waters."

On September 6th, 1958, *People*, the official newspaper of the Central Agency of the Communist Party of Vietnam, reported in a prominently featured on its front page the statement of the government of the PRC on China's territorial sea. On September 7th and 9th, the same newspaper commented on the statement about the territorial sea of the Chinese government from an supportive perspective.

More importantly, on September 14th, 1958, Phạm Văn Đồng, the Premier of the Vietnamese government, met with Zhou Enlai, the Premier of China, acknowledged and endorsed on behalf of the government of the Democratic Republic of Vietnam the statement of the government of the PRC about its territorial sea. Pham wrote that "The Government of the Democratic Republic of Vietnam respects this decision, and will instruct all national agencies to strictly adhere to the provision that the territorial sea of the People's Republic of China is 12 nautical miles wide in all maritime relations with the People's Republic of China." This letter was submitted to Ji Pengfei, the Vice Minister of Foreign Affairs of China, by Nguyễn Khang, the Vietnamese Ambassador in China on September 2nd, 1948. And it served as a formal commitment made by the head of government of one country to another.

The facts above indicate that according to the letter from the North

Vietnamese Premier Phạm Văn Đồng to the Chinese Premier Zhou Enlai on September 21st, 1958, as well as the Republic Act No. 3046 of the Philippines approved on June 17th, 1961, there is no dispute about sovereignty over South China Sea Islands between China and either Vietnam or the Philippines.

However, it should be noted thatthe southern regime in Saigon did not cease its infringement on South China Sea Islands of China. In 1962, Saigon naval vessels from Southern Vietnam. On May 19th and 20th, 1963, they occupied Nanwei Dao and Duoanbona Dao (Amboyna Cay), followed by the occupation of Didu Dao (Thitu Island), Luoaida Dao along with the northeastern reef and the southwestern reef, where they erected so-called "sovereignty stone pillars."

Furthermore, the Filipino president issued a "presidential announcement" on March 20th, 1968, declaring the country's sovereignty over the continental shelf, stipulating that "all mineral deposits and other natural resources on the continental shelf and seabed, which are adjacent to the Philippines and allow for deep utilization outside its territorial sea, belong to the Philippines."

From 1970 to 1973, the Philippines successively occupied Mahuan Dao (Nanshan Island), Zhongye Dao, Xiyue Dao, Beizi Dao, Nanyao Dao, Feixin Dao (Flat Island), Nanzi Dao in China's Nansha Qundao, dispatching a marine corps company to Mahuuan Dao, Zhongye Dao, Xiyue Dao, Beizi Dao and Nanyao Dao. The company's headquarters, with around 110 men, was set in Zhongye Dao,

On July 28th, 1966, Malaysia issued *the Act on Continental Shelf* (Parliament Act No. 57 of July 28th, 1966), stipulating that the seabed and subsoil in the areas adjacent to the states of Malaysia, located beyond the territorial sea of each state and with a water depth of less than 200 meters or within permissible depths for exploitation, along with their resources, belong to Malaysia. Additionally, "mining zones" are established in the East and West Seas of Malaysia, which will be leased to foreign companies for exploration and extraction. Part of the "mining zones" mentioned therein are involved in the South China Sea of China.

According to the Act above, the Malaysian government designated the waters of over 80 thousand square kilometers within the range of Nansha Qundao as its "mining zones", and leased them to Sarawak Shell Berhad, a subsidiary of Shell USA Inc., for exploration. From October, 1947 to October, 1975, Malaysia carried out large-scale mining operations in the waters around Nansha Qundao and acquired vast quantities of gas and oil products.

On December 21st, 1979, Malaysia published *the Map of Malaysian Continental Shelf*, which placed the area in Nansha Qundao south of the line of Nanle Ansha (Glasgow Shoal), Xiaowei Ansha (North East Shoal), Siling Jiao (Commodore Reef), Polang Jiao (Gloucester Breakers), Nanhai Jiao (Mariveles Reef), Anbo Shazhou (Amboyna Cay) in the territory of Malaysia, thus lodging territorial claims over Nansha Qundao. This provoked protests against Malaysia, first from Vietnam and then from the Philippines, Indonesia, Singapore successively. China, while primarily focused on curbing the ambition of Vietnam at that time, chose to voice its stance via private protest towards the publication of the Malaysian map above.

When it comes to the sovereignty over Nansha Qundao, Malaysia tends to resort to real action to occupy the islands and reeds in Nansha Qundao, establishing a factual possession of these territories in the sovereignty dispute. From 1981 to 1982, Malaysia began to planning the occupation of Danwan Jiao (Swallow Reef). In 1983, taking advantage of the conferences and naval exercises relevant to "the Treaty of Five Power Defence Arrangements" Malaysia occupied Danwan Jiao (Swallow Reef) on August 22nd and dispatched garrison there. However, Malaysia failed to provide any evidence to support that action. Again, the Chinese government resorted to a low-profile treatment, launching a declaration on September 14th, 1983, to protest against the illegal act of "a certain foreign army" to occupy Danwan Jiao (Swallow Reef) in Nansha Qundao. China reiterated in the declaration that "all the archipelagos in the South China Sea - including Nansha Qundao, Xisha Qundao, Zhongsha Qundao and Dongsha Qundao - have always been part of China's territory from time immemorial. China brooks no violation on its legal sovereignty over Nansha Qundao by any country under any pretext or in any manner."

In November, 1986, Malaysia sent troops to occupy Nanhai Jiao (Mariveles Reef) and Guangxingzai Jiao (Ardasier Reef) in Nansha Qundao; again, in May, 1999, the country took Yuya Ansha (Investigator Shoal) and Boji Jiao (Erica Reef), yet provided no legal evidence for its encroachment in Nansha Qundao. Ever since its occupation of islands and reefs in Nansha Qundao, Malaysia has undertaken a series of factual operations to increase its economic and military investments therein. For instance, Malaysia established a tourist resort center on Danwan Jiao (Swallow Reef), thereby continuously promoting its opening up to the outside world, and increase developmental efforts to internationalize the reef; reinforced naval equipment and the construction of military facilities on the occupies islands and reefs; purchased armament from countries like France, England, Russia, the United States, Spain, etc.; stirred up fishery disputes in relevant waters, showcasing its alleged "sovereignty" via its jurisdiction to legalize its occupation of the islands and reefs in discussion; and more importantly, stepped up its exploration and exploitation of the gas and oil resources in the waters around the occupied islands and reefs. Among the four countries that have invaded in relevant waters of Nansha Qundao, Malaysia is the one deprives most of China's oil resource in the South China Sea, whose drilling wells account for half of the total number established by these four countries. Also, 70% of Malaysia's exported oil was from the waters of Nansha Qundao. In 1997, the total oil and gas reserves of Malaysia reached 3.9 billion barrels and 2.27 trillion cubic meters respectively, with its total oil export volume surpassing 20% of the country's GDP.

Brunei is still another peripheral country in the South China Sea to claim islands and waters of Nansha Qundao.Once a British protectorate, Brunei became independent on January 1st, 1984, and has since become one of the most affluent countries in the world. Being the major oil-producing nation in Southeast Asia and the prime liquified-natural-gas-producer in the world, Brunei views oil and natural gas as its main source of revenue. 90% of Brunei's oil production and almost all of its natural gas come from offshore oilfield. In Brunei, oil and gas exploration and extraction are mainly conducted by foreign corporations. For example, Royal Dutch Shell not only take the grip of the exploration and exploitation rights for nearly ten thousand square kilometers of oil and natural gas, but also holds the rights to refine and sell the country's crude oil. In early 2001, the government of Brunei tendered a deep-water area of 10,000 square kilometers and a land area of 2,624 square kilometers within its self-defined 200-nautical-mile Exclusive Economic Zone. In March, 2003, the National Oil Corporation of Brunei signed contracts on behalf of the government of Brunei with three foreign corporations from France, England and the United States. In total, Brunei has encroached on almost 50 thousand square kilometers of waters of China in Nansha Qundao, an equivalence to 8.6 the total area of Brunei. What's more, two of Brunei's eight oil fields lie within the dashed-line of China.

To date, Malaysia has occupied five reefs in Nansha Qundao, including Danwan Jiao (Swallow Reef), Boji Jiao (Erica Reef), Yuya Ansha (Investigator Shoal), Guangxingzai Jiao (Ardasier Reef) and Nanhai Jiao (Mariveles Reef), and claimed sovereignty over Nantong Jiao (Louisa Reef). Both Malaysia and Brunei base their claims on provisions relevant to continental shelves and exclusive economic zones in *the United Nations Convention on the Law of the Sea*, asserting their territorial sovereignty over the islands with maritime jurisdiction. Nonetheless, the dashed-lines of China were established prior to *he United Nations Convention on the Law of the Sea*. And according to the principle of "inter-temporal law", the islands and reefs in Nansha Qundao were restored by China as a major victorious nation according to *the Cairo Declaration* and *the Potsdam Declaration*, which, without doubt, are beyond the jurisdiction of *the United Nations Convention on the Law of the Sea* approved in 1980s. Nonetheless, as Malaysia and Brunei had both agreed to settle disputes through negotiation, a solid foundation was laid for China to resolve disputes with the two countries with regard to the islands in the South China Sea.

There is no dispute between China and Indonesia over the sovereignty of islands. Yet in terms of the boundaries of waters, the "nine-dashed line" of China overlap with the maritime boundary of Kabupaten Natuna, Indonesia. Despite some past issues over fishing right, the two countries managed to settle their maritime disputes through negotiation owing two the friendly ties between them.

II. The establishment of Chinese administrative institutions for the governance and jurisdiction over South China Sea Islands

After the establishment of the PRC, China went on to set up administrative institutions the governance and jurisdiction over South China Sea Islands.

Since 1950, South China Sea Islands has been placed under the jurisdiction of Hainan Administrative Region of Guangdong Province. In March, 1959, Hainan Administrative Region set up the Office of Xisha Qundao, Nansha Qundao and Zhongsha Qundao, reinforcing its leadership in the development of the three archipelagos. On March, 1969, these offices were altered into "the Revolution Committee of Xisha Qundao, Zhongsha Qundao and Nansha Qundao of Guangdong Province". Besides, institutions like people's armed forces department and police station were established in Xisha Qundao for the betterment of the administration therein. On February 22nd, 1981, "the Office of Xisha Qundao, Zhongsha Qundao and Nansha Qundao of Guangdong Province" was set up as the agency of the People's Government of Guangdong Province, which is directly led by the Office of Hainan Administrative Region.

On May 31st, 1984, the Second Session of the Sixth National People's Congress (NPC) reviewed the State Council's proposal to establish the People's Government of Hainan Administrative Region and decided to establish the Hainan Administrative Region, which would govern Haikou City, Qiongshan, Qionghai, as well as the reefs and maritime areas of Xisha Qundao, Nansha Qundao, Zhongsha Qundao and their relevant waters.

On April 13th, 1988, the First Session of the Seventh NPC reviewed the State Council's proposal to establish the Hainan Province and approved the establishment of Hainan Province, abolishing the Hainan Administrative Region, with the People's Government of Hainan Province located in Haikou City. The NPC officially confirmed that the islands and waters of Xisha Qundao, Nansha Qundao and Zhongsha Qundao would be placed under the jurisdiction of Hainan Province.

On July 24th, 2012, Sansha City was officially established as a prefecture-level city, with its government located in Yongxing Dao. Covering an area of 2.3 square kilometers, Yongxing Dao is not only the largest island in South China Sea Islands, but the political, military, economic and cultural center of Sansha City. On the island, there are constructions like offices, post offices, banks, shops, weather stations, marine research stations, fishery stations, barns, power plants and hospitals. Also, the island is equipped with airports allowing Boeing 737 takeoffs and landings, as well as docks for large steamers.

III. The publication of the name list of the islands in the South China Sea

To standardize the geographical names all over the country to meet the needs of China's socialist modernization and development of maritime undertakings, China Committee on Geographical Names conducted a survey of the geographical names of the South China Sea islands according to the uniform requirements of the national geographical names census. This was carried out in accordance with the spirit of *the Interim Regulations of the State Council on the Naming and Renaming of Geographic Names* and involved standardization processing. On April 25th, 1983, under the authorization of the State Council, the China Committee on Geographical Names published 287 standardized geographical names in South China Sea Islands on the fourth page of China Daily, of which the content included serial numbers, archipelagos, standardized names, Chinese pinyin, geographic coordinates (north latitudes and east longitudes) and names of fishermen. This was also the third time the Chinese government had announced the geographical names in South China Sea Islands to exercise its jurisdiction over them, following the announcements in 1935 and 1947.

IV. China's counter-attack to defend its territory

From January 15th to 19th, 1974, the Saigon authorities of South Vietnam outrageously sent troops to invade in China's Xisha Qundao, dispatching warships and planes to encroach on the territorial sea and airspace of China's Xisha Qundao, occupying China's islands and firing upon the Chinese fishermen engaged in production activities and naval vessels on their normal patrol duties. This was a brazen violation of China's territorial sovereignty and provocation act to the Chinese military and civilian personnel.

At about 1 p.m. on January 15th, the Saigon authorities dispatched military vessels to harass the production activity of fishing vessel No. 402 of China near Ganquan Dao (Robert Island), shelling on the island where the Chinese national flag was displayed and unreasonably demanding that our fishing vessels leave.

At about 8 a.m. on January 17th, the troop of the Saigon authorities took possession of China's Jinyin Dao (Treasure Island) and blatantly tore down the national flag of China.

In the afternoon of January 18th, two vessels of the Saigon authorities crushed on fishing ships No. 402 and No. 407, destroying the bridge of the latter.

In the morning of January 19th, the Saigon troops made another attempt to forcibly occupy China's Chenhang Dao (Duncan Island), going so far as to shoot the Chinese fishermen, killing and wounding many on spot.

Confronted with the invasion of the Saigon troops of South Vietnam, two submarine chasers and two minesweepers arrived in waters around Yongle Dao on January 17th and 18th successively, forming a four-on-four confrontation with the warships of Saigon. The total tonnage of these four Chinese vessels, however, was still less than that of a single warship of Saigon.

Saigon had hoped for a quick battle due to its superiority in force at that time. Nonetheless, the Chinese navy seized the chance to engage with the Saigon navy with superb maneuverability and flexibility. During the battle, a seriously damaged Chinese vessel rushed in between two rival ships, sinking an escorting gunboat of Saigon while managing to reach the shore without sinking. 18 Chinese naval officials lost their lives in this naval battle, whose memorial tombs were set up on Chenhang Dao (Duncan Island). During this battle, the Chinese navy sank a escorting gunboat (the "Nhat Tao"), wounded three destroyers and killed 53 to 100 people of Saigon, South Vietnam. After the recovery of Ganquan Dao (Robert Island), Shanhu Dao (Pattle Island) and Jinyin Dao (Treasure Island), China gained full control over of Xisha Qundao and the nearby waters.

In the wake of China's recovery of Xisha Qundao via the Battle of the Xisha Qundao, another skirmish occurred in 1988 between China and Vietnam for the grip of the islands and reefs in the South China Sea. This conflict stemmed from March, 1987, when the Intergovernmental Oceanographic Commission of the United Nations Educational, Scientific and Cultural Organization (UNESCO) decided in the 14th Assembly to commission China to build marine observation station No. 74 in the waters of Nansha Qundao.

The 14th Assembly of the Intergovernmental Oceanographic Commission of the UNESCO was held in Paris, France from March 17th to April 1st, 1987, where approved *the Program of Global Sea Level Observation*, confirming the locations, code and countries of 200 oceanic observation points all over the world. Among them, five are located in China, including three coastal observatories and one in Xisha Qundao (already established), and still one in Nansha Qundao to be built - i.e., Station No. 74. After the assembly, Yan Hongmo, the Director of the State Oceanic Administration reported to the State Council and met at once with Liu Huaqing, the then Commander of Chinese Navy.

On May 6th, 1987, the Nansha Comprehensive Scientific Expedition Team conducted a comprehensive survey in Nansha Qundao. After months of investigation, the team completed a report entitled *On Issues Regarding the Construction of Maritime Observatories in Nansha Qundao*, which was signed by Liu Huaqing and Yan Hongmo, and submitted it to the State Council as well as the Central Military Commission. The report points out that the establishment of the maritime observatory in Nansha holds strategic significance, which is a perfectly justifiable chance for China to get entrenched therein. Also, it is suggested in the report that the observatory be built on Yongshu Jiao (Fiery Cross Reef), which is located on the wide-open sea and close to the mainland. There were two plans for the construction of the observatory: one is to build an automatic unmanned observation station, and the other is to establish a permanent manned observation station. Both Liu Huaqing and Yan Hongmo preferred the latter.

On November 6th, the Central Military Commission of the State Council launched *the Official Reply on the Construction of the Maritime Observatory in Nansha Qundao*, approving that a manned maritime observatory be built on Yongshu Jiao (Fiery Cross Reef) in Nansha, which will be responsible for maritime observation according to international requirements. Besides, the observatory should carry out reconnaissance and surveillance in the surrounding waters to guarantee its own security.

Also, the Reply specifies that the construction of the maritime observatory on Yongshu Jiao (Fiery Cross Reef) be overseen by the Chinese Navy with the assistance of the State Oceanic Administration, and necessary support from the dedicated engineering vehicles dispatched by the Ministry of Transport.

It is emphasized in the Reply that the establishment of the maritime observatory in Nansha Qundao is a major step for China to safeguard its territorial sovereignty. The task is strenuous and highly policy-oriented, necessitating strengthened leadership and meticulous organization, with the aim of essentially completing the construction of the observatory and rendering it operational by 1988.

On February 3rd, 1988, the Chinese Navy held an oath-taking ceremony for the construction of the observatory on Yongshu Jiao (Fiery Cross Reef) in the military port of Zhanjiang. Subsequently, a massive engineering fleet composed of 11 vessels, laden with engineering personnel and construction equipment in the escort of combatant fleets, arrived on the construction spot on Yongshu Jiao (Fiery Cross Reef) on February 7th.

Around the New Year's Day of 1988, the Vietnamese Navy had repeatedly dispatched vessels to Yongshu Jiao (Fiery Cross Reef) in an attempt to forcibly seize the island. After being intercepted and gravely warned by the Chinese Navy, they shifted their focus to successively occupying Xi Jiao (West Reef), Dong Jiao (East Reef), Riji Jiao (Ladd Reef), Wumie Jiao (Pigeon Reef) and Daxian Jiao (Discovery Great Reef) in the adjacent waters, thereby encircling Yongshu Jiao (Fiery Cross Reef).

Such an insolent act of the Vietnamese authorities stimulated extraordinary indignation and vigilance in Commander Liu Huaqing. In the evening of February 12th, 1988, Liu made a detailed report on the present situation of the Nansha dispute during his appointed talk with leaders of the Central Military Commission. The leaders of the Central Military Commission took an adamant stand that China should make clear its sovereignty over the territorial sea of Nansha, reinforce its military presence and heighten patrols in the region so as to manifest our national and military dignity.

Liu Huaqing, along with senior leaders of the Central Military Commission, analyzed the situation in Nansha Qundao and proposed a combat deployment plan, noting that "the driving interest of the Vietnamese authorities' actions is the crux of the issue." He indicated that in the short term, Vietnam had occupied islands and reefs in Nansha Qundao and drilled for oil recklessly, which was indeed an act of excessive offense; and in the long run, China's fight in the Nansha region shall be viewed with extreme strategic significance. Also, Liu pointed out that the essence of the fight in the Nansha region was that China's territorial sovereignty is being violated, its maritime areas are being divided, and our marine resources are being plundered. This is a fundamental issue that directly relates to our national status and dignity. It is an unshakable responsibility of the People's Liberation Army (PLA) to defend the national sovereignty and territorial integrity of China. After much discussion, a plan on the situation and combatant deployment in Nansha Qundao was drafted and finalized under the management of Liu Huaqing, and was swiftly submitted to the leaders of the Central Military Commission. On February 29th, the leaders of the Central Military Commission reviewed the plan and approved it with the comment "Agreed".

In the first lunar month of 1988, the transport vessels and armed fishing ships of the Vietnamese Navy, loaded with building materials and engineers, headed directly to Yongshu Jiao (Fiery Cross Reef) from Xi Jiao (West Reef) in an attempt to land the former. Li Shuwen, the Chief of Staff of the South Sea Fleet (SSF), ordered the frigate "No. 508" to dispatch six soldiers to board a small boat. On the afternoon of January 31, 1988, under the leadership of Duan Chengqing, the Deputy Missile and Mine Commander, the six landed on Yongshu Jiao (Fiery Cross Reef) and raised the Chinese national flag there, marking the first time the Five-Star Red Flag was hoisted on the reefs of Nansha Qundao.

On February 17th, 1988, the first day of the Lunar New Year, Li Shuwen received a wireless order from the SSF that the Vietnamese Navy was attempting to seize Huayang Jiao (Cuarteron Reef). At this, Li ordered destroyer "162" and South Tug 147 to immediately set sail for Huayang Jiao (Cuarteron Reef). While Li arrived on Huayang Jiao, the Vietnamese troops were unloading their building materials on the western side of the reef for their intended occupation. Li commanded a combat group of 12 men to land on the reef. At 3:40 p.m. that day, a Five-Star Red Flag was firmly inserted into the soil of Huayang Jiao (Cuarteron Reef). Overwhelmed by the mutual confrontation, the Vietnamese Navy consequently fled from Huayang Jiao

(Cuarteron Reef) by water at 9:40 p.m.

On February 25th, the Chinese naval vessels marched towards Zhenghe Qundao (Tizard Bank) in the middle of Nansha Qundao, and landed on Nanxun Jiao (Gaven Reef).

In early March, 1988, naval formation under the command of Chen Weiwen, the Chief of Staff of a base of the SSF, together with fleet sent by the East Sea Fleet (ESF), arrived successively in the waters of Nansha Qundao and joined the fleet led by Li Shuwen for patrol and reef protection in the region. This fleet from the SSF had previously been patrolling Nanxun Jiao (Gaven Reef).

At 6 a.m. on March 13th, the fleet received an order to send corvette 502 to Chigua Jiao (Johnson South Reef) area for vigilance and corvette 503 to Anda Jiao (Eldad Reef) for patrol.

On the arrival on Chigua Jiao (Johnson South Reef), the radarmen of Chen's fleet discovered two batches of Vietnamese vessels were sailing towards the reef. Soon, the two sides drew closer, and the Chinese side shouted at the Vietnamese vessel: "This is the territory of China. You are required to leave immediately!" At the same time, Chen Weiwen received an order from the ESF to defend Chigua Jiao (Johnson South Reef). Soon after that, frigates 556 and 531 were ordered to reach Chigua Jiao (Johnson South Reef) at a high speed and join corvette 502.

On the 14th before dawn, when the Vietnamese troops began to land on Chigua Jiao (Johnson South Reef), Chen also commanded his men to land. By 7:29 a.m., there were 58 Chinese soldiers and 43 from the Vietnamese side on the reef. In the operation to remove the flag (of Vietnam) and protect the reef, the Vietnamese troops fired first, wounding Chinese soldierYang Zhiliang, who was forced to return fire. When shots rang out, real engagement between the two sides began. Before long, transport HQ-604 of the Vietnamese troop exploded in the gunfire of the Chinese navy, and sank to the bottom of the sea in 12 minutes. During the battle, two Vietnamese transports - HQ-604 and HQ-605 - were seriously damaged or bombed by the Chinese navy, both buried at sea ultimately.

The triumph in the Chigua Jiao skirmish inspired every Chinese individual. General Liu Huaqing was also profoundly invigorated. This general, who had fought for 60 years for the liberation of the nation and the strength of his motherland, could not tolerate the long-standing foreign occupation of the blue oceanic territory established by his ancestors. Neither could he sit by and watch any reckless plunder of the maritime rights and valuable resources of China. He would never allow the Nansha issue to be wantonly internationalized, complicated, and escalated by the surrounding claimants in the South China Sea.

Liu had a hunch that the Nansha issue has not yet been settled, and that Vietnam was still unreconciled to their failure, poised to attack at anytime. Hence he warned the Chinese navy that all possible preparation must be made. "We will by no means provoke others. But in the event of any offense, we must allow ourselves no respite to annihilate them.""

Conforming to Liu Huaqing's order, the Chinese Navy controlled Dongmen Jiao (Hughes Reef) of Jiuzhang Qunjiao (Union Banks and Reef) on March 15th, 1988; on March 25th, the Chinese vessels landed Zhebi Jiao (Subi Reef). This was how the Chinese Navy managed to deploy permanent garrisons on the six islands and reefs in the south, middle and north of Nansha Qundao.

V. The construction of right protection base in Nansha through sand-blowing land reclamation

From the end of 2013 to June, 2015, China engaged in its sea reclamation project in the "seven old reefs" - that is, Meiji Jiao (Mischief

Reef), Yongshu Jiao (Fiery Cross Reef), Chigua Jiao (Johnson South Reef), Zhebi Jiao (Subi Reef), Huayang Jiao (Cuarteron Reef), Dongmen Jiao (Hughes Reef) and Nanxun Jiao (Gaven Reef). The land reclamation project employs a natural simulation method, where the process of blowing sand to fill the sea is actually a mimicry of the natural evolution of coral gravel and other biological debris into a marine oasis after being struck and transported by storms. The project only imposed a partial, temporary, controllable and reversible influence on the environment, since it has been repeatedly discussed by relevant academicians and experts majoring in civil engineering, marine engineering, marine ecology, environmental protection, geology, hydrology and so on.

Meiji Jiao (Mischief Reef), located in the eastern sea of Nansha Qundao, is an oval atoll with ideal environment, extending 9 kilometers from east to west and 6 kilometers from south to north, covering an area of about 46 square kilometers. The lagoon in the atoll is 36 square kilometers and 20-30 meters deep. There are three entrances in the south and southwest of the atoll. The western waterway of the south entrance is 37 meters wide, 275 meters long and over 18 meters deep. Allowing large ships to enter the lagoon at a high tide, this entrance becomes a natural safe haven.

China gained control of Meiji Jiao (Mischief Reef) through fisheries development, which is quite different from the armed struggle for the recapture of the six islands and reefs mentioned above. Early in 1987, the Chinese Academy of Sciences Nansha Comprehensive Scientific Expedition Team has conducted comprehensive scientific investigation on Meiji Jiao (Mischief Reef). On December 18th, 1994, China dispatched a couple of official vessels to Meiji Jiao (Mischief Reef) for investigation, who built the first batch of stilt houses therein at the end of the month for the development of long-range fishing and cage aquaculture. Thus Meiji Jiao (Mischief Reef) has become a significant fishery base of China in the Nansha region. On

December 15th, 2012, Meiji Village of Nansha Area, Sansha City was established. In 2013, the jurisdiction over Meiji Jiao (Mischief Reef) was transferred from the Ministry of Agriculture to military control.

The northwestern reef flat of Meiji Jiao (Mischief Reef) is about 3,000 meters long, 800 meters wide, while the southeastern one 4,000 meters long and 300 meters wide, both located along-wind, appropriate for airport construction. Meiji Jiao Airport is underway. Due to the better condition for runway construction, the airstrip of the airport is designated on the northwestern reef flat. The airstrip, which is over 2,600 meters in length, has witnessed successful flight tests.

Yongshu Jiao (Fiery Cross Reef), situated in the confluence of the central course of the South China Sea (from Hong Kong, China to Singapore) and Nanhua Shuidao, has a long oval reef flat that is 26 kilometers in length and 7.8 kilometers in width. Covering an area of 108 square kilometers, Yongshu Jiao (Fiery Cross Reef) is the political and military center of Nansha Qundao. Since the skirmish on March 14th, 1988, Yongshu Jiao (Fiery Cross Reef) has witnessed the establishment of a tablet of sovereignty, maritime observatory, 3G base-stations for mobile phone and beacon lights. The project of sand-blowing reclamation began in 2014. Up to now, the total land area of Yongshu Jiao (Fiery Cross Reef) has reached 2.8 square kilometers, surpassing that of Taiping Dao (Taiping Island), which makes it the largest island in Nansha Qundao. Also, there is an airport on the island. *Jane's Defence Weekly* described that the airstrip of the airport, including helipad and runway markers, measures a total length of 3,125 meters. Haikou Meilan International Airport in Hainan Island and landed in Yongshudao Airport after a flight of over two hours. At 2 p.m. on the same day, the plane returned from Yongshu Airport, proving that the airport has been well equipped for the take-off and landing of civil airliners.

Chigua Jiao (Johnson South Reef) is a drying rock with a reef flat of 5 kilometers long and about 2 kilometers wide, covering an area of 7 square kilometers. There is a 3-square-kilometer lagoon within, which is 10-20 meters deep, with its water surface accounting for 70% of the reef. On the artificial island created by land reclamation, there is a helipad and a 50-meter tall lighthouse built alongside Huayang Jiao (Cuarteron Reef) to serve vessels from various countries passing through the South China Sea.

Zhebi Jiao (Subi Reef) is located in the central-eastern part of Nansha Qundao, just 26 kilometers from the southwest of Zhongye Dao (Thitu Island), which is now occupied by the Philippines. Zhebi Jiao, stretching northeast and southwest, is 6.5 kilometers long and 3.7 kilometers wide, with its reef flat covering 16.1 square kilometers. This island is well-conditioned in terms of the establishment of massive naval and air base. In 1988, China built the first generation of stilt houses on the reef, and later expanded to the third generation of stilt houses in the late 1990s, along with the establishment of a radar station. The reclamation project of Zhebi Jiao (Subi Reef) began in January, 2015. By June that year, the land area of the reef has reached 4.1 square kilometers, making it one of the three major bases where stationed by China in Nansha Qundao. Zhebi Airport, upon its completion, will form a triangular configuration along with the airports on Yongshu Jiao (Fiery Cross Reef) and Meiji Jiao (Mischief Reef), creating a triad.

Huayang Jiao (Cuarteron Reef) is situated at the east end of Yinqing Qunjiao (London Reefs). 5.5 kilometers in length and 2 kilometers wide, this is a platform-shaped reef covering a total area of 7.6 square kilometers. Huayang Jiao (Cuarteron Reef) is the southernmost reef among the islands stationed by the Chinese army in Nansha Qundao, serving as an surrounding and protective outpost for Yongshu Jiao (Fiery Cross Reef). The man-made island formed by reclamation of Huayang Jiao (Cuarteron Reef) has already encompasses constructions like office buildings, living rooms and tall blockhouses. At present, Huayang Jiao (Cuarteron Reef) has become the seventh largest island in Nansha Qudao.

Dongmen Jiao (Hughes Reef) is a hidden reef in the northeast of Jiuzhang Qunjiao (Union Banks and Reef) in Nansha Qundao, named after the entrance at the east end of its central lagoon. This oval reef is 2 kilometers long from south to north and 1.9 kilometers wide from east to west, covering an area of 2 square kilometers. In 1988, the Chinese Navy was stationed there and built defensive facilities. There are still eight first-generation stilt houses on the island; later, third-generation stilt houses were added. Since the end of 2013, land reclamation projects have been carried out on the reef. At present, with artillery assistance, the Chinese navy on Dongmen Jiao (Hughes Reef) is able to control Ximen Jiao (McKennan Reef) 1.4 kilometers to its west, together with Anle Jiao (Hallet Reef) 2.4 kilometers to its east. In 2000, the Chinese Navy stationed in Dongmen Jiao (Hughes Reef) successfully thwarted -through artillery warning - Vietnam's attempts to occupy Ximen Jiao (McKennan Reef) and Anle Jiao (Hallet Reef). The artificial island in Dongmen Jiao (Hughes Reef), formed by sand-blowing reclamation, has greatly improved the living condition of the soldiers stationed therein.

Nanxun Jiao (Gaven Reef) is a drying rock in the southwestern part of Zhenghe Qundao (Tizard Bank) consisting of two reef bodies situated to the north and south, with the northern one being larger. Generally speaking, Nanxun Jiao refers to the northern reef body. The smaller southern reef body is generally referred to as "Minor Nanxun Jiao". It was on February 2nd, 1988 that the Chinese garrison entered Nanxun Jiao, where there is the third-generation stilt houses and a supply platform.

VI. The organization of the production and construction in the waters of the South China Sea

Since the establishment of the PRC, the central and local governments of China have resorted to a string of measures for the continual development and construction in both the waters of the South China Sea and South China Sea Islands. The overall idea of China's development and construction in the waters of the South China Sea is to comprehensively initiate it with fishery leading the way. From 1950 to 1952, counties like Wenchang, Qionghai and Lingshui in Hainan Island organized a cohort of fishermen to carry out fishing production in Xisha Qundao and on Nansha Qundao.

In September, 1956, the Department of Fishing Industry of Guangdong Province conducted investigation on the aquatic resources in Xisha Qundao and Nansha Qundao, establishing a central station on Yongxing Dao (Woody Island) which included institutions like supply and marketing cooperatives, health clinics, clubs and power plants.

From the winter of 1959 to April, 1960, the Department of Fishing Industry of the Administrative Region of Hainan commanded the Xisha Fisheries Production Command of Hainan District to mobilize 131 fishing boats and a total of 1,752 people from various coastal counties in eastern Hainan Island to conduct fishing activities in the waters of Xisha and Nansha Qundao.

Since 1979, with the opening up of China and the reform of economic mechanism in the rural areas nationwide, fishermen in various districts of Hainan Island, Guangxi and Guangdong provinces promoted the recovery and development of fishing vessels and traditional production in the South China Sea. At that time, fishing boats of both private possession and state-run companies reaped good economic benefits from fishing activities. According to surveys, fishermen in Qionghai County, Hainan Island, invested in over 250 fishing boats from 1985 to 1990, producing 3,500 tons of fish valued at 25 million yuan, yielding remarkable economic benefits. The development and utilization of fishery resources in the South China Sea have become the primary focus for the fishermen in this county. The Marine Fisheries Company of Beihai, Guangxi first ventured to the Nansha Islands to develop trawl fishing grounds in 1989. In just three years, it made 157 trips, capturing 4,936 tons of fish with a value of 14.285 million yuan, achieving higher benefits than any other fishing grounds in Beibu Wan (Gulf of Tonkin) and waters nearby. From March to June, 1990, the Maritime Fisheries Company of Guangzhou operated 8 bottom trawl fishing boats and made pilot production on 17 trial fishing trips, catching a total of 636 tons of fish with a value of 1.6 million yuan. Compared to fishing boats operating in Beibu Wan (Gulf of Tonkin) during the same period, five performance indicators of this company — daily output per boat, average catch per net, proportion of high-quality fish, average price per ton of fish, and average daily output value per boat — were all about 31% higher. Its average profit per trip was 12,824 yuan, while boats operating in Beibu Wan (Gulf of Tonkin) during the same time incurred a loss of 1,335 yuan.

At present, apart from the maritime observatory in Yongshu Jiao (Fiery Cross Reef) of Nansha Qundao, there are third-generation masonry stilt houses on islands and reefs like Meiji Jiao (Mischief Reef), Zhebi Jiao (Subi Reef), Chigua Jiao (Johnson South Reef), Dongmen Jiao (Hughes Reef) and Nanxun Jiao (Gaven Reef). Moving into the 21st century, facilities have been established like tall buildings, docks, roads, vegetable gardens and meteorological observatories on some of the islands. Yongshu Jiao (Fiery Cross Reef) has an airport capable of accommodating large passenger planes, while Zhebi Jiao (Subi Reef), Meiji Jiao (Mischief Reef), and Chigua Jiao (Johnson South Reef) have also established airports and lighthouses of varying grades and sizes. These facilities not only meet the production, living, and combat readiness needs of the stationed personnel but also provide necessary services for international sailors navigating through this sea area.

While attaching importance to the development of traditional industries in the South China Sea, China also pays exceptional heed to tremendous resource advantage herein, i.e. the exploitation and construction of oil and gas industry. The eight Tertiary basins, including the Sino-Vietnamese Basin, the west Wan'an basin, the Zengmu Ansha basin, the Brunei-Sabah basin, the Andutan basin, the Zhenghe Basin, the Liyuetan Basin, and the western Palawan basin, cover a total area of approximately 410,000 square kilometers, with about 260,000 square kilometers fall within China's traditional territorial lines (i.e., the "nine-dash line"). Currently, the explored recoverable reserves amount to 1.1821 billion tons of oil and 3.296 trillion cubic meters of natural gas.In order to maintain the legal rights and interests of China in the waters of Nansha Qundao, the headquarters of China National Offshore Oil Corporation (CNOOC) signed a contract on oil exploration in north Wan'an with Crestone Energy Corporation of the United States, agreeing to carry out joint exploration and exploitation within an area of 25,255 square kilometers. But due to the intervention of the Vietnamese authorities, China National Offshore Oil Corporation suffered substantial losses during the process. In this regard, the spokesman of the Ministry of Foreign Affairs of China pointed out in his speech in June 16th, 1994, that China owns indisputable sovereignty over Nansha Qundao and its adjacent waters, with Wan'an Tan being part of the region. In recent years, Vietnam has designated blocks in this area for international bidding, repeatedly interfering with China's normal scientific research and fishing activities. Now, it has even gone so far as to enter this region for oil and gas exploration and development. It must be pointed out that these activities seriously infringe upon China's sovereignty in the waters of Nansha Qundao and significantly sabotage the contract for the "Wan'an North-21" project in this area signed between CNOOC and the U.S.-based Crescent Energy Company.

In June 27th, 2012, the official website of the Chinese Ministry of Foreign Affairs, together with China News Service, published a notification issued by CNOOC, noting that CNOOC would open up nine maritime blocks for the collaborative exploration and development between China and foreign companies. The official CNOOC website also announced the geographic coordinates of the nine blocks, which cover a total of 160,124.38 square kilometers.

And on the previous day, i.e. June 26th, Hone Lei, the spokesperson of the Ministry of Foreign Affairs in China, stated that it is a normal entrepreneur behavior for Chinese enterprises to announce oil and gas bidding blocks, which conforms to relevant Chinese legislation and international practices. China has not changed its stance on the disagreements and disputes in the South China Sea, and will carry on its commitment to settling them through negotiation and proactively promoting joint development and cooperation.

The oil platform Hai Yang Shi You 981 (Ocean Oil 981) of China began building a southern basin in Xisha Qundao on May 2nd, 2014 for deep-sea exploration of oil and gas.

This platform is a sixth-generation deep-sea semi-submersible drilling platform designed and built independently by China for the first time. The rig can operate 3,000 meters below the sea, with a maximum drilling depth of up to 10 thousand meters, representing the highest level of technology in marine oil drilling platforms in the world today. Hai Yang Shi You 981 (Ocean Oil 981) is a project under the "863 program" initiated in 2006, focusing on the "Key Technology Research for 3,000-meter Semi-Submersible Drilling Platforms" in the field of marine technology, jointly undertaken by China National Offshore Oil Corporation Research Center, Waigaoqiao Shipyard, and more than a dozen other enterprises and research institutions. The construction of the platform commenced on April 28th, 2008, and was finished on May 23rd, 2011, costing nearly 6 billion yuan. Lately and delivered to CNOOC later on.

The deep-sea semi-submersible drilling platform Hai Yang Shi You 981 (Ocean Oil 981) is 114 meters in length and 89 meters in width, covering an area surpassing that of a standard football pitch. In the middle of the platform lies a drilling derrick reaching up to 5-6 stories, with a weight of 30,670 tons and a load capacity of up to 125,000 tons. It allows for the take-off and landing of large helicopters, and is equipped with functions for exploration, drilling, completion, and workover operations This drillship began operations on-site on May 4th, 2014, with an original plan of 100 working days, and was scheduled for completion by August 15th. Due to meticulous design and the absence of geological hazards and typhoons during operations, the exploration task was completed in just 75 days. As the data and samples in the exploration were supposed to be processed indoors, it was necessary for Hai Yang Shi You 981 (Ocean Oil 981) to be transferred to a new spot for on-site operations. In this sense, the transfer was neither the result of any "resolution" approved by the U.S. Congress, nor the consequence of any Vietnamese interruption on spot.

However, during its service in the southern basin of Zhongjian Dao (Triton Island), Hai Yang Shi You 981 (Ocean Oil 981) indeed suffered from enormous interruption from Vietnam. On May 3rd, 2014, the Maritime Safety Administration of the PRC issued Navigation Warning No. 0033, announcing that from May 2nd to August 15th of that year, Hai Yang Shi You 981 (Ocean Oil 981) would conduct drilling operations centered at the coordinates 15°29'58" N latitude and 111°12'06" E longitude, with a radius of one nautical mile, prohibiting the entry of unrelated vessels. Soon after that, a couple of vessels of the Vietnamese coast guard entered into the said area to disturb the drilling operation of China. On May 5th, the Maritime Safety Administration of the PRC issued Navigation Warning No. 0034, warning that the radius of the maritime exclusion zone had expanded to 3 nautical miles, with multiple vessels of the Chinese coast guard entering the related sea region.

On May 4th, Le Hai Binh, the spokesperson of the Ministry of Foreign Affairs of Vietnam, claimed that "the operational location of the 'Hai Yang Shi You 981' drilling platform mentioned in the navigation warning issued by the Maritime Safety Administration of the PRC is entirely within Vietnam's exclusive economic zone and continental shelf", requiring China to withdraw all of its explorations from the relevant waters. Also, some oil and gas corporations in Vietnam issued similar declarations. Vietnam employed dozens of governmental vessels for the disturbance, which triggered several chases and even crashes between vessels of Chinese coast guard and Vietnamese law-enforcement vessels. Vietnam even had a mass of fishing boats and frogmen engaged in this harassment. China deployed various types of ships to protect Hai Yang Shi You 981 (Ocean Oil 981), regularly rotating vessels to be on site for guard duty each day, and also utilizing maritime monitoring and aviation aircraft that took off daily. This fully demonstrated China's resolution and faith in safeguarding the territorial sovereignty over the South China Sea and exploiting the resources therein.

VII. The establishment of maritime observatory

In March, 1987, the 14th Session of the Intergovernmental Oceanographic Commission of UNESCO came up with a resolution, where China was required to build a maritime observatory in Nansha Qundao. After the approval of the State Council, the construction of the required maritime observatory began in February, 1988 on Yongshu Jiao (Fiery Cross Reef). Under substantial support from relevant institutions, the People's Navy completed the construction task in August, 1988. Upon its completion, the observatory covered a mere land area of over 800 square meters.

Through land reclamation, apart from an ocean weather station that reports marine meteorological data to meteorological organizations in

Beijing and the UN, Yongshu Jiao (Fiery Cross Reef) is also furnished with plants, playgrounds, basketball course, underground reservoir, post office and other facilities. The observatory is equipped with some state-of-art hydrometeorological observation instruments available domestically and internationally. It features a high degree of automation and a wide range of observation parameters, allowing for comprehensive data collection. Apart from conducting all-weather observations and reporting various hydrometeorological parameters in the Nansha waters, the observatory also provides the Pacific Sea Level Monitoring Organization of the United Nations with the monthly average water levels in the Nansha area, thereby offering timely navigation support for vessels traveling through these waters. The establishment of this observatory provides significant scientific data for the research of the alteration rules of sea level in the Pacific Ocean, crust changes, the hydrology-weather condition of tropical sea, the formation of typhoons in the South China Sea and the southwestern Pacific Ocean, as well as the marine resources and geological environment of the South China Sea. To this end, on August 3rd, 1988, the State Council and the Central Military Commission issued a telegram to commend all comrades involved in the establishment of the station at Yongshu Jiao in Nansha Qundao, expressing the hope that they remain humble and diligent, and continue to continue to contribute to the defense and development of Nansha Qundao.

VIII. The organization of scientific expeditions

To safeguard the integrity of China's sovereignty over South China Sea Islands, the Chinese government had repeatedly organized scientific expeditions for expeditions to Nansha Qundao and its adjacent waters. This has deepened the scientific understanding of the South China Sea and South China Sea Islands, preparing for the development of the South China Sea. Since the 1980s, the following surveys were carried out in the South China Sea:

(1) From July, 1984 to April, 1986, the South China Sea Institute of Oceanography (SCSIO) of the Chinese Academy of Sciences (CAS) organized relevant personnel for a specific survey in the basin of Zengmu Ansha (James Shoal), the southernmost part of the South China Sea. Consequently, they published *The Report on the Comprehensive Investigation and Research of the Southern Border of China - Zengmu Ansha* after the investigation on the geology, geomorphology, deposit, hydrological phenomena, optics of sea water, seawater chemistry and marine organism of Zengmu Ansha (James Shoal) and its peripheral waters (within the range of 442 square kilometers).. The Report is considered a significant achievement of the first ever investigation and research in Zengmu Ansha (James Shoal) and its adjacent waters in China's history. It is of weighty theoretical and practical significance as it fills the gap of the comprehensive surveys in the southern border of China, while also providing favorable evidence for the reasonable utilization and exploitation of the resources in the South China Sea.

(2) In March, 1987, with the approval of the State Council, a comprehensive survey team from the CAS was formed, led by the Academy and in collaboration with the Ministry of Education, the Ministry of Agriculture, the Ministry of Energy, the State Oceanic Administration, the State Bureau of Surveying and Mapping, and other departments. This team conducted a comprehensive survey of Nansha Qundao and their adjacent waters, focusing on ten reefs, including Pengbo Ansha, Xianbin Jiao (Sabina Shoal), Niuchelun Jiao (Boxall Reef), Ren'ai Jiao (the Second Thomas Shoal), Meiji Jiao (Mischief Reef) Xinyi Jiao (the First Thomas Shoal), Haikou Jiao (Investigator Northeast Shoal), Jianzhang Jiao (Royal Captain Shoal), and Banyue Jiao (Half Moon Shoal). The survey covered ten disciplines, primarily focusing on oil and gas resources, biological resources, marine environment, and the land of the reefs. Over a period of five years,

more than 400 scientists from over 40 research institutions made five trips to the South China Sea aboard survey vessels. They conducted 10 survey voyages, covering nearly 50,000 nautical miles and spending over 350 days at sea. They visited and surveyed 26 reefs, conducted approximately 20,000 kilometers of comprehensive geophysical measurements, surveyed fishery resources in 28 areas covering over 200,000 square kilometers, and completed and published more than 400 papers and reports, totaling several million Chinese characters. Among these publications, the first and second volumes of the book *The Comprehensive Investigation and Research in Nansha Qundao and its Adjacent Waters* consist of up to 1.18 million Chinese characters. Moreover, works like *The Chorography of Nansha Qundao and its Peripheral Sea Area* were also published in 1990.

Meanwhile, the Second Institute of Oceanography of the SOA conducted surveys in the middle area of the South China Sea, with special reports published afterward. Also, the South China Sea Branch of the SOA has carried out activities like a second investigation in the South China Sea.

(3) In 1993, China yielded new accomplishment in the geological exploration in Nansha Qundao. According to reports, by 1993, China had completed the fully geophysical investigation in Nansha waters, and carried out evaluations of six trap structures in the Wan'an Basin of the Nansha area, providing valuable data for further exploration and development of oil and gas resources in the Nansha sea area.

It was also reported that since 1987, China's geological and mineral departments have successively dispatched the vessels called "Haiyang IV (Ocean IV)" and "Fendou V (Strive V)" to the Nansha sea area for geological surveys. They completed a comprehensive geological and geophysical reconnaissance plan over four survey voyages in the Zengmu Basin and Wan'an Basin, conducting geological measurements over 20,000 kilometers, as well as related detection work, including gravity and magnetic measurements, attaining a number of research findings. The SCSIO also conducted independent geophysical investigation in part of the Nansha waters and acquired a considerable amount of data, laying necessary foundation for the knowledge and development of Nansha Qundao.

IX. The proposal for the resolution of disputes in the South China Sea that "sovereignty belongs to China, disputes can be shelved, and we can pursue joint development"

The Chinese government upholds the principle on the issues on Nansha Qundao that Nansha Qundao has been an integral part of China's territory all through the ages, for which China has indisputable sovereignty over Nansha Qundao and its adjacent areas. But given the actual condition at home and abroad, in order to strengthen the friendly tie between China and its peripheral countries and continue to promote regional peace and stability, the Chinese government repeatedly reiterates and is committed to the peaceful settlement of the boundary disputes and historical issues between China and its neighboring countries, advocating the idea that "sovereignty belongs to China, disputes can be shelved, and we can pursue joint development".

The situation in Nansha Qundao is far more intricate than that of any existing precedent. Firstly, the core of the Nansha Qundao issue lies in the dispute on the sovereignty over this archipelago, but not dispute over any individual island, continental shelf or special economic zone. Secondly, the disputes over Nansha Qundao involve rights over an area of 800,000 square kilometers. Hence it will be an extremely audacious process to settle the issue over Nansha Qundao through the idea mentioned above. This settlement process not only includes diplomatic negotiations with relevant countries but is also not ruling out the possibility of armed conflict that may be necessary to uphold territorial sovereignty. At the same time, it is imperative for us to make further research and elaborate discussion for specific and feasible resolution.

In September, 1975, the Chinese leader Deng Xiaoping pointed out to the Vietnamese leader Le Duan, who was then visiting China, that The Chinese side has ample evidence proving that Xisha Qundao and Nansha Qundao has been the territory of China since ancient times. However, adhering to the principle of resolving disputes through friendly consultation, Deng stated that "negotiations can be conducted in the future".

In April, 1988, Deng Xiaoping, when meeting with Lady Aquino, the President of the Philippines, said when he mentioned issues over Nansha Qundao that upon the recognition of China's sovereignty, both sides will not dispatched troops and will carry out joint development. Meanwhile, the English telegraph of the French News Agency on April 18th, 1988 stated that Lady Aquino reached consensus with Deng Xiaoping that "Since China and the Philippines are friends, we will shelf this issue for the time being."

On May 12th, 1988, the Ministry of Foreign Affairs of China issued *The Memorandum about Xisha Qundao and Nansha Qundao*, reiterating that China has always been holding the sovereignty over Xisha Qundao and Nansha Qundao, and refuting Vietnam's claim of its sovereignty over the two archipelagos. The declaration pointed out that "China has always advocated for the peaceful resolution of disputes between nations, including with regard to the Nansha issue. It is in this spirit that China proposes to temporarily shelve the issue of Nansha Qundao and discuss a resolution in the future."

In the days that followed, China's national leaders and the Ministry of Foreign Affairs consistently upheld this position regarding the South China Sea issue and the sovereignty disputes over Nansha Qundao with Vietnam and the Philippines.

On July 21st, 1992, Qian Qisen, the State Councilor and Minister of Foreign Affairs of China, attended the diplomatic conference of ASEAN in Manila. Speaking on Nansha Qundao, Qian stated, "Countries that have disputes with us regarding the Nansha issue are all friendly neighbors of China. We value our friendly and cooperative relationship with these countries and do not wish to see conflicts arise due to differences, which could affect the development of friendly relations between nations and the peace and stability of the region. We propose the stance that 'sovereignty belongs to China, disputes can be shelved, and we can pursue joint development' and we are willing to negotiate with the relevant countries to seek solutions when conditions are ripe. If conditions are not mature, the issue can be temporarily shelved without affecting state relations. We believe that through joint effort of the countries in this region, the South China Sea will not become a new 'hotspot' of conflict, and there is hope for extensive cooperation with mutual benefits among the coastal nations."

Ever since Deng Xiaoping put forward his idea of "sovereignty belongs to China, disputes can be shelved, and we can pursue joint development", the ground rule of "sovereignty belongs to China" has been adhered to and developed. Yongshu Jiao (Fiery Cross Reef), Zhebi Jiao (Subi Reef), Meiji Jiao (Mischief Reef), Chigua Jiao (Johnson South Reef), Huayang Jiao (Cuarteron Reef), Nanxun Jiao (Gaven Reef) and Anda Jiao (Eldad Reef) in Nansha Qundao have been occupied and guarded by the Chinese Navy, with airports with airstrips of about 3000 meters long established in the first three islands, and a helipad in Chigua Jiao. Also, lighthouses standing 50 meters tall have been built on Chigua Jiao and Huayang Jiao to serve vessels passing through international shipping routes in the South China Sea. The occupation and development of these reefs have greatly improved China's passive situation in the South China Sea.

Bibliography

1.**CHEN Tianxi.** *Compilation of Cases Concerning the Xisha and Dongsha Islands* [G]. Shanghai: Commercial Press, 1928.

2.**CHEN Dongya.** Essential Understanding of the Xisha Islands [J]. *Foreign Affairs Review*, 1933, 2(10).

3.**LIN Xiushi, PING Tian Mozhi.** Past and Present of the New Southern Islands [N]. *Taiwan Times*, 1939-05-20.

4.**LING Chunsheng.** Geography of the Small Islands in the South China Sea Occupied by France [J]. *Journal of Local Records*, 1934, 7(5).

5.**HU Huanyong.** The Paracel and Spratly Islands Coveted by France and Japan [M]. LING Chunsheng. *China's Border Issues Today*. Nanjing: Cheng Chung Book Co., 1934.

6.**CHEN Jitang Dispatches Warship to Investigate Coral Island Case** [N]. *Shen Bao (Shanghai News)*, 1933-08-02 [page number unknown].

7.**Guangdong Provincial Government Investigates Truth of French Occupation of Nine Islands (Reuters Telegram from Guangzhou, August 3)** [N]. *Shen Bao (Shanghai News)*, 1933-08-04 [page number unknown].

8.**ZHANG Junran.** Record of the Chinese Navy's Stationing in the Southwest Sand Islands (Xisha and Nansha) in 1946 [G]. *Compilation of Materials on the Xisha Islands*. Internal material, 1988.

9.**SHAO Xunzheng.** China's Sovereignty over the Nansha Islands is Inviolable [N]. *People's Daily*, 1956-06-05 [page number unknown].

10.**WU Qingyu, LÜ Shengzu, SU Dushi.** True Record of the Chinese Navy's Recovery of the Nansha Islands after the Victory of the War of Resistance [M]. Nansha Integrated Scientific Expedition Team, Chinese Academy of Sciences. *Monograph on the Historical Geography of the Nansha Islands*. Guangzhou: Sun Yat-sen University Press, 1991.

1.陈天锡.西沙岛东沙岛成案汇编［G］.上海：商务印书馆，1928.

2.陈东亚.西沙群岛应有之认识［J］.外交评论，1933，2（10）.

3.林修史，平田末治.新南群岛之今昔［N］.台湾时报，1939-05-20.

4.凌纯声.法占南海诸小岛之地理［J］.方志月刊，1934，7（5）.

5.胡焕庸.法日觊觎之南海诸岛［M］‖凌纯声.中国今日之边疆问题.南京：正中书局，1934.

6.陈济棠派舰调查珊瑚岛案［N］.申报，1933-08-02.

7.粤省府调查法占九岛真相（广州 8 月 3 日路透社电）［N］.申报，1933-08-04.

8.张君然.1946 年中国海军进驻西南沙群岛纪实［G］‖西沙群岛资料汇编.内部资料，1988.

9.邵循正.我国南沙群岛主权不容侵犯［N］.人民日报，1956-06-05.

10.吴清玉，吕胜祖，苏读史.抗战胜利后中国海军奉命收复南沙群岛实录［M］‖中国科学院南沙综合科学考察队.南沙群岛历史地理研究专集.广州：中山大学出版社，1991.

Chapter 5
A Brief History of the Relationship Between China and Countries Around the South China Sea

Section 1 Overview

Countries like Vietnam, Cambodia, Thailand, Malaysia, Indonesia, Brunei, the Philippines are situated around the South China Sea, which had maintained connection with China long before recorded history.

In early Chinese works like *Zhu Shu Ji Nian* (*the Bamboo Annals*) and *Yue Jue Shu* (*End of the kingdom of Yue*), there are records about historical figures like Shennong, Zhuanxu, Yao and Shun "pacifying Jiaozhi in the South" or "arriving at Jiaozhi in the South".

After unifying the six states in 221 BC, Qin Shi Huang dispatched troops to pacify southern Vietnam, and set up commanderies of Nanhai, Guilin and Xiang. Therefore, the area in the south of Nanling at that time and the north of central Vietnam in the present day is called southern Vietnam. The Nanhai Commandery roughly corresponds to present-day Guangdong, with Guilin Commandery located in the eastern part of Guangxi, and Xiang Commandery including present-day northern and central Vietnam. At that time, middle and northern Vietnam belonged directly to the central government of China, being a component part of the Chinese territory. This situation remained unchanged throughout the Han, Jin, the Southern and Northern dynasties, Sui and Tang periods, until China entered the Five Dynasties and Ten Kingdoms period, during which Annam still belonged to the territory of the Southern Han. In the 12th year of Dayou of Southern Han Dynasty (939 AD), Ngô Quyền defeated the Southern Han and established an independent kingdom. From Qin Shi Huang's pacification of Annam in 214 BC to Ngô Quyền's establishment of his own state in AD 939, northern Vietnam was under Chinese rule for a total of 1,153 years. After Ngô Quyền's death, there was great chaos within the region, leading to the concept of the "Twelve Warlords" dividing the territory until 989 AD, when Đinh Bộ Lĩnh managed to unify northern Vietnam again. Over the course of the subsequent Đinh, Early Lý,

Lý, and Trần dynasties, Vietnam maintained close political relations with China's Song Dynasty. Although there were short-term wars between the two countries during the three hundred years, both of them still maintained friendly exchanges most of the time.

The Tang Dynasty witnessed dramatic prosper of trades between China and countries around the South China Sea. During the seventh century, the Kingdom of Sri Vijaya on Sumatra Island thrived as a trading port due to its strategic location on the essential maritime route between China and India. It was in this place that the famous monk Yijing of the Tang Dynasty had ever stayed and translated Buddhist sutras, gradually making it the center of Buddhist research.

The Song Dynasty saw a gradual increase in the trades of China with Southeast Asian countries along the coastal area of the South China Sea. One of them that maintained close relationship with China was Samboja, a kingdom established on Java and Sumatra.

During the Yuan Dynasty in the 13th century, China waged war against Jiaozhi and Java. By the end of the 13th century after Kublai Khan's death, China altered its diplomatic policy and adopted the attitude of maintaining friendly relationship with its neighboring countries.

In the fourth year of the Yongle reign (AD 1406) of the Ming Dynasty, troops were directly dispatched to occupy Annam, establishing commanderies and counties there, which lasted until the second year of the Xuande reign (AD 1427), for a total of 21 years. China and Annam maintained their friendly relations during the majority of time in the Ming Dynasty, with Annam sending envoys to the Ming court more than 100 times, while the latter dispatched envoys to the former over 30 times.

During the Qing Dynasty, the relationship between China and Vietnam was similar to the feudal vassal relationship of the Ming Dynasty. From the first year of the Shunzhi reign (AD 1644) to the 54th year of the Qianlong reign (AD 1789), the Vietnamese government was effectively controlled by two opposing feudal factions: the Trịnh in the north and the Nguyễn in the south. The Trịnh held nominal authority over the Lê court, serving as a symbol of a unified Vietnam, while maintaining a feudal vassal relationship with the Qing court, which recognized and conferred the title of King of Annam upon the Lê court. In 1789, the Lê court was overthrown by the rebels of the Tay Son revolt led by Nguyễn Văn Huệ. But before the regime of the Tay Son rebels could last long, it was soon replaced by the Nguyễn regime - i.e. the Nguyễn dynasty, the last imperial dynasty in the history of Vietnam.

After the establishment of the Nguyễn dynasty in AD 1802 (i.e. the seventh year of Jiaqing's reign in the Qing Dynasty, or the first year of Jialong in the Nguyễn dynasty), the Nguyễn court immediately sent envoys to the Qing court according to custom, asking for the conference of titles. "In the year of Renxu, the 11th month of the first year of the Jialong reign, Lê Quang Định, the Deputy Minister of War, was appointed as the Minister of War... The emperor commanded Lê Quang Định and others to carry the national decree and gifts to request a royal title. They also requested to change the national title to Southern Yue."

At this, the Grand Secretariat Booning rotested against the national title of Southern Yue on December 23rd in the seventh year of Jiaqing (AD 1802), proposing that "...Annam was anciently called Nanjiao, which was known as Jiaozhi during the Zhou dynasty. When Zhao Tuo took control, he first claimed the title of King of Southern Yue, but was soon defeated by the Han, which then established commanderies and counties in that region. Today, Nanhai, Cangwu, Yulin, and Hepu all belong to Guangdong and Guangxi provinces. By the Five Dynasties period, the local leader Khúc Thừa My had taken control of Jiaozhou and was merely appointed as the jiedushi (Military Commissioner) of Jinghai Commandery. In the third year of Kaibao during the reign of Emperor Taizu of Song (AD 970), Đinh Bộ Lĩnh was appointed as the king of Annam Commandery. In the first year of Tianxi during the reign of Emperor Zhenzong of Song (AD 1017), Lý Công Uẩn was titled the king of Anping Commandery. By the first year of Chunxi in the reign of Emperor Xiaozong of Song (AD 1174), Lý Thiên Tộwas granted the title of King of Annam, marking the beginning of Annam as an independent kingdom. This title was followed throughout the Yuan and Ming dynasties, all the way to the Qing dynasty today.　Actually, the territory of Annam only occupies a corner of Southern Yue. Thus, it is not appropriate for Annam to hastily claim the title of Southern Yue as a mere part of the region. Besides, Guangdong and Guangxi were the past component of Southern Yue, which have long been the territory of China since the Han Dynasty. So, if Annam were to use the name Southern Yue again, not only will it be inconsistent with reality, but its system would be particularly discordant. Therefore, there should be no further discussion regarding the request from that kingdom to be granted the name Southern Yue." In the eighth year of Jiaqing (AD 1803), an imperial edict declared, "As for the request to name the country Southern Yue, this nation initially occupied the land of the Yue people and later gained the entirety of Annam. The Celestial Empire bestows a royal title upon this country, specifically using the two characters for 'Yue' at the forefront, retaining the territorial domain of its ancestors, while placing the character for 'Southern' below to indicate the newly conferred fief. Moreover, situated to the south of Baiyue, it will not be confused with the ancient Southern Yue. With the name being correct, the meaning of the characters is also auspicious, ensuring a perpetual blessing from the Celestial Empire." This historical fact was also recorded in *Chronicle of Greater Vietnam*, a historical record composed by the Vietnamese, "In the first place, the emperor of the Qing Dynasty had intended not to approve the request because the name Southern Yue was literally similar to Eastern and Western Yue (present-day Guangdong and Guangxi). After further reconsideration, the Qing emperor eventually granted the name 'Vietnam' for fear that he should lose the loyalty of Annam if its request (or conference of title) were denied. Hence the letter from the Qing Dynasty stated that the region of Yuechang was previously pacified and referred to as Southern Yue. Now that we have annexed the entire territory of Annam, it is only appropriate to harmonize names with reality and bestow a commendable title that encompasses the territories established both before and after. Thus, it is decided to place the character 'Yue' at the forefront, indicating that our nation continues the legacy of its predecessors and inherits their honors, while placing 'Southern' beneath it to signify that our nation has expanded southward and received new imperial favor. This name is both honorable and auspicious, and is distinct from the old designations used in both Guangdong and Guangxi." Though the two accounts differ in their specific details, the name of the nation "Vietnam" was indeed established from this point onward, its vibrant history well-documented and beyond dispute.

In 1858 (during the Nguyễn dynasty of Vietnam), France and Spain launched a joint offensive against Da Nang for the governmental ban on trade and slaughter of clergymen in Vietnam. In 1861, the Anglo-French forces seized the three provinces of Định Tường, Biên Hòa and Vĩnh Long. In 1862, a treaty was signed in which Vietnam ceded Biên Hòa, Gia Đinh and Định Tường provinces in the eastern part of Cochinchina, along with Côn Đảo Island, to France, granted French nationals the freedom to practice their religion, and opened the cities of Da Nang, Ba Ria and Quảng Yên as trading ports. Faced with the fastening invasion of France, the imperial dynasty of Vietnam sent envoys to China requesting for assistance, for which the Qing court sent troops to its rescue. During the Sino-French war from 1883 to 1885, the Black Flag Army had delivered an immense blow to the French forces. Under the victorious circumstance of China, Li Hongzhang signed an unequal treaty - *The Treaty of Tianjin* - on behalf of the Qing government in

June, 1885. Since then, Vietnam was reduced to the France colony, marking the end of the suzerain-vassal relations between China and Vietnam lasting for nearly a thousand year.

Throughout the written history of over 2,000 years, China had basically been maintaining friendly exchanges with its neighboring countries in the South China Sea. Except for the war waged against Jiaozhi and Java during Emperor Shizu of Yuan's reign, there was not a single record of war between China and the peripheral nations in the South China Sea. Moreover, there were continuous records of exchange of envoys between China and various Southeast Asian countries. In *A Study of Ancient Navigation in Kunlun and the South China Sea*, a book by the French scholar Gabrel Ferrand, there was a chapter entitled "Envoys to the Chinese court" with historical accounts of envoys from the various countries of the South China Sea paying tribute to China, utilizing Chinese historical sources. The text details the number of tribute missions and offerings from countries such as Java, Fu'nan, Champa, and the Philippines to China, noting that Champa dispatched envoys to China over 160 times. As a matter of fact, the statistics offered by Mr. Ferrand is incomplete for the omitted data at the end of the 15th century, when the relations between China and its neighboring countries in the South China Sea bloomed during the Ming and Qing dynasties. Added that Mr. Ferrand was exposed to limited amount of historical accounts, there could be a great deal of omission in his book. As he himself mentioned, "If one were to examine the Chinese historical texts in detail, there might be even more tributes than this number."

Ever since the "Age of Discovery", the European colonial system has posed dramatic influence on the development of the world. Due to its location at a crucial crossroads of East-West trade, the South China Sea and its surrounding areas became a destination of colony seizure for Western colonial empires. Among the major colonial powers in the West, Portugal was the first to enter Southeast Asia. In 1511, with its formidable maritime strength, Portugal occupied Malaka - the center - for maritime trade in the first place. Subsequently, another major colonial power in the West, Spain, intruded upon the manor of Portugal in 1521. This led to drastic conflicts were sparked between the two countries, who signed *The Treaty of Zaragoza* through negotiation in 1529 to divide their sphere of influence. In accordance to the treaty, Spain expanded eastward and Portugal westward. In 1571, Spain took the Philippines and converted the latter into its colony.

In the wake of Portugal and Spain, the Netherlands, yet another major colonial power, rose to prominence as "Sea Coachman". During its occupation of Java since 1595, the Netherlands had suffered from the attack of Portugal. But ultimately, it got the grip of Java in 1602 and established Batavia Port (present-day Jakarta) on Java Island in 1619, thereby conquering several regions of present-day Indonesia gradually, and maintained its colonial rule there until after World War II.

Early in 1612, the British had entered Southeast Asia and began to vie with the Netherlands for spice trade. In the 18th century, with the decadence of the Netherlands as a commercial empire, Britain embarked on its establishment of hegemony in Southeast Asia. After taking Penang in 1786 and controlling the passage of the strait by occupying Melaka in 1795, Britain continued to seize Singapore in 1824. Since the beginning of the 19th century, Britain turned Myanmar and Malaysia into its colonies successively.

Compared with other colonial powers, France was much of a late-comer in Southeast Asia. But early in 1858 when Britain and France forced the Qing government to sign *The Treaty of Tientsin*, the French warships had entered Da Nang, forcing Tự Đức, the king of Vietnam (then a subject of China), to sign a treaty ceding three provinces in the eastern Cochinchina to France. In 1867, France turned Cambodia into its colony. Then in June, 1885, France completely turned Vietnam into a colony through *the Treaty of Tianjin*, and subsequently made Laos a colony as well.

At the end of the 19th century, the United States took advantage of Spain's decline and seized the Philippines from the Spaniards, establishing it as an American colony.

During World War II, Japan had occupied the entire Southeast Asia rapidly. Until the end of the war, countries around the South China Sea achieved independence through different processes and in various ways, which posed different influence on those independent countries in politics, economy, culture and so on.

Overall, throughout the historical process of the common development among the countries surrounding the South China Sea, other nations either became part of Chinese territory (such as northern Vietnam) or were regarded as vassal states (such as central and southern Vietnam, Malacca, Brunei, etc.). They maintained a friendly political relationship with China, engaged in mutual economic exchanges, actively developed trade, and broadly absorbed advanced Chinese ideas, culture, and production techniques in their social and cultural spheres. Be it the national strength, productivity level or navigation equipment and technology, China was then second to none when compared to other countries around the South China Sea. It was against such historical backdrop that the forefathers of China became the first to develop, name and continue its administration in South China Sea Islands. Therefore, with the South China Sea being the sea of the Chinese forebears, South China Sea Islands - including Nansha Qundao undoubtedly - is the legacy bestowed to us by our Chinese ancestors.

Section 2 A brief Introduction to the Sino-Vietnam relation

Located to the South of China, Vietnam was once known as Jiaozhi in the ancient times, with its name changed for several times. In the first year of Tiaolu during Emperor Gaozong of Tang (AD 679), the Tang Dynasty set up Annam Protectorate, with its administrative center in Jiaozhou, for which it was also called Annam. After the establishment of an independent feudal dynasty in Vietnam, the kingdom was given names such as Đại Cồ Việt, Đại Việt, Đại Vu and the like. In late 1802 (the seventh year of Jiaqing), Nguyễn Phúc Ánh, the first king of the Nguyễn dynasty - the last dynasty of Vietnam - sent envoys to the Qing court in request of title conference, "positioning to change the country title to Southern Yue". But the Qing court disapproved, only to entitle Nguyễn Phúc Ánh as the king of "Vietnam", hence the country's name whichis still used today.

I. The age of legends

The Vietnamese originated from Luoyue, one of the branches of Baiyue people widespread in South China. Distributing in the middle and lower reaches of the Red River, they led primitive lives along the coast of rivers and seas.

According to Chinese and Vietnamese historical records related to the age of legends, the first ever dynasty of Vietnam should be Hong Bang Dynasty. The first Vietnamese monarch was called King of Kinh Dương, said to be a descendant of the Yan Emperor Shennong. "The third-generation grandson of the Yan Emperor, named Emperor Ming, toured the Five Ridges to the south, married the Wuxiannv and had a son named Diyi, who was granted the title of King of Kinh Dương. The King married Shenlong, the daughter of the Lord of Dongting, and had a kid named

Chonglan, i.e. the Dragon Lord of Lạc. Later, Dragon Lord of Lạc married Yuji. It is said that she gave birth to a hundred sons from a single pregnancy, which is considered a sign of great fortune. One day, the Lord said to Yuji that 'I am the descendant of dragon while you are the offspring of celestial beings, just like water and fire that restrict and contradict with each other.' Thus, 50 sons followed their mother back to the mountains, while 50 sons followed their father to the sea. The throne was left to their eldest son, Hùng King, who took Fengzhou as capital. Hùng King established a kingdom called Yuechang, or Văn Lang, which was divided into 15 regions..." Since then, there were legends about Hùng King, lords and generals of Hung, spirits in the mountains and waters in historical accounts like *Complete Annals of Đại Việt: the Treatise of Hong Bang*. Despite the ridiculous statements in this book, it still reflects the affiliation of the Chinese and Vietnamese people.

But in 1971, *The History of Vietnam*, a chronicle compiled by the Social and Science Committee of Vietnam, presented a statement that was poles apart. In the first part of the chronicle, which is entitled "The Period of Kingdom Establishment and National Defense", the first chapter begins with records of the Kingdom of Văn Lang. Yet the Văn Lang here has no connection to China, but a kingdom "with dozens of tribes living in the plain and hill regions in the north of Vietnam... Due to the demand of water control and resistance against foreign invasion, as well as the ever-increasing economic and cultural exchanges... the trend of unification gradually unfolded among those tribes." Among them, in the tribe of Văn Lang characterized by its ferocity, "its leader" stood out for the unification of the tribes in Luoyue, thus establishing the Văn Lang kingdom. This leader claimed himself to be an emperor, who was historically known as "Hùng King".

In *The History of Vietnam*, the story of Hồng Bàng Dynasty was missing in the section about ancient legends, with an extra legend about "Thánh Gióng ". As recorded in this book, during the times of Hùng King, Văn Lang Văn Langwas vulnerable to foreign invasion for its crucial location... The legendary invaders included "Man", "the Red-Nosed" and "An". In Phu Dong village, there was a child lying on a stone bed "incapable of speech or smile" though being three years old. But at the news of the intrusion of foreign invaders and the sound of wooden fish calling for talent to resist against aggression, he "experienced a growth spurt like a blowing balloon", and was able to consume "seven baskets of rice and three baskets of eggplants, drinking up an entire river." He rushed right to the An invaders and "killed the leader of those aggressors, flattening his army eventually." The book hailed *Thánh Gióng* as an excessively excellent myth.

Meanwhile, there are records in ancient Chinese texts about Vietnam (known as Jiaozhi in ancient times) during the age of legend.   According to the *Book of Documents: Canon of Yao*, "Shen commanded Xishu to reside in southern Jiaozhi." And in the *Huainanzi: Zhushu Xun* (*The Writings of the Huainan Masters: Craft of the Ruler*), "When Shennong ruled the world in the past, ... his territory extended south to Jiaozhi, north to Youdu, east to Yanggu and west to Sanwei, none disobeying his order." According to *Wudibenji (The Basic Annals of the Five Emperors)*, the first chapter of *Shiji*, "King Zhuanxu ruled Gaoyang, ... which extended to Jiaozhi in the south, Liusha in the west, and Panmu in the east. ... All places radiated by sun and moon were its subjects." According to the *Mozi: On the Economy of Expenditure*, "In the ancient times when Yao was the ruler of the world, he pacified Jiaozhi in the south and conquered Youdu in the north. Places where the sun rises in the east and sets in the west were all obedient to Yao's reign." Another record in *Shiji: Wudibenji (The Basic Annals of the Five Emperors)* goes that "Emperor Shun pacified Jiaozhi in the south, ... leaving all his achievements recorded within the range of the Four Seas." While legend can by no means be regarded as true history, they still reveal the fact that among the mass of countries around the South China Sea, Vietnam was the earliest one to get in touch with China.

II. The period of the administration of prefectures and counties in China

It is unlikely that the true history of Vietnam began earlier than the Qin Dynasty. There is a relatively reliable record about the early society of Vietnam *Records from the Outer Region of Jiaozhou* in the fourth century, "In the past when there was no commandery or county in Jiaozhi, there was a land called Luo field (雒田， Luo Tian) where the fields relied on the rising and falling tides. The people there assarted and were fed by the fields there, thus being called the Luo people. The king of Luo was designated, with the lords of Luo governing various prefectures and counties. And in the counties, there were a cohort of generals of Luo..." The character "Luo" (雒) here was referred to as "nac" in ancient Vietnamese texts and "nuuc" in modern Vietnamese, meaning "water"; it could also be referred to as "Lo" or "Lua", meaning "rice". By "the fields relied on the rising and falling tides", the text means that the fields were irrigated by the ebb and flow of tides. Such a farming method is called "plowing with a knife and mowing with water" or "plowing with fire and mowing with water". But neither Chinese nor Vietnamese historical accounts include any records about the social organization at that time. However, judging from the traces of language and folk-customs left by the long-standing Vietnamese rural communes, we can infer that the early social structure of Vietnam took the form of rural commune. At that time when there was no private land, all of the plowlands, mountains, forests, rivers and ponds belonged to rural communes. The princes, lords and soldiers of Luo could be the mere leaders of rural communes or their relevant unions. There was no such thing as real nation or language in Vietnam at that time when it was "on the threshold of civilization".

In 214 BC, Qin Shi Huang pacified Southern Yue and ventured deep into Lingnan, establishing the prefectures of Guilin, Nanhai, and Xiang after seizing Luliang. It is commonly recognized that the Xiang Prefecture refers to the region in the north and middle of Vietnam as well as southwestern Guangxi of China. The establishment of Xiang Prefecture during the Qin Dynasty marked the beginning of China's promotion of the system of prefectures and counties in Vietnam.

Masses of migrants from the Qin court "lived together with the Vietnamese", facilitating the social advancement of Vietnam, and accelerating its economic and cultural exchange with the Central Plains of China. At the end of the Qin Dynasty when the Central Plains were plagued by turmoil, Zhao Tuo, the county magistrate of Longchuan (who was also a native of Zhending, taking over Ren Xiao's position as the deputy prefect of Nanhai Prefecture), took the advantage to "attack and annex the prefectures of Guilin and Xiang". After that, Zhao established the separatist power - Nanue Kingdom centered on Guangzhou, setting up the prefectures of Jiaozhi and Jiuzhen in the central and northern area of present-day Vietnam. The ancient history of Vietnam once listed Nanyue as one of its dynasties and named Zhao Tuo "King Wu of Zhao", revering him as the founder of the nation. But in *The History of Vietnam* compiled by the Social and Science Committee of Vietnam, Zhao Tuo has been portrayed as an "invader". Zhao's governance of Jiaozhi and Jiuzhen was "arranged according to their local customs", only dispatching "two envoys" for the management of affairs in these two commanderies.

In 111 BC, Emperor Wu of Han annihilated nine commanderies of Nanyue and set up Nanhai, Cangwu, Yulin, Hepu, Jiaozhi, Jiuzhen, Ri'nan, Zhuya and Da'er. Among them, Jiaozhi, Jiuzhen and Ri'nan were located in the north and middle area of present-day Vietnam under the jurisdiction of the Central Government of Han. Counties were established under the commanderies. And above the nine commanderies, there was the Jiaozhi region, which was overseen by a regional inspector. This administration deployment, which is more rigorous than that of the past, laid foundation for the administrative division both in the dynasties to come and after the establishment of the autonomous feudal dynasties of Vietnam.

During the Western Han Dynasty, though there were three commanderies established in Nanyue, they were classified as "elementary commanderies". Those three commanderies were "governed according to their original customs" with the lords and generals of Luo "maintaining their original subordinating relations", immune from all taxes. This policy conformed to the lagging social and economic situation of Jiaozhou. It was recorded in *Hou Han Shu (The Book of the Later Han)* that "all of the precincts of Jiaozhi, despite the establishment of commanderies and counties therein, differed from each other in languages, which could only be understood through translation." "People in Jiuzhen primarily engage in hunting and do not know about plowing with oxen"; "the people of Luoyue have no marriage customs or laws; they form unions based on their desires without specific partners, unaware of the surnames of fathers and sons or the relationships between husbands and wives." With the influx of immigrants from the Central Pains, this unenlightened situation gradually changed. Specially at the turn of the Eastern and Western Han dynasties, the measures taken by the "honest officials" dispatched to Jiuzhen by the central government acted as a significant stimulus for the society there. Ren Yan, the governor of Jiuzhen, promoted the advanced cattle-plowing technique of the Central Plains, ordaining people to cast iron farming implements and expand plowlands. These measures altered the original "slash and burn methods" of farming, resulting in bumper harvests for years running and "enabling people to live in abundance". Ren Yan, together with Xi Guang, the then governor of Jiaozhi, "established schools in their precincts and taught people with etiquette. Besides, they set up matchmaking customs and acquainted people with the concept of marriage, cleansing the remnant of collective marriage of the primitive society by practicing monogamous marriage, thereby empowering the progress of the entire society.

At the end of the Western Han and the beginning of the Eastern Han, as the three commanderies including Jiaozhi no longer enjoyed the privilege of "the elementary commanderies" any longer, local officials began to rule their local people directly and levy taxes. Such am alteration of ruling policy landed the inherent system of clans and tribes at risk of collapse, depriving the lords and generals of Luo of their original status, and thus igniting the conflicts between them and the central government. Meanwhile, the atrocious and corrupted specimen of those local officials further intensified the conflicts between feudal rulers, tribal leaders and the people, ultimately triggering off "the Rebellion of the Two Trungs" in AD 40. In AD 42, the court of Eastern Han sent Ma Yuan, General Fubo, to suppress the uprising, which he successfully quelled the following year. During the process of suppression, Ma Yuan "established administrative cities and towns in the areas he passed through, constructed canals for irrigation to benefit the people, and proposed more than ten Yue rules that went against the laws of Han, clarifying the old customs and restrain the Yue people. From then on, the Yue people followed the practices of General Ma." (cr. *The Book of the Later Han*) After the Rebellion of the Two Trungs, lords and generals of Luo stepped down from history. Most of the Chinese and Vietnamese acholars believe that Vietnam had entered the feudal society since the Rebellion of the Two Trungs. The historical facts above demonstrated that it was the rule of the feudal dynasties of China that led Vietnam through the "threshold of civilization" and entered the feudal society, bypassing the devastating slavery society in human history. And it was also due to its being led into the feudal society by

China that the interior revolution of Vietnam was not thorough enough, leaving a great deal of feudal remnants in the country. The main manifestation is the long-standing existence of rural communes and the serious remnants of slavery, which is an important characteristic of the feudal society of Vietnam.

During the late Eastern Han Dynasty, the Central Plains were in turmoil, leading to the Three Kingdom period with frequent wars. Fortunately, Shi Xie, a local of Cangwu, defended Jiaozhi for nearly 40 years (AD 187-226), allowing the region to remain "peaceful and free from conflict, with the populace not losing their livelihoods," thus maintaining a precarious peace in a corner of the world. Shi Xie, "with his humble attitude towards scholars", welcomed numerous distinguished intellectuals from the South. He also "established schools, taught the texts of Zhongxia, translated their meanings, and educated the local people, who then began to understand the importance of learning," which greatly enhanced and developed the cultural education in Jiaozhi (cr. *San Guo Zhi (The Records of the Three Kingdoms)*. Shi Xie's remarkable political achievements had always been complimented by Vietnamese historians, thereby revered as "King Si" and earning the reputation of "the learning pioneer of Jiaozhi in the south".

From the end of the Three Kingdoms period until the Sui and Tang dynasties, China exercised effective rule over Vietnam. Since the reign of Sun Quan, King Wu of the Three Kingdoms period, China had made several adjustments in the administrative division of Jiaozhi region. By the end of the reign of Wu, Jiaozhou exercised jurisdiction over commanderies including Jiaozhi, Xinchang, Jiuzhen, Jiude, Wuping, Ri'nan, which was followed by the two Jin dynasties. During the Jin Dynasty, Jiaozhou encompassed the north and middle region of present-day Vietnam (i.e. Thanh Hóa and Nghệ An). (cr. *The Book of Jin: Treatise on Geography*)

During the Sui and Tang dynasties, the central government of China still had long-term military and political institutions established in Vietnam, with frequent changes in organizational system during the Tang Dynasty, In the fourth year of Wude (AD 621), Jiiaozhou was designated as a general prefecture, which was soon altered to Jiaozhou Commandery. In the fifth year of Wude (AD 622), the whole nation was divided into 10 circuits, with Jiaozhou under the jurisdiction of Lingnan Circuit. In the first year of Tiaolu (AD 679), Jiaozhou Commandery was converted into Annam Protectorate, whose jurisdiction was way broader than that in the Three Kingdom period and the Southern and Northern dynasties. After the An Lushan rebellion, the Tang Dynasty altered Annam Protectorate to Protectorate General to Pacify the South in the second year of Zhide (AD 757), after which the name of Jiaozhou experienced several changed. At the end of the Tang Dynasty, in the seventh year of the Xiantong era (AD 866), it was promoted to Jinghai Military Commissioner.

The Tang Dynasty implemented direct and effective rule over Annam through the aforementioned military and political institutions and officials appointed by the central government. Economically, it changed the practice of the Three Kingdoms to the Southern and Northern Dynasties of collecting tribute in the form of rare and exotic goods, and instead introduced a unified system of Zuyongdiao (tax paid in grains, corvée and textiles) as well as the Semiannual Tax System. This indicates that Annam had been regarded as an interior prefecture of China both politically and economically at that time. At the end of the Tang Dynasty, the Nanzhao regime of the ethnic minorities in Yunnan raided Annam and captured Jiaozhou twice. Despite being in its declining years, the Tang court still dispatched the valiant general Gao Pian to lead an army to drive out Nanzhao and maintain central control over Annam and the unity of the state. Gao set up garrisons in Annam for the consolidation of border defence, created tax registers for tax collection, and rebuilt Daluo City by the banks of the Suli River, and dredged the submerged rocks in various rivers to facilitate navigation. Due to his well-run governance in Annam, Gao Pian was honored as "King Gao" by the Vietnamese.

During the time when China ruled Annam through the system of prefectures and counties, the major jurisdiction of Annam was in the northern region of present-day Vietnam. Lâm Ấp in the middle became independent early in the Eastern Han Dynasty, becoming an ancient civilization that was "Indianized". Fu'nan in the south and the later Chenla were only annexed by Vietnam late in the 18th century.

During the ages of prefectures and counties that lasted for over a thousand years, Vietnam was closely intertwined with China in various aspects. The first evidence of this is that the southward migration of the people in the Central Plains and the northward movement of part of the Jiaozhou people. This ramped up the economic and cultural exchange and ethnic integration through intermarriage. For instance, Ren Yan, the Governor of Jiuzhen, taught the Vietnamese people to plough with cattle and produce iron farm implements; Ma Yuan "dug canals for irrigation to benefit the people" in Vietnam. Since Ren Yan started "the practice of cattle-plowing, for over six hundred years, the techniques of fire weeding and farming have been similar to those of the Chinese. Fields called 'Bai Tian (White Fields)' were used for planting white grains, which were sowed in July and harvested in October. Fields called 'Chi Tian (Red Fields)' was used for planting red grains, which were sowed in February and harvested in April; this was what is referred to as the two-crop rice system." (cr. *Shui Jing Zhu* (*The Commentary on the Water Classic*) This indicates that under the influence of the Central Plains, the farming technique based on rice cultivation had reached maturity in Annam. The people of Annam "were ignorant of the way of wheat cultivation", for which Governor Zhao Chang of the Tang Dynasty "taught them how to grow it". In turn, tropical fruits like bananas, coconuts, longan and lychee were spread into the Central Plains, enriching people's life therein.

Apart from farming technology, the cutting-edge process technology was also spread southward to Jiaozhou. At the archaeological site of Han tombs in northern Vietnam, many ceramics, jade artifacts, bronzeware, ironware, lacquerware, and Wuzhu coins were unearthed, indicating that these items had already been introduced to Jiaozhou during the Han Dynasty. In the Eastern Han Dynasty, the Chinese invented papermaking technology that spread southward. During the third century, the people of Jiaozhou produced paper with the bark of incense trees abundant in the local area, hence its name "incense paper". This kind of paper is tinted with brown, featuring spawn-shaped stripes with fragrance and resilience, "which does not rot when soaked in water". The weavers of Jiuzhen employed fine and tender bamboos to make bamboo cloth while those in Jiaozhi used the stems of plantain to make "Ge (ko-hemp cloth)", which became famous as "Jiaozhi Ge" or "Jiao Ge".

During the long period of the prefectural and county system, the ruling feudal dynasties of China and their officials actively promoted Central Plains culture in Annam, facilitating local cultural progress. The language, customs, superstructure and various aspects of Vietnam were extensively and deeply influenced by Han culture, making it one of the neighboring countries most profoundly permeated by Han culture.

Before China established prefectures and counties in Annam, there was no writing in the region. As Chinese officials and migrants arrived one after another, the local people "gradually learned to speak and slowly became enlightened". The Vietnamese accepted Chinese characters and used it for a long time. Vietnamese words borrowed from Chinese are called "Chinese Vietnamese", accounting for approximately 60% in modern Vietnamese. The broad application of Chinese characters was favorable for the transmission of Han culture.

There are generations of officials and scholars contributing to the spread of Han culture in Vietnam, whose legacies are well documented in literature. As mentioned earlier, Ren Yan and Xi Guang "imparted the Vietnamese with rites", and "the Chinese vogue in Vietnam began with these two governors" (*The Book of the Later Han: Biography of Southern Barbarians*). Besides, Shi Xie also proactively promoted Han culture. It is recorded in the *Complete Annals of Đại Việt,* "We (Vietnam) are well-versed in poetry and literature, practices rites and music, and is known as a land of literature. Since the time of the sage kings, the virtues and achievements have not only influenced their own time but have also extended to future generations. Is this not magnificent indeed?" During Shi Xie's governance, "only Jiaozhou was in modest peace while the entire world was in turmoil," (cr. *The Records of the Three Kingdoms: Biography of Shi Xie*) "where hundreds of scholars from the Central Plains came for refuge." Among the refugee were the famous doctor Dong Feng and Master Mou Bo, the representative of Buddhism. At that time, Confucianism, Taoism and Buddhism were transmitted and were thriving remarkably.

From the Three Kingdom period to the Wei, Jin, Southern and Northern dynasties, the Chinese culture exerted continuous influence on the Vietnamese culture, with the Tang Dynasty, known for its cultural prosperity, having a particularly significant impact. The officials sent by the Tang Dynasty to Annam were highly cultured themselves and were enthusiastic about promoting education and literature. Take the Governor Gao Pian, who "was fond of literature"; his poem "Sending off to Annam to Write to the Governor" is included in *Quan Tang Shi* (the *Complete Tang Poems)* (Volume 598). Another governor Ma Zong, "taught the local customs using Confucian principles. And his governance was praised for its grace." He "can be said to have excelled in both literature and politics". Wang Bo, one of the Four Masters of Early Tang, had a father named Wang Fujiao, who once served as the magistrate of Jiaozhi and was a renowned scholar of classical texts and elegant prose. During his tenure, he "greatly promoted education and culture, earning the respect of the scholars and the people." Wang Bo had visited Jiaozhi to pay a family visit, during which he wrote the famous "Preface to the Tengwang Pavilion," in which there are many passages related to Jiaozhi. Other renowned poets like Du Shenyan, Shen Quanqi, Liu Yuxi and Han Wo had once lived in Annam, leaving poems that celebrated the region. Overall, the Tang poems serve as the major influence of the development of Vietnamese poetry in later generations. Even in modern times, many Vietnamese people continue appreciate and can compose poems in classical Chinese.

During the time of prefecture and county, the cultural and educational systems and talent selection policy promoted by the central government of China were similar to those in the mainland. Early in the Eastern Han Dynasty, Vietnamese scholars like Lý Tan, Lý Cam and Truong Tuong were already held in great esteem. The most notable figure was Jiang Gongfu from Junning County of Ai Chau (modern An Đinh County, Thanh Hóa Province, Vietnam) during the Tang Dynasty, who passed the imperial examination and was promoted to Prime Minister by Emperor Dezong (AD 780–805), reaching the pinnacle of power among his peers. This all illustrates the profound influence of Han culture on Vietnam. Feng Chengjun, an expert in the history of the exchange between the East and West in China, holds that "among all the regions influenced by Chinese culture, none has been more deeply affected than Vietnam."

III. The Sino-Vietnamese Relations During the Period of Autonomous Feudal Dynasty

After the perish of the Tang Dynasty, China stepped into the chaotic period of the Five Dynasties and Ten States period (AD 907-960), when the feudal lords of Annam took the advantage of the division and turbulence of the

Central Plains, each establishing their own independent factions. Over the course of almost half a century, the five families of Khuc Thua Du, Duong Đinh Nghe, Kieu Cong Tien, Ngô Quyền and Đinh Bộ Lĩnh emerged successively, known as the "Little Five Dynasties." The families of Khúc, Đường, and Kiều all claimed the title of *jiedushi* (Military Governor). In AD 939, Ngô Quyền claimed himself king. But after his death in AD 944, 12 provinces under his jurisdiction were landed into huge turmoil, triggering "the Anarchy of the 12 Warlords" that lasted for 22 years. Until AD 968, Đinh Bộ Lĩnh defeated the 12 warlords and established Great Viet. Later in AD 975, Đinh was enthroned by Emperor Taizu of Song, with the Great Viet deemed as "one of the several vassal states". Traditional historiography of Vietnam classifies the families of Khúc, Đường, Kiều and Ngô among the "External Chronicles" or "Five Dynasties Observations," viewing them as "stealthy usurpers" during the Five Dynasties; while only the Đinh family is hailed as the beginning of the "Đinh clan" or "Đinh Chronicles." Therefore, it should be the year AD 968 that marks the establishment of the autonomous feudal dynasty of Vietnam.

After this, Vietnam entered into the brand-new period of independent feudalism, undergoing the development of the Đinh Dynasty, the Early Lê dynasty, the Lý Dynasty, the Trần Dynasty, and the Hồ dynasty. In the early 15th century, it briefly came under the control of the Ming Dynasty of China (the Ming period), but soon restored its independence and reached the peak of feudal dynasties during the Later Lê dynasty. Later on, Vietnam was plagued by long-lasting division and civil wars, experiencing dynasties and regimes like the Mạc dynasty, the Trinh lords, the Nguyễn lords and the Tây Sơn dynasty until it was unified at the beginning of the 19th century. In 1802, Nguyễn Phúc Anh proclaimed himself king and established the Nguyễn dynasty, the last feudal dynasty in Vietnamese history.

The independent feudal states of Vietnam completely modeled

themselves on China in various aspects, including its system of governance. The Đinh dynasty (AD 968-980) the subsequent Early Lê dynasty that replaced it (AD 980-1009), established a system of centralized monarchy from the very beginning. During the Lý dynasty (AD 1010-1225) and the subsequent Trần dynasty (AD 1225-1400), Vietnam was consolidated and developed as a centralized feudal country. In 1174, the Southern Song Dynasty converted Jiaozhi Prefecture to be the Kingdom of Annam, crowning Lý Anh Tông as the King of Annam, thereby further recognizing the independence of Vietnam. The Lý dynasty modeled its central and local administrative systems after those of the Song Dynasty, significantly strengthened its military forces, formulated new laws, established Confucian temples, and instituted a system for selecting scholars. The Trần dynasty further improved upon the various systems of the Lý dynasty, leading to Vietnam's flourishing national strength. In terms of culture, the indigenous script—Chu Nom—and Chu Nom works emerged. In 1227, the earliest official historical book of Vietnam, *Annals of Đại Việt*, was compiled.

The early years of the Lê dynasty (AD 1428-1784) was the heyday of the feudalism of Vietnam, which reached its peak during Lê Thánh Tông's reign (AD 1460-1497). At that time, when the centralized political system was further fortified as the state apparatus of Vietnam, the local court reduced the power of local officials dramatically, set up investigating censors to supervise local governments, and established a great standing army. During the Hong Duc era, *the Decree of Hong Duc* was issued. In the early years of the Lê dynasty, the equal-field system was established, leading to some adjustments in land relations. The government showed concern for the hardships of the people, emphasized production, appointed officials to promote agriculture and manage dikes, constructed irrigation systems, and rewarded land reclamation efforts. Handicrafts and commerce saw significant development compared to before, with commercial towns such as

Xiannan (Xing'an) emerging apart from the capital. With regard of culture, the *Complete Annals of Đại Việt* was compiled in 1479, being the definitive edition of Vietnamese history, along with bunches of other works coming into being.

Ever since the establishment of its independent feudal dynasty, Vietnam had been maintaining suzerain-vassal relation with the Chinese feudal dynasty until the former was reduced to a French colony. The "suzerain-vassal relation" reflects feudal affiliation in international relations; however, this relationship differs in social nature from the relationships of modern capitalist imperialism and colonialism, and should not be conflated.

The relation between China and Vietnam during this period could be inspected from the perspectives as follows:

1.Tribute payment

The feudal rulers of Vietnam were obliged to pay tribute to the feudal court of China "in conformity with the courtesy of a vassal" to show allegiance. Since the first year of Kaibao period of the Song Dynasty (AD 968), Vietnam had begun to pay tribute to China, which had been uninterrupted during its entire independent feudal period except for the times when the two countries became enemies or engaged with each other. In the case of the Song Dynasty, Li You's *Song Chao Shi Shi (Facts of the Song Dynasty)* recorded 25 tributary missions from Vietnam during the Northern Song period from the Kaibao era to the first year of the Yuanfeng era (AD 968–1078). The tribute items included trained rhinoceroses, elephants, local Vietnamese products, gold artifacts, rhinoceros horns, dragon and phoenix chairs, umbrella handles and so on. This record might not be complete, but still provides an overview of Vietnam's tributary missions to the Northern Song during a certain period. Zhou Qufei from the Song Dynasty recorded of Vietnam's tributary missions in the Southern

Song Dynasty that "during the Jianyan period, Lý Thiên Tố requested to pay tribute, for which the (Chinese) court appreciated his sincerity and responded with a gracious decree. In the 26th year of the Shaoxing era (AD 1156), Lý requested to pay tribute again, and was granted permission. He then sent envoys to reach the central court via Qinzhou. The chief envoys were Li Yisi, the Right Martial Gentleman　of Annam, and Guo Ying, the Martial Official of Annam. They brought five elephants as the supplement of regular categories of tribute, thus elevating the level of his tributary practice. Li Guo, the governor of Taiping Prefecture in Annam, was appointed as envoy. The goods he presented were in profusion, with all the official documents inscribed in gold characters. The gold artifacts in the tribute totaled more than 1,200 taels, with half of them adorned with jewels. The tribute included pearls, among which the three largest were the size of eggplants, followed by six smaller ones the size of jackfruit seeds, 24 the size of walnuts, 17 the size of plum pits, and 50 the size of jujube seeds, totaling one hundred pearls presented in a golden vase. Also, there were 1,000 *jin* of agarwood, 50 pieces of green feathers, 850 bolts of deep yellow silk with a dragon pattern, and six imperial horses, along with saddles and bridles. According to the common practice, eight horses and five trained elephants shall be presented, with 50 officials from each of the two departments... In the ninth year of the Qiandao era (AD 1173) ... five elephants were offered as a grand tribute... and ten more were sent to congratulate the ascension to the throne... In this tribute, in addition to the elephants, gold and silver wash basins, rhinoceros horns, elephant tusks, agarwood, and paper were included, with a total value of no less than 20 to 30 thousand strings of cash. This seems less grand compared to the tributes during the Shaoxing era, but was what a country could merely gather from what was available from its treasury..." The tribute in the 26th year of Shaoxing can be said to be the most abundant of all. Apart from the "regular" categories of tribute, "irregular" ones were also presented. While the tribute in the ninth year of Qiandao was "inferior to that in Shaoxing period", it still derived from "sweeping the treasury". So, would it be an extremely tremendous burden for Vietnam? In the same record, Zhou Qufei pointed out that Vietnam was politically "received the favor of the granted nation" and economically "bestowed by the court generously, receiving repeated exceptional grace," thus "the envoys returned satisfied".

The regular tributes of Vietnam were "all useless items like rhinoceros and elephants", while the granted objects from China were daily necessities that "provide for livelihood". Moreover, considering the value of the return gifts, Vietnam consistently made a profit. In July of the first year of Qianxing period of Emperor Renzong's reign in the Song Dynasty (AD 1022), "According to Sansi (the Financial Bureaus), Jiaozhou tributary envoys like Li Kuantai each presented local products... The merchants calculated the value at 1,682 *guan*. But the court granted return gifts of 2,000 *guan* to surpass in value, demonstrating goodwill and fostering distant relations. In March of the sixth year of Tiansheng period (AD 1028), "According to Sansi (the Financial Bureaus), it was estimated by the material warehouse of the workshop that the value of the tribute from Jiaozhou, consisting of incense and medicinal herbs, was 3,060 *guan*, with granted return money of 4,000 *guan*." (cr. *Song Government Manuscript Compendium: Foreigners and Barbarians*)

The Song Dynasty, like other feudal dynasties in China, consistently adopted a policy of "generous gifts in return for minimal tribute" towards the "vassal" states including Vietnam, only to "commend their sincerity" without seeking profit, and even regarded it as a burden. Particularly, feasts and entertainment activities were held for the porters at great expense in the counties and towns that received the elephants contributed by Vietnam. In addition, the tribute envoys extorted along the way, leading even the Song emperor to remark: "The elephants are useless objects, causing significant disturbance to my people along the roads. Yet we do not accept them." Therefore, the Song Dynasty was not proactive regarding the tribute from Vietnam; instead, it rejected the tribute more than once, suggesting that envoys from Annam should be exempted from visiting the court, and the local products presented, except for those of extravagant value, were not accepted. The rest will be judged based on the established customs and returned accordingly." It was only after repeated requests from Vietnam that permission was granted for them to "visit the court" (cr. *Wenxian Tongkao (Comprehensive Examination of Literature)*, Vol. 330).

The reason why the feudal rulers of Vietnam repeatedly "requested tribute" in such a proactive way is that tribute was profitable for them. Under the excuse of tribute and envoy exchange, they were allowed to pass onto China their ferocious exploitation on their own people, thus reaping the benefits like a wolf watching the quarrel of shepherds. Soon after the establishment of Vietnam as a kingdom, the king Lê Hoàn "used the tribute as an excuse to impose taxes", and thus selling out his people. More importantly, tribute is a crucial way of international trade. "Tribute is but a way that benefits trade and promotes gift granting," (cr. *Wenxian Tongkao (Comprehensive Examination of Literature)*, Vol. 331), bring huge profits to Vietnamese rulers. When describing the tributary team of Vietnam, Zhou Qufei said, "There were a hundred of envoys and government officials in the team with almost none to carry tributes. Thus the goods were all brought to the cities by the envoys." In this light, rather than a diplomatic corps, the team was more of a caravan of international trade. Therefore, tribute payment is also referred to as "tributary trade".

During the Song Dynasty, Vietnam's tribute to China was as described above; and the tribute during the Yuan, Ming, and Qing dynasties was generally similar.

2.Title conference

The feudal rulers of Vietnam received titles from the Chinese emperors with their allegiance and tribute, thus gaining strong political support as a means to consolidate their reign domestically. Whereas the Chinese emperors, in turn, retained their titular suzerain position as the "great celestial country". Therefore, envoys from both countries continuously traveled back and forth, with a variety of requests for tribute such as seeking titles, royal seals, memorial ceremonies, congratulations for birthdays, celebrations of the crown prince's accession, official reports, requests for crowns and garments, and expressions of gratitude for bestowed crowns and garments, all of which became the main content of interactions between the two countries during Vietnam's period of autonomous feudalism.

In the eighth year of Kaibao of Emperor Taizu's reign of Song (AD 975), Đinh Bộ Lĩnh was initially granted the title of King of Jiaozhi, gradually resulting in a system whereby "upon the initial establishment of a king, he would be titled King of Jiaozhi; after some time, he would be promoted to King of Nanping; and upon his death, he would be posthumously honored as Shizhong and King of Nanyue". Such promotion of crown title was intended for "the demonstration of special courtesy", which was also a policy of conciliation and preference towards Vietnam adopted by the Song court. At that time, however, Vietnam's "petitions and documents only referred to as Annam Circuit", which "did not clearly indicate that it was a separate nation". Until the first year of Chunxi era of Emperor Xiaozong of the Southern Song (AD 1174), the name "the Kingdom of Annam" was granted to Vietnam, when Lý Anh Tông (Lý Thiên Tố) was also appointed as King of Annam. In the second year of the same period (AD 1175), a seal was granted to this Kingdom, and in the third year (AD 1176) its own calendar day. It was not until then that the Chinese court admitted the Kingdom of Annam and referred to it as a kingdom from then on. Hence the world "no longer recognized it as a county of China". (cr. Yujiaoji (Records on Taming

Jiaozhi), Vol. 2)

After that, in the third year of Jingding era under Emperor Lizong of the Southern Song (AD 1262), Trần Nhật Cảnh was conferred by edict as the Chief Minister and Grand Prince of Annam, **with** Trần Thái Tông **(**Trần Cảnh **) as the Chief General and King of Annam**.

In the sixth year of Xuande era under Emperor Xuanzong of Ming (AD 1431), Lê Lợi (Thái Tổ of the Lê dynasty) was appointed to "be in temporary charge of affairs of the Kingdom of Annam".

In the 19th year of the Jiajing era of Ming (AD 1540), an edict was issued to alter the Kingdom of Annam to the Office of Commanders-in-chief in Annam, and appointed Mạc Đăng Dung the Commander-in-chief.

In the 14th year of Emperor Qianlong's reign in the Qing Dynasty (AD 1789), Nguyễn Huệ was designated as the King of Annam.

In the eighth year of Jiaqing era under Emperor Renzong of Qing (AD 1803), Nguyễn Phúc Ánh, the founding emperor of the last ever dynasty of Vietnam, was made the king of Annam, with the name of the kingdom designated as "Vietnam".

Since the establishment of Vietnam, generations of its emperors had all received title conference from Chinese emperors.

3.Wars

Since its establishment, Vietnam maintained peaceful official relations with various dynasties of China through tribute and conference reception for most of the time. Meanwhile, there were continuous friendly exchanges and frequent economic and cultural interactions between the peoples of China and Vietnam, which was the mainstream of their relations between these two countries. Yet there were still several wars between them, being a mere branch or an ephemera amid the long history of Sino-Vietnamese relations.

As mentioned before, due to the long-standing rural communes in the Vietnamese society as well as the dispersive land occupancy pattern, there were not many massive peasant rebellions in this country. Despite the Tay Son revolt that overthrew the old dynasty and established a new one, the alterations of most of the dynasties of Vietnam were achieved through palace coup - the internal adjustment of the ruling class. While China, the suzerain, tended to crusade against the revolt for the maintenance of its suzerainty. In the fifth year of Taipingxingguo era (AD 980), Emperor Taizong of Song dispatched troops against Vietnam for Le Hoan's usurpation of the throne of the Đinh clan. According to Emperor Taizong of Song, this was "a war against the rebel, which was on reasonable grounds but not without justice cause. Recently, in one region, there has been a succession of usurpations. The transport commissioner of Guangxi has submitted a memorial stating that Đình Toàn's family has been wronged by bandits. If the chaos has no end in sight, the people are likely to seek out a protector. Moreover, since ancient times, tributes from the people have been continuously submitted; how can those in power bear to remain indifferent and not provide assistance?" (cr. *Annan zhilüe (Concise records of Annam)*, Vol. 5) From the perspective of ethic moral in a feudal society, it can be said that this war was waged to uphold "righteous cause" on a justice ground. Subsequently, the Ming Dynasty waged war against Vietnam in 1407 under the pretext of restoring the Trần dynasty; and during the Qianlong period of the Qing Dynasty, war was waged against Vietnam in 1789 due to Nguyễn Huệ's expulsion of the Lê Emperor Lê Duy Kỳ. Both belong to this category of wars.

Due to the enduring debility of the Song Dynasty, the powerful feudal Ly dynasty of Vietnam offended the border unceasingly, encroaching on Song territory and seizing the inhabitants of the border to be slaves. Subsequently, the ruler of the Lý dynasty waged a massive war against the Song court from the end of 1075 to early 1076. The Lý court dispatched the Grand Assistant

Commandant Lý Thường Kiệtand others to lead an army of 100,000 men, advancing through both land and water routes to invade the border areas of Guangxi and Guangdong, capturing places such as Qinzhou, Lianzhou, and Yongzhou. The intruding army slaughtered hundreds of thousands of border inhabitants and took a mass of citizens in these three regions back to Vietnam. The Song court was forced to send Guo Kui and others to launch a counterattack in self-defence, retaking the lost territory in Guangdong and Guangxi and advancing to Fuliang River (modern Red River) which was 30 *li* from the Vietnamese capital. Upon defeat, the Vietnamese army was forced to conduct peace negotiation, after which the Song army withdrew from Vietnam.

The losses inflicted upon the peoples of both countries by war went without saying. However, once the conflict ended, the Vietnamese side often send envoys to apologize and earnestly request recognition, leading to the restoration of normal relations between the two countries.

IV. A Brief Statement on the Contemporary Sino-Vietnamese Relation

In the later period of the 16th century, the western colonists successively embarked on their invasion in Vietnam. At the end of the 18th century, Bishop Pedro of France had tried to assist Nguyễn Phúc Anh for reinstatement, harboring blatant ambition of aggression towards Vietnam. In 1858, France, in collaboration with Spain, formed a joint fleet and launched a colonial invasion of Vietnam. From that point on, Vietnamese history was cast into a period of eighty years of resistance against French colonialism.

Plagued by the invasion, oppression and exploitation of colonialism and imperialism, the peoples of China and Vietnam were inseparably bound up by their shared destiny, and fostering an enduring friendship with each other during their fight against imperial invasion for national liberation. Early in

1873 when the French colonists invaded Tonkin, The Black Flag Army led by Liu Yongfu of China had joined hands with civil and military forces of Vietnam to launch counterattack. In Cau Giay on the outskirts of Hanoi, the Black Flag Army had killed Garnier, the head of the French army, thereby dealing the French invaders a mighty blow. On April 29th, 1882, the French army captured Hanoi again. In May, the Black Flag Army maul heavily on the French army during yet another battle in Cầu Giấy, killing Rivière, the ringleader of the invasive force, marking remarkable achievements in battle. However, the invaders shifted their assault on the Vietnamese capital Huế, forcing the Nguyễn court to bow and surrender. Eventually, the Nguyễn court signed the Treaty of Huế in 1883 and accepted the French "protection" in Vietnam.

The purpose of the French colonists was not restricted to the encroachment on Vietnam, but also to further infringe on South China. After occupying Tonkin, they posed direct threat to the security of South China, sparking the Sino-French War in 1884. During China's fight against aggression, Feng Zicai, a general from Guangxi, utterly defeated the French force. When the news of defeat reached Paris, the cabinet of Jules Ferry of France collapsed as a result. Nonetheless, the incompetent Qing government engaged in negotiations with France in Tianjin and signed *the Treaty of Tientsin* in June 1885, ending the "tributary relationship" between the Chinese feudal dynasty and Vietnam. Since then, Vietnam had been reduced to a colony of France.

From the day of the French invasion of Vietnamese territory, the struggle of the Vietnamese people against French colonialism had never ceased. And these struggles had consistently received sympathy and support from the Chinese people. At the beginning of the 20th century, with the development of the capitalist factors in the Vietnamese society, some enlightened intellects appeared among the scholar-officials of Vietnam -

with Phan Boi Chau and Phan Chau Trinh as their representatives. In 1904, Phan Boi Chau created "Vietnam Modernization Association" with the tenet of "restoring Vietnam and establishing independent government". In order to strive for foreign aid and emulate the Meiji Restoration of Japan, Phan also founded "journey to the east" that encouraged oversea study in Japan. In Japan, Phan got acquainted with Liang Qichao and met with Sun Yat-sen, both of whom exerted huge influence on him. After the outbreak of the Xinhai Revolution of China in 1911, Guangzhou had gradually become the overseas base of the Vietnamese revolution. In 1912, Phan Boi Chau convened Vietnamese patriots for a meeting in Liu Yongfu's house in Guangzhou, establishing the "Restoration League of Vietnam" and organizing the "Restoration Army" to fight for the banishment of French imperialism, the restoration of Vietnam and establishment of the Republic of Vietnam.

Since the victory of the great October Revolution in 1917, Vietnam's struggle against the French invasion had entered a new phase of proletarian party. In 1921, Nguyễn Ái Quốc (aka. Hồ Chí Minh) joined the French Communist Party. In 1925, Quoc created the "Vietnamese Revolutionary Youth League" in Guangzhou, the origin of revolution in China, and organized the "League of Communists" as the core of this mass organization, making the ideological and institutional preparation for the establishment of the communist party in Vietnam. On February 3rd, 1930, Hồ Chí Minh held a meeting in Hong Kong, merging three dispersive communist organizations in Vietnam into the unified Vietnamese Communist Party. In October of the same year, the First Assembly of the Central Committee of the Communist Party of Vietnam was held, during which the *Political Theses* was adopted as the guiding principle for the party in the stage of the bourgeois-democratic revolution, with the party renamed the Indochinese Communist Party. Upon its establishment, the party led the extensive and in-depth revolutionary movement of workers and peasants from south to north Vietnam.

From the 1930s to 1945 before the independence of Vietnam, a cohort of Vietnamese revolutionists carrying on their revolutionary activities in China acquired the support and assistance from both the Chinese Communist Party and the Chinese people in various aspects. Regions like Guangxi and Yunnan bordering Vietnam had become the base of their activities that laid the foundation for Vietnamese revolution. As early as the late 1920s, a cadre of Vietnamese revolutionaries, including Hoàng Văn Thụ, were active in Longzhou, Guangxi. In the 1930s, Hoàng Văn Thụ, Hoàng Văn Hoan, Trường Chinh, Hoàng Quốc Việt, Chu Văn Tấn and others were also active in Longzhou. The border inhabitants provided them with food, accommodation, transportation and liaison, helping them to purchase firearms, ammunition and other resources, as well as ensuring their safety. There were many Vietnamese expatriates in Yunnan. In 1935, the Communist Party of Vietnam established a party organization among the expatriates, followed by the formation of the "Yunnan-Guizhou Branch." During China's fight against the Japanese aggression, Hồ Chí Minh, the prominent leader of Vietnam, carried out revolutionary activities in China together with some other revolutionists. In 1938, Ho arrived in Yan'an through Xinjiang and Xi'an from the Soviet Union. He had followed Comrade Ye Jianying once and been active as a soldier of the Eighth Route Army. In February 1940, Hồ reached Kunming and assembled with Fung Chi-kin, Võ Anh, Hoàng Văn Hoan and others of the overseas branch of Vietnamese Communist Party. There, Hồ gave detailed instruction on the activities of the party and held training classes to cultivate backbones of revolution. In February, 1941, Hồ Chí Minh returned to Pác Bó, Vietnam from Jingxi, directly leading the Vietnamese revolution. In May, under the leadership of Hồ, the eighth Assembly of the Central Committee of the Vietnamese Communist Party was held, and the united front organization the "League for Independence of

Vietnam" (Việt Minh) was established to unite the people of the nation, carry out armed struggle, and seize national power. Hồ was once captured in Guangxi and wrote the renowned *The Prison Diary* during his imprisonment, and was back in Vietnam after being released. At that time, the French troops, who had already surrendered to the Japanese, periodically conducted sweeps in the Sino-Vietnamese border region, brutally suppressing the revolutionary masses in Vietnam. To ensure Hồ's safety, the underground organization of the CPC in the border region of Guangxi brought him to live with a poor peasant family in Pingmeng Town, Napo County, in August 1944. It was there that Hồ wrote a great deal of important instructions which were sent back to Vietnam as the guide for revolutionary fights.

China and Vietnam had supported each other throughout their revolutionary struggle, which means the Chinese revolution was also backed by the Vietnamese people. During China's fight against the Japanese invasion, the Communist Party organization of Vietnam in Yunnan actively mobilized Vietnamese expatriates to support China's resistance, establishing the "Rearguard Committee of Vietnamese People's Support for China's Anti-Japanese Fight," abbreviated as "Anti-Japanese Committee." The "Anti-Japanese Committee" once organized a strike by Vietnamese expatriate railway workers, forcing the Yunnan Railway Company to transport supplies for the anti-Japanese power of China. On September 2nd, 1945, the Democratic Republic of Vietnam was established upon the triumph of the "August Revolution" in Vietnam. Consequently, the Chinese people, who were engaged in the liberation war, received support from the Vietnamese people. The Communist Party organizations and revolutionary armed forces in the border regions of China regarded Vietnam as their rear base, frequenting Vietnam to carry out revolutionary activities. Besides, quite a few Vietnamese comrades directly participated in the revolutionary struggle of the Chinese people.

Immediately after the establishment of the young Democratic Republic of Vietnam, French colonialists returned in September, 1945, attempting to restore their colonial rule, which forced the Vietnamese people to engage in an arduous and desperate war against the French. To this, the Chinese people showed extreme sympathy and provided substantial support.

In 1949, the People's Republic of China was established, entering into a new era of the Sino-Vietnamese relations. On January 18th, 1950, the diplomatic relations between China and Vietnam were fully established. Thus China became the first country in the world to acknowledge the Democratic Republic of Vietnam. This day was designated by the Vietnamese government as a day of diplomatic victory. Since then, over a very long period of time, the relations between the two countries and the traditional friendship between their peoples saw all-round and unprecedented development under the leadership of the Communist Parties of the two countries and on the basis of proletarian internationalism. As is put by President Hồ Chí Minh, "The deep friendship between China and Vietnam are as comrades and brothers."

In the difficult circumstances of a newly founded nation facing numerous challenges, the Chinese government and its people still provided substantial and selfless assistance to Vietnam in its war of resistance against French colonialism. During Vietnam's war against the French invasion, China was the only country providing military assistance to Vietnam. The weapons, ammunition and military supplies of Vietnam were all furnished by China. The Central Committee of the CPC had dispatched Comrade Chen Geng to Vietnam to assist in training cadres and organizing command, which resulted in the victory of the border campaign. This opened several major transportation routes along the China-Vietnam border, linking the liberated areas of northern Vietnam with China, allowing for a continuous flow of large quantities of aid materials from China to the front lines in Vietnam. Also, the

Committee sent military counsels led by Comrade Wei Guoqing to provide long-term assistance for Vietnam to fight against the French invasion. Besides, a political advisory group was dispatched to assist Vietnam in work in the financial, economic and political sections, as well as helping the country to mobilize its masses. Chinese military advisors helped organize a series of battles, including the Central Plains Campaign and the Northeast Campaign, which eliminated the effective fighting force of the French Army. Among these battles, the decisive Battle of Điện Biên Phủ in 1954 is specially worth mentioning. From the determination to launch the attack on Điện Biên Phủ to the formulation of specific tactical guidelines, the organization and command of the battles were all carried out with the advice and assistance of the Chinese military advisory group, and all weapons, ammunition, food, and military supplies were provided by China. The impressive victory in Điện Biên Phủ forced France to sign on the ***Agreement on the Cessation of Hostilities in Indochina***, completely liberating the entire Northern Vietnam. It is no exaggeration that but for the substantial help provided by China, there was barely hope for Vietnam to succeed in its fight against the French invasion.

After peace restored in Indochina, Northern Vietnam embarked on its journey to economic and cultural development. During this period, the Chinese government and its people, amid their own economic difficulties, still provided huge and effective assistance to Vietnam according to its demand for revolution and construction. China helped Vietnam to forge the guidelines and course of economic recovery and development, supporting Vietnam notably in transportation recovery and improvement, water-control projects and agricultural production, funding the country at the same time. From 1955 to 1959, China donated a sum of 800 billion yuan together with some technology to assist in the construction of a number of industrial enterprises in Vietnam. Due to China's assistance coming from all aspects in enormous scale, it only cost Vietnam three years to triumph in its mission of economic recovery. Meanwhile, both countries maintained close exchanges and cooperation in economy, trade, culture and diplomacy.

While Northern Vietnam was peacefully restoring and building its society, the American imperialists, in the stead of French colonizers, ferociously stamped on *the Geneva Agreement* in Southern Vietnam, vigorously supporting a pro-American puppet regime, turning the region into a new type of American colony and military base. Hence the people in Southern Vietnam were forced to rise to opposition. On December 20th, 1960, National Liberation Front of South Vietnam was established, leading its people to fight against America and save their country. In 1961, the U.S. launched a "special war" commanded by American military advisors, with the Saigon puppet troops of South Vietnam serving as cannon fodder. After this failed, in August 1964, they fabricated the "Gulf of Tonkin incident", whence they began bombing and attacking North Vietnam. On March 8th, 1965, the United States Marine Corps (USMC) landed in Da Nang, escalating its invasive war against Vietnam to a "localized war" through direct military involvement. However, by fighting against the U.S. to save their country, the enduring Vietnamese people won the "localized war" and crushed the American policy of "Vietnamizing wars". On January 27th, 1973, the U.S. was forced to sign the *Paris Agreement* with the Saigon regime of South Vietnam, agreeing to end the war in Indochina and recover peace therein. Thus the U.S., along with its vassal countries, was forced to withdraw from South Vietnam, yet leaving a large quantity of military advisers. Nonetheless, under the connivance and support of the U.S., the Nguyễn Văn Thiệu regime in Saigon, South Vietnam, rampantly undermined the *Paris Agreement*, continuously encroaching on the liberated areas. Thus, the Vietnamese people rose up against them and launched a general attack in spring in March, 1975, liberating the entire South Vietnam on May 1st, which marked the victory in their war of national salvation against the U.S.

Just as they did during the Anti-French war in Vietnam, the Chinese government and its people provided enormous support to Vietnam during its fight against the U.S. for national salvation. The Chinese government and its leaders had loudly denounced the aggressive movement of the U.S. on many occasions and on behalf of the Chinese people, thereby significantly bolstering Vietnam's struggle against the U.S. for national salvation. "The 700 million Chinese people will be a strong support for the Vietnamese people, and the vast Chinese territory will be the reliable rear of them"; "the Chinese people will take every possible measure - even at any cost of the nation - to spare no effort to support the Vietnamese people throughout their combat against the U.S. for national salvation." The Chinese government and people were true to their word, delivering the most comprehensive, resolute, substantial, and effective assistance to Vietnam. In the first place, China admitted the National Liberation Front of South Vietnam. From 1962 to 1966, China supplied 270,000 firearms, over 5,400 artilleries and more than four million square meters of cloths of all kinds. Moreover, China had signed various aid agreements with North Vietnam. From June, 1965 to March, 1973, China sent over 320,000 support troops to Vietnam, including air defense, engineering, railway, and logistics units. Among them, tens of thousands sacrificed their precious lives or were injured and disabled on Vietnamese soil, forging a bond of militant friendship between the peoples of China and Vietnam with their blood. It was estimated that from 1950 to March, 1978, the total value of the supplies provided by China for Vietnam surpassed 20 billion dollars, topping all of the supplies from other countries. Among them, there were light and heavy weapons, ammunition, and other military supplies sufficient to equip over two million personnel across the Army, Navy, and Air Force, hundreds of production enterprises and repair factories, more than 300 million meters of fabric, over 30,000 vehicles, hundreds of kilometers of railway along with all tracks, locomotives, and carriages, more than five million tons of grain, over two million tons of gasoline, over 3,000 kilometers of oil pipelines, as well as foreign currency that China itself urgently needed. Notably, many military supplies were reassigned from Chinese troops, newly produced and not yet used by them, or even specially imported. Besides, many civilian supplies were diverted from domestic projects or provided by the Chinese people who still lived frugally to support Vietnam. Evidently, the Chinese people made tremendous national sacrifices for Vietnam's independence and liberation.

During the honeymoon of the Sino-Vietnamese relations, both countries were diplomatically in line with each other and maintained mutual support. Vietnam acknowledged that Taiwan is an inseparable part of the Chinese territory, and supported the restoration of China's legitimate seat in the United Nations; backed China in settling the revolt in Tibet and carrying out democratic reform, agreeing with China's position on the issue of the Sino-Indian boundary; condemned the encroachment of American military planes on the territorial air of China; supported China's diplomatic policy on friendly relations with neighboring countries; reiterated its acknowledgment of China's contribution to world peace, heartily congratulated China for its success in the test of atomic bomb and hydrogen bomb, and spoke highly of their significance in safeguarding world peace; promoted policies friendly to overseas Chinese in Vietnam; acknowledged that Xisha Qundao and Nansha Qundao are the territories of China, etc.

After winning the national salvation war against the U.S. and fulfilling the unification of North and South Vietnam, Vietnam held a national popular vote on April 25th, 1976 and established a unified congress, altering its name into the Socialist Republic of Vietnam. Unfortunately, incited by the then Soviet government, the Le Duan bloc in power diverted to the track of regional hegemonism, expressing hostility and opposition against China. In

December, 1978, Vietnam sent a troop of 200 thousand men for military aggression in Cambodia, domestically expelling and persecuting overseas Chinese at the same time with the slogan "all for the defeat of China". Due to Vietnam's unceasing provocations on the Sino-Vietnamese border and repeated encroachment on the Chinese territory, the Chinese border troops, beyond endurance, launched counter-attack for self-defence from February 17th to March 16th, 1979. However, after the withdrawal of the Chinese force, Vietnam proceeded its provocation and encroachment on the Sino-Vietnamese border. To defend its sacred territory, the Chinese army fought back again and restored Faka Mountain and Koulin Mountain on the border of Guangxi in 1981.Three years later, another battle was sparked for the restoration of strategic sites like Laoshan on the borderline of Yunnan.

From the 1970s, the sovereignty of Xisha Qundao and Nansha Qundao became the focus of the Sino-Vietnam relations. As a matter of fact, be it in the suzerain-vassal era or the French colonial period, Vietnam harbored no conception of intruding in South China Sea Islands, with but one French colonist Chabrier proposing in December, 1898 to set up a supply station for fishermen in "Paracel". Yet the French Governor-General Dounei believed that "this attempt will never work". Later, when the Nanko Enterprise of Japan sent a request letter about the exploitation of guano on Nansha Qundao, Remy, the Colonel of French Navy, still insisted in his reply on September, 24th, 1920, "There is not a single document in the files of the Navy that can decide the territorial entitlement of Paracel. But I can assure you that it does not belong to France." In Telegraph No. 569 to the Saigon Navy on January 23rd, 1921, the Paris Navy still asserted that "In 1909, the Chinese claimed their ownership of the Xisha Qundao. This is the only available information at present."

But on January 12th, 1929, Pasquier, the French Governor-General of Indochina, purported in a letter to the French Resident-Superior of Annam in

Huế, Annam that "the Annam government might have confirmed its sovereignty over this archipelago... They told me that the survey was going on, and that Annam will manage to establish its sovereignty over Paracel. Favorable evidence shall be sought for this purpose - and not a single trace of it shall be spared."

At this, the French Resident-Superior of Annam replied in his letter to the Governor-General of Indochina in Hanoi on January 22nd, 1929, that the director of the Research Institute of Marine Fisheries in Nha Trang had been studying this issue since 1926, acknowledging that "from then on, however, no new material had been found to resolve the issue of sovereignty in discussion." The Resident-Superior of Annam could do nothing but to restate the facts found in the past investigations. The following record was published in an article named "Additional Notice on the Geography of Cochinchina" in 1883 by Bishop Jean Louis Taberd, "In 1816, Emperor Gia Long went with solemnity to plant his flag and take formal possession of these rocks." In addition, Vietnamese historical records like *Dai Nam Comprehensive Encyclopaedia (Vol.6)*, and *the Geography of Annam, (Vol.2)* mention that "in the old dynasties, the Vĩnh An Society recruited a 70-man team to garrison Paracel, which was called the 'Hoàng Sa (Yellow Sand) Team.' Under this team, there was another one called the 'Bac Hai (North Sea) Team.' Gia Long had reorganized the garrison at Paracel but later canceled it. Since then, it seems there has been no establishment of garrison in Paracel again". "Gia Long repeatedly dispatched officials and teams to explore the archipelago (Paracel), one of which discovered a temple with Chinese characters. In 1835, the emperor sent workers to Paracel again for the transportation of various construction material, building towers, erecting monuments and leaving permanent marks. When digging for the foundations, they found various items in two thousand *jin*, including copper sheets, iron and wrought iron. This was an evident testimony of the occupation of this island." Even the Resident-Superior of Annam admitted that "Annam seems to have nothing to do with Paracel at present. The fishermen and ship owners in the coastal area of Annam know nothing about the existence of these island, let alone any soul having been there," and explicitly indicated that, "As a matter of fact, these islands are the natural extension of Hainan Island," with the signature "Fol" at the end of the statement.

In 1970s, relying on the alleged "evidences" coined by the French colonists above for the sake of invading in Xisha Qundao, Vietnam compiled four "white books" in the name of its Ministry of Foreign Affairs, including the *White Book About Hoàng Sa (Paracel) Islands and Trường Sa] (Spratly) Islands* published by the Ministry of Foreign Affairs of the Saigon regime on May, 1975; *Vietnam's Sovereignty over Hoàng Sa and Trường Sa Islands* published by the Ministry of Foreign Affairs of Vietnam on September 28thm 1979;*Hoàng Sa and Trường Sa Islands: the Territory of Vietnam* by the Ministry of Foreign Affairs of Vietnam on January 18th, 1982; along with *Hoàng Sa and Trường Sa Islands and the International Law* by the Ministry of Foreign Affairs of Vietnam in April, 1988. While widely spreading and promoting anti-China and China-phobic rhetoric, they also took the opportunity to occupy as many as 29 islands and reefs in Nansha Qundao, the largest number among all the claimant countries surrounding the South China Sea. In January 1974, the Saigon authorities of South Vietnam brazenly dispatched warships and aircraft to infringe upon China's territorial waters and airspace around Xisha Islands, forcibly occupying islands and injuring Chinese fishermen. The Chinese navy retaliated and regained control of Xisha Islands. Around New Year's Day in 1988, the Vietnamese navy attempted to forcibly and militarily occupy islands and reefs in the South China Sea. On March 14th, a battle broke out between the two sides at Chigua Jiao (Johnson South Reef). Consequently, the Chinese navy won the battle and restored six islands and reefs in Nansha Qundao, establishing standing garrison since then.

Section 3 The Brief History of the Sino-Philippines Relations

China and the Philippines face each other across the sea, and the two peoples have a long history of friendly exchanges. Records of friendly interactions between the peoples of China and the Philippines began to appear in ancient Chinese texts as early as the 10th century. According to *Song Shi (the History of Song)* and *Wenxian Tongkao (Comprehensive Examination of Literature)*, in the seventh year of Taipingxingguo era of the Song Dynasty (AD 982), a merchant from an ancient Philippines state called Mait "carried treasure goods to Guangzhou" for trade with China. This is the earliest historical account about the trade between China and the Philippines. In fact, the large number of Chinese cultural relics excavated on the islands of the Philippines, including coins and porcelains from the Tang Dynasty, is a good indicator of the close trading relations between China and the Philippines by the Tang Dynasty (7th to 9th century) at the latest. Statistics show that there are as many as 200 sites in the Philippines where ancient Chinese porcelain has been unearthed, with over 20 sites specifically yielding Tang Dynasty porcelain, most of which are located along the western coast of the Philippines. During the Song, Yuan, Ming dynasties, there were an ever-increasing amount of porcelain being imported to the Philippines. From 1950s to 1960s alone, Chinese ancient porcelain found in the Philippines was no fewer than 40 thousand pieces, originating from provinces like Fujian, Guangdong, Jiangxi and Hubei in various categories. Currently, the Philippine museums and private collectors hold tens of thousands of ancient porcelain and ceramic pieces, of which 80% were produced in China The earliest pieces date back to the mid-Tang Dynasty, the latest to the early Qing Dynasty, with the majority from the Ming Dynasty. Thus, it can be seen that the time when the Chinese merchant traded in the Philippines was about 800 years earlier than that of the establishment of the Spanish colonial rule therein. Therefore, some historians propose that the historical period of the Philippines before the Spanish rule, i.e. from the 8th to 16th century, should be designated as the Age of Porcelain. The Philippines cherish Chinese porcelain a lot, using it not only in their daily life as domestic ornament, but also in activities like marriage, funeral, ceremonies and religious events.

During the Tang Dynasty, the maritime route in the South China Sea, known as "Guangzhou Tonghai Yidao" served as a channel for exchanges between China and the Philippines. After the Song Dynasty, the maritime route between Quanzhou, Fujian Province and the Philippines was opened, which greatly shortened the voyage between the two countries. Compared with the past, Chinese merchants conducted more trade in the Philippines in large sailing boat, heading south during winter and spring by the northeastern monsoon, and returning by southwestern monsoon before the typhoon season in summer, making this round trip once a year. Before the Spanish rule in the Philippines when there were divisions among the Filipino tribes, the Chinese merchants visited and traded with those tribes one after another, spending a total of three to four months in the Philippines. At that time, there was no coin but barter trade, they carried with them some Chinese products to exchange for Philippine specialties before they returned north. Chinese products popular among the Philippines included porcelain, pottery, silk and cotton textures, ironware, bronze ware, pewter ware, tripod stove, fishing net, plumment, and five-colored glass beads. While the Philippine specialties brought back by the Chinese merchants included pearls, gems, shells, ceiba, Areca triandra, and coconut pulp. The trade between China and the Philippines at that time was restricted to the coastal area of the Philippines where there were chiefs of tribes in various parts. They were gifted porcelain, textiles, and other items to maintain good relations. The chiefs, seeing the economic benefits brought the Chinese, did their utmost to provide protection.

Whenever the Chinese merchants arrived at a tribe and anchored their ship a considerable distance from the shore, the Philippines would carry some specialties for trade in their boats. Later, some of those Chinese merchants set up stalls on shore with their goods and traded with the Philippines, and gradually converting their temporary stalls into constant shops. When returning, any unsold goods were stored in the shop, and some merchants would remain behind to continue trading when the ship headed north.

In the Ming Dynasty, the friendly relationship between China and the Philippines developed further, with envoys dispatched by both sides for mutual visits. From the Hongwu years at the beginning of the Ming Dynasty to the Yongle era (AD 1368-1424), the relations between both countries remained considerably friendly. In the third year of Yongle era (AD 1405), the Ming court sent an embassy to Luzon. At the end of July in 1417, the leader of the Sultanate of Sulu (an ancient state of the Philippines) led a large embassy with over 340 people for a visit in China, carrying a huge number of gifts and staying in Beijing for 27 days. The Ming court returned lavishly to every one of the Philippine foreign missions, dispatching officials for escort on their way back. During their return voyage, East King of Sulu died for serious illness and was buried in Dezhou, Shandong Province, where his descendants are still living around this region up to now.

The Ming Dynasty had dispatched envoys to various countries in the Philippine Archipelago many times. During Zheng He's Seven voyages to the western seas from AD 1405-1433, the Ming court sent officials to visit the Philippines three times and was friendly received by the country. The envoy exchange prominently promoted the development of trade between the two countries, enabling the Chinese merchant ships to sail directly to places like Luzon, Pangasinan, Sulu Archipelago. Between 1571 and 1580, the number of Chinese merchant ships sailing to the Philippines surged from three or four per year to thirty to forty, continuing into the 17th century. These sailing ships, each with a carrying capacity of 100-300 tons, carried Chinese items like farm animals, farm implements, porcelain and pottery wares, bronze wares, iron wares, coins, silk and cloths to the Philippines, and importing yellow wax, pearls and condiments from the Philippines to China.

With trade flourishing, there were an ever-increasing number of Chinese merchants staying in the Philippines. Some of them went all the way to the Philippines for a living and lived there for generations. By the beginning of the 17th century, when the Spanish rule was established in the Philippines for only 30 years, there were already 30,000 overseas Chinese inhabiting Parian (an overseas Chinese zone designated by Spain) in Manila. There are two major reasons for the relatively large population of overseas Chinese in this place: above all, due to the domestic chaos at the end of the Ming Dynasty and the beginning of the Qing Dynasty, an increasing number of coastal residents in Fujian ventured abroad for a living. The Philippines, located only across the sea, is relatively close to Fujian, hence the rising amount of arrivals there. The second reason was the proliferation of Chinese products in the Philippines. Before the Spanish rule in the Philippines, the Chinese merchants conducted trade with the Philippine residents by exchanging goods. Owing to the limited amount of Philippine specialties, the sales of Chinese goods were greatly restricted.   While the arrival of the Spaniards gave a boost to Chinese goods, which was resulted by the following reasons: First, the Spaniards arriving in the Philippines were all financially capable, while the products produced in the Philippines could not meet their needs. Chinese goods, especially porcelain and silk, were highly favored by the Spaniards, who purchased them in large quantities and transported them to Mexico for sale on colossal sailing ships. Second, Mexico produced a large amount of silver, with about 300,000 pesos shipped to the Philippines each year as a medium for trade. Most of these silver coins were collected by Chinese merchants and transported back to China.   Before World War I, these pesos were widely used in markets along the Chinese coast.

Apart from merchants, there were an army of Chinese carpenters, masons, blacksmiths coming to work in the Philippines. Since the local workers in the Philippines failed to meet the Spaniards' demands for skilled labor, the latter brought in a large number of Chinese laborers, which was one of the reasons for the rapid increase of Chinese people in the Philippines during this period.

The advent of the Chinese in the Philippines prospered the local economy and satisfied the needs of the Spaniards. But as the Spaniards were outnumbered by overseas Chinese by many times, the colonial authorities deemed it a hindrance to their rule. Worse still, it was impossible for the Spanish merchants to compete with overseas Chinese who had almost controlled all of the local bazaars. Therefore, the Spanish ruler began to adopt racial discrimination policy towards overseas Chinese, going so far as to persecute and massacre those people. During the 327 years of Spanish rule in the Philippines between 1571 to 1898, a total of five massive massacres were imposed on the overseas Chinese therein.

In the later period of Spanish rule, the authorities encouraged intermarriage between Chinese and Filipinos to strengthen their control. The Spanish rulers did not manage to assimilate overseas Chinese through religious methods, but found it easier to do so among the Mestizo. After adopting Catholicism, the Filipinos were more easily loyal to Spanish rule. When the Spanish rulers massacred the Chinese immigrants, many Chinese-Filipinos stood by and even sided with the Spanish authorities. In 1979, Chinese-Filipino accounted for about one fifth of the total population of 44 million in the Philippines.

The turmoil in China caused by the Opium Wars led to a significant increase in the number of Chinese immigrants to the Philippines after the mid-19th century. During this period, the Chinese population in the Philippines was about 10,000, which rose to 90,000 by 1898 (the end of the 19th century). Overseas Chinese in the Philippines tended to center around Manila, with more than a half of them crowding the Parian. After the mid-19th century, they spread all over the Philippines, with the majority of them engaging in business, providing various kinds of food and daily necessities to urban and rural residents. While a considerable part of them worked as craftsmen like tailors and masons, still quite a few of them entered into agricultural, animal husbandry and fishery industries, all closely related to the daily life of the Philippine people.

Statistics from 1991 showed that there were 151 thousand overseas Chinese and 1.1 million ethnic Chinese in the Philippines, totaling 1.251 million people. The trade and cultural exchanges between China and the Philippines in the history, as well as the influx of ethnic Chinese into the Philippines, have exerted profound and proactive influence on the social, economic and cultural development in the Philippines. The overseas Chinese arriving in the Philippines in early times had brought into the country some techniques regarding agriculture, gardening, iron casting, ceramic making, jewelry processing, gunpowder preparation, civil construction, weaving, paper-making and painting. Until the 19th century, the Philippines still plowed with Chinese-style ploughs. The overseas Chinese also brought grafting techniques for fruit trees and methods of sugar production from sugarcane, along with sugar-making tools. In some regions of the Philippines, these sugar-making tools are still used under their original Chinese names.

China's impact on the Philippines is also reflected in language, writing, social life, and customs, even including the impact of the mixed-race children from intermarriages between Filipinos and Chinese on the development of Philippine identity and society.

The Philippine historian Alip pointed out in his *Philippine Political and Cultural History* that the Philippine people had benefited from the business, social and political tie between China and the Philippines in more ways than one. It was through this tie that the Philippine people learned about porcelain manufacture, metallurgy and mine exploitation, even adopting loose-fitting clothes as well as some business-related and economic terms, with 521 words in this field originating from China indeed. Manuel, a linguist from University of the Philippines, listed 381 words from Chinese in his book *The Chinese Components in Tagalog.*

In their social life, the Philippine people drew on and imitated the Chinese ethical ideas like revering parents and the elderly as well as the custom for the siblings to call each other according to their sexuality and ages, maintaining them for hundreds of years before gradually altering them in modern times.

In the Philippines, there are quite a number of mixed-race children born to Chinese fathers and indigenous mothers, and their descendants are also considered to be of mixed-race Chinese. Those who marry Chinese individuals or mixed-race persons, the mixed-race children they have, as well as their descendants, are all registered as mixed-race Chinese.

In 1850, there were 240,000 mixed-race Chinese in the Philippines, with the indigenous population rising to above four million. In six provinces, mixed-race Chinese accounted for over one-third of the overall local population. At the end of the 19th century, there were approximately five million mixed-race Chinese, with 46 thousand of them living in Manila.

As is noted by the Chinese-Filipino historian Chen Shouguo in his book *Mixed-race Chinese and the Formation of the Philippine Nation*, it is imperative to take into considerations the contribution of mixed-race Chinese to the development of the Filipino nation; otherwise, the understanding of the recorded history of contemporary Philippine society will be incomplete.

After the Philippines being reduced to a colony, mixed-race Chinese held a social status far more important than mixed-race Spaniards. In addition to their larger numbers, mixed-race Chinese took delight in assimilating into local social organizations, playing more significant roles in the economic and social life of the Philippines. By the latter half of the 19th century, their considerable population and influence led the Spanish in the Philippines to commonly refer to them as "Mestizo".

From 1850s to 1950s, the growth of mixed-race Chinese entrepreneurs paved the way for the development of the middleclass in the Philippines. Inheriting the economic activities from their Chinese ancestors, those mixed-race entrepreneurs were more motivated, enterprising, prudent and initiative, thus more adaptable to trade and business.

The increase of financial wealth was a tremendous booster of the living standard and social status of the mixed-race Chinese, who in turn stood better chance of opening the door to higher education for their children. In 1970s, those middle-class families were capable of sending their children to Manila, Spain, France, England, Austria, Germany and developed European countries alike for education. The middle-class individuals among the mixed-race Chinese, despite their modest population, were well-educated; combined with their financial wealth and social reputation, they were not only prone to dominate the development of local economy and society, but had also witnessed the leap of some members to be celebrities, holding prominent positions at the highest levels of government.

As a vital element of development, mixed-race Chinese had played significant roles in many ways like the formation of the middle-class in the Philippines, the encouragement of reformation, the 1898 Revolution, as well as the formation of the present Philippine nation. Even to the modern days, they are still playing major parts in the national construction of the Philippines.

Section 4 A Brief History of the Sino-Malaysian Relations

Situated in the middle of Southeast Asia, Malaysia is south of countries like Thailand, Myanmar, Vietnam and Cambodia, facing the Philippines to its northeast and Indonesia to its south and southwest across the sea. Being well located, it has become the gateway of business and tourism for immigrants. Chinese travelers to Indonesia or Myanmar usually pass through Malaysia. Ancient Arab and Indian traders traveling to China and Southeast Asia also had to go through Malaysia. With navigation highly developed today, the Malacca Strait is still the channel for the exchange between the Indian Ocean and the Pacific Ocean.

Due to its crucial location, Malaysia has not only been an immigration port since ancient times, but a focus of conflicts between multiple political powers.

Archeological materials reveal that the Malay Peninsula had been inhabited as early as ten thousand years ago, witnessing the Paleolithic and Neolithic ages of the primitive society as well as the Bronze and Iron ages of the hierarchical society. At the beginning of the 2nd century, ancient states like Langkasuka and Kedah were established on the Malay Peninsula. In the 6th century, Langkasuka became a major power in the north of the peninsula. Many Indian merchants arrived in Kedah for trading, when the region was deeply affected by the Buddhist culture from India. At the end of the 6th century and the beginning of the 7th century, Kedah broke away from Langkasuka as an independent state, Thriving in business at that time, Kedah was the trading hub of items like agarwood, camphor, santal, ivory and tin. Between the 9th and the 10th century, Sri Vijaya) gained Kedah as a vassal. As Sri Vijaya went downhill since the 12th century, the northern part of the Malay Peninsula was dominated by Siam. At the end of the 14th century,

Majapahit conquered Sri Vijaya, dominating the Malay Peninsula while controlling the Malacca Strait. In 1402, Parameswara founded the Malacca Sultanate (AD 1402-1511, formerly known as "Manlajia" in Chinese, with Malacca as its capital), the first ever feudal kingdom embracing Islam in Malaysian history. Since the occupation of Malacca by the Portuguese colonists since 1511, the king of Malacca led his people to retreat to the inland area for long-term resistance, and founded Johor Sultanate. From then on, Malaysia fell into a period of colonial rule, with Portuguese dominance lasting for over 100 years. In 1641, the Dutch colonists defeated the Portuguese army and began their colonial rule in Malacca. In 1771, British colonizers began their invasion of Penang and gradually brought the various states of Malaysia under their rule, establishing the Straits Settlements in 1826 and then directly administering them as British colonies in 1867. In 1914, the United Kingdom converted its possessions in Malaysia into Unfederated Malay States. Under this historical condition, the Malaysian people underwent uphill battles against the British colonial rule for a long time, and going through unswerving war against Japanese invasion during World War II. After the end of World War II, the Federation of Malaysia officially gained independence on August 31, 1957, and officially announced its establishment on September 16th, 1963. (In August, 1965, Singapore announced its exit from the federation and became an independent country.)

Since the ancient times, China and Malaysia have been closely related to each other. Early in the Neolithic Age, stepped stone adzes, originated from Guangdong and Fujian, had been brought to Malaysia. It is recorded in *the Book of Han: Treatise on Geography* that Chinese ships arrived in countries like Pisang, Duyuan and the Pagan Kingd. Historical records have it that during the Southern Liang dynasty, Langkasuka dispatched envoys to China for four times; while in the second year of the reign of Emperor Gaozong of the Tang Dynasty (AD 671), the monk Yijing traveled through Langkasuka on his journey to India to obtain Buddhist scriptures. On the other hand, the Malacca Sultanate (AD 1402-1511) had sent envoys to China a total of 30 time, five of which were led by the Sultan himself. Since Yin Qing's visit to Malacca in 1403, the Ming court had dispatched envoys to Malacca for 14 times. Thus, both countries had conducted high-level exchanges in terms of production technology and materials. Meanwhile, there were overseas Chinese migrating to Malaysia. In West Malaysia, Malays make up 53% and Chinese account for 35.6%; in Sarawak, the Chinese also make up 30.1%. Such a concentration of Chinese people is rarely seen in places other than Singapore.

The Tang Dynasty marked the height of China's national power. With China's advancement in ship-building technology and navigation expertise, there were an increasing number of people sailing to Nanyang (Southeast Asia) for business, giving rise to the title of "Tangshan" and "Tangren" at that time. Chinese merchants trading here exchanged Chinese products for Malaysian specialties. Finishing the exchange, they would immediately returned north by sea, seldom living there.

The shipbuilding technology during the Song Dynasty showed significant advancements compared to the Tang Dynasty. Due to the development of overseas trade, which could increase tax revenue, the government encouraged merchants to engage in international trade, leading to a more developed foreign trade system with an increased number of vessels. Shibosi (maritime trade bureau), initiated in the Tang Dynasty, was designated in ports like Guangzhou, Quanzhou, Ningbo and Hangzhou. Among those regions, Guangzhou and Quanzhou boasted the most developed foreign trade and the greatest amount of vessel entry and exit. Moreover, the number of overseas Chinese from Guangdong and Fujian who settled in Nanyang (Southeast Asia) via Guangzhou and Quanzhou was also quite substantial. At that time, Sri Vijaya, the largest kingdom in Malaysia, paid regular tribute to and was tightly knit with China. After the annihilation of the Southern Song by Yuan, a fleet of Chinese residents fled abroad, part of which arriving in Malaysia.

The Yuan Dynasty attached great importance to foreign trade, with more shibosi (maritime trade bureau) set up than before. During that period, Quanzhou proved to be the busiest and the most significant port for foreign trade in China. Due to the government's encouragement of foreign trade, merchants found it profitable to engage in barter trade abroad, leading to an increase in maritime trade compared to before. During the early period of Zhizheng era of Emperor Shun's reign in the Yuan Dynasty (AD 1341-1349), Wang Dayuan sailed abroad passing a couple of countries, after which he composed the book *Dao Yi Zhi Lüe (A Brief Account of the Islands)*. Many places mentioned in the book locate exactly in present-day Malay Peninsula, including Tambralinga (Kuantan), Pengkeng (Pahang), Dingjialu (Terengganu), Kelantan, Temasek (Singapore) and Dongxizhu (Johor).

At the beginning of the Ming Dynasty, the Malay Peninsula was actually under the domain of the Malacca Sultanate centered on Malacca. Boasting a superior location, Malacca had been a vital station during Zheng He's seven voyages into the Western Seas. Legend has it that the residents of Malacca lived on water in wooden houses on stilts with inconvenient transportation, for which Zheng He taught the local aboriginals to move to the land and learn farming. Furthermore, due to the lack of water on land, he also taught them the method of digging wells to obtain water. Evidence shows that Zheng He's fleet had docked in the port of Malacca five times, stationing his command in this place as well. The present-day Bukit China in the suburb of Malacca is exactly a place where Zheng He had once stationed his troop. And the Well of Perigi Raja at the foot of the hill was said to be the earliest well in Singapore and Malaysia. To provide water for his troop, Zheng He had dug dozens of wells in Bukit China, with only two left to this day. In 1795, Poh

San Teng Temple was built beside the Well of Perigi Raja. In the courtyard of the Temple, a stone statue of Zheng He, about one meter in height, was erected in memorial of him.

Malacca is not only the capital of the Malacca Sultanate, but the hub of trade in Nanyang (Southeast Asia) as well. Chinese merchants would set sail from Quanzhou Port during the autumn and winter seasons, using the northeast monsoon to travel south, carrying Chinese products such as porcelain, silk, cotton textiles, and metal goods to Malacca in exchange for Southeast Asian products like pearls, glass, unusual stones, spices, and medicinal herbs. Then, during the summer, they would return north with the southwest monsoon. Apart from the Chinese merchants coming and going by sea, the overseas Chinese settling down in Malacca were also on the rise, constituting the merchant class of the local society. At Zheng He's arrival in Malacca, there had already been a great number of overseas Chinese living in the region. Most of them came from Fujian, with the buildings in their cities all characterized by Chinese-style bungalows, resembling those in Quanzhou or Zhangzhou in Fujian.

The Malacca Sultanate was closely related to the Ming Dynasty, revering the latter as its suzerain, receiving titles from and paying tribute every year to it as well. Additionally, other small countries like Pahang and Kelantan in the Malay Peninsula also paid tribute to China, during which there were officials and members of the imperial households were dispatched as envoys, with the kings themselves appearing in the embassy at times. The close relations between the Malacca Sultanate and the Ming court both stepped up the trade between the two countries, and increased the overseas Chinese residing in Malacca on a yearly basis, who in turn transplanting the Chinese customs in the local area.

During the Portuguese occupation of Malacca for over 130 years, the monopoly policy and ferocious taxation imposed by the Portuguese government cast Malacca into dramatic economic decline, thereby discouraging Chinese merchant ships to Malacca. As a result, the population of Chinese residents in Malacca plummeted instead of rising.

After replacing Portugal as the colonizer in Malaysia, Netherlands retained the policy of monopoly, bringing about little change in the economy of the overseas Chinese. Later, discovering the overseas Chinese's hardworking nature and skillfulness in business, which was beneficial for local development and economic prosperity, the Dutch shifted to a policy of attracting overseas Chinese, leading to an increase in their numbers and new developments in urban construction.

Since the decline of Malacca, the port of Pattani had replaced China as the trade partner of the peninsula of Malacca. In 1786, the United Kingdom took control of Penang and opened up the business of this island. After that, Malacca was soon eclipsed in terms of its business significance, with the number of Chinese merchants plunging in the region.

Taking Malacca from the Dutch in 1825, the United Kingdom implemented a policy of free trade, advocated exploitation and leveraged the power of overseas Chinese for the development of Malaysia. When the Chinese came to Malaysia seeking a livelihood, they found the society relatively stable with opportunities for development, leading to a significant increase in the number of immigrants. The number of Chinese in Malaysia grew to 6882 in 1842, reaching 10,608 in 1852 - up from a thousand or so at the beginning - which registered an unprecedented speed of population growth. Taking Penang Island as the sole example, it was nothing more than a desert island with not more than a hundred residents when it was taken by the United Kingdom. The British authorities encouraged the Chinese to reclaim the desert island, boosting the population to 12 thousand people, 40% of whom were overseas Chinese. The majority of those overseas Chinese engaged in business or worked as craftsmen like carpenters, plasterers or metal workers, transforming Penang from a desert island to a prosperous city. Apart from conducting business in ports like Malacca, Penang and the later developed Singapore, overseas Chinese also entered into the inland regions of Malaysia and participated in business, agricultural and mineral sectors.

The Chinese has contributed significantly to the development of economy and culture of Malaysia. They brought new mining technology of tin to the country, thereby promoting the development of the local tin-mining industry. In terms of agricultural development, overseas Chinese brought in Chinese foods, crops and vegetables, meanwhile promoting the advanced farming methods of farmers in southern China. Moreover, industries like sugar-making, brewing and brick-making were also operated by Chinese in the first place.   By connecting with the local Malays, overseas Chinese had played a major part in improving the living standards of the local people. The Chinese silk has greatly improved the clothing of the local residents, with Chinese porcelain exerting even larger influence on their lifestyle. Before the import of Chinese porcelain, the locals in Malaysia still used banana leaves as plates and coconut shells as cups and bowls. Those tableware, fortunately, were converted after Chinese porcelain was brought in by the Chinese merchants. The locals placed great importance on porcelain, associating it with activities such as ancestor worship and wedding and funeral ceremonies, and traces of porcelain can be seen in temples and graves. Many vegetables were also introduced from China; even today, many vegetables and foods in Malaysia still retain their Chinese names.

In the early days, overseas Chinese would always transfer their own culture to wherever they went by establishing schools, building Buddhist or Taoist temples, and setting up temples for Guanyu, Dabogong and Mazu. They also founded clan organizations and halls to worship their ancestors.

Currently, the Chinese accounts for 32% of the total population of Malaysia, who have their own political parties and schools, and enjoy the basic human rights to use their mother tongue and reserve their own culture, religions and customs. In the multinational society of Malaysia, the local Chinese retain their cultural features, which has acted a major role in the modernized development of the society and economy in Malaysia.

Politically, the Malaysian government allows the existence of three Chinese political parties: the Malaysian Chinese Association, the Malaysian People's Movement Party, and the Democratic Action Party, which occupy certain quotas in the composition of the government cabinet. Among them, the Democratic Action Party is an opposition party. In the Chinese-dominated Penang state, the administrative head is sometimes held by a Chinese.

In culture and education, the Malaysian government accepts the cultural and educational policy of the Chinese people, regarding Confucian, Islamic and Christian cultures as the three major cultures in the world that should be highly valued. Also, the local government believes that the diverse culture in Malaysia can strengthen the country. In 1994, with the encouragement of the Malaysian government, some Malaysian scholars translated into Malaysian some ancient Chinese books like *Daxue (The Great Learning)*, *Zhongyong (The Doctrine of the Mean)* and *Tao Te Ching*. Meanwhile, the local government adopted an opening policy towards Chinese education, allowing students from countries like Malaysia and India to study in Chinese elementary or middle schools, which in turn boosted the development of overseas Chinese education.

Section 5 A Brief History of the Sino-Bruneian Relations

Brunei has maintained a time-honored connection with China, with political exchanges between both countries in the Southern and Northern Dynasties at the latest. At that time, Brunei was still referred to as "Poli" in the Chinese historical records. In AD 473, Poli dispatched envoys to pay tribute to the Liu Song dynasty, which might well be the earliest tribute paid by the envoys of Poli in the records of ancient Chinese historical accounts. In the Liang dynasty, the political relations between China and Poli was further strengthened. Specifically, Poli paid tribute to the Liang court three times - in AD 511, 517 and 522 respectively. The tributary objects in the third tribute included dozens of native products like white parrots, caterpillars, ancient helmets, glass wares, cotton, gastropod shell goblets and miscellaneous herbs. In just over a decade, Poli had paid tribute to the Liang court three times, indicating a rather close relationship between the two countries. It was a time when Poli boasted vigorous national strength and the Southern China was in a relatively stable situation in the Southern and Northern Dynasties, featuring more developed handicraft industry, business and foreign trade than the previous dynasties.

However, after the third year of Putong era in the Liang dynasty (AD 522), the relations between the two countries experienced a stagnation for a time, with the two sides recovering their official relations until the third year of Daye in the Sui Dynasty (AD 607). In the 12th year of Daye in the Sui Dynasty (AD 616), Poli sent envoys to pay tribute to the Sui court.

The communications between the two peoples and governments entered a new phase. In the fourth year of Zhen'guan in the Tang Dynasty (AD 630), Poli dispatched envoys to pay tribute to the Tang court, receiving a warm welcome from the Tang court, where the great painter Yan Liben personally created portraits for them. This was the only political interactions between the two countries found in the chronicles, a consequence of Poli's submission to the newly risen Sri Vijaya, which led to a breakdown in political relations between China and Poli. Nonetheless, the economic ties and non-governmental exchanges between China and Poli were unaffected. Archeological evidence showed that the estuarine delta region of Sarawak was proved to be a famous international port as well as a nucleus of small retailers. This was also a region where merchants from China and Arab conducted business and other productive activities. The Chinese merchants brought ceramic products like bowls, plates, bottles, large jars, together with objects like glass beads, stonewares, iron wares, gold wares and coins, to exchange for native products in Poli. Objects unearthed in Santubong at the estuary of Sarawak - including ceramic pieces, stone wares, glass beads, gold wares and coins from the Kaiyuan era of the Tang Dynasty - indicate that there was still ongoing trade between the Tang court and Poli. There were also tombs of overseas Chinese, crucibles for smelting, iron bracelets and anklets, and a mass of iron wares unearthed in the Santubong region. These objects are a good indication that apart from Chinese merchants, there had also been Chinese craftsmen arriving in Poli for productive activities like smelting. With the development of the Tang Dynasty and Poli, especially in terms of non-governmental trade, there were already Chinese immigrants residing in Poli during the Tang period, forming small settlement communities therein. Since the end of Tang, Chinese chronicles converted the name "Poli" into "Boni", using this title for quite a period from then on.

With foreign trade flourishing in the Song Dynasty, Chinese merchants frequently visited and returned from Boni by sea, which marked a relatively significant development in the political and economic exchanges between the two countries as well as the business activities of overseas Chinese.

At the end of the Tang and the beginning of Song, due to the domestic turmoil in China and Sri Vijaya's grip on Brunei, the relations between China and Boni was severely undermined. In the middle of the 10th century, when the Song Dynasty unified China and promoted foreign trade, Boni got rid of the manipulation of Sri Vijaya, thereby actively recovering its relations with China. In 997 AD, Xiangda, the King of Boni, sent a large embassy with the Chinese merchant Pu Luxie to pay tribute to the Song court. Emperor Taizong of Song attached great importance to the Brunei embassy and rewarded a great deal of presents to them. The Brunei king Xiangda had proposed sending envoys to China annually in his credential to Emperor Taizong of Song, which revealed the considerably friendly relations between Boni and the Song court. In AD 1082, King Xilimanuo of Boni sent envoys to the Song court for tributary visit again.

The friendly political relations between the Song Dynasty and Boni were beneficial for the development of economic tie between the two countries. Boni attached great importance to its trade with China, with its kings and officials directly participating in the whole trade process. Both sides conducted trade on the basis of the principle of equality and mutual benefits. At that time, the products brought in by Chinese merchants mainly included gold, silver, silk floss, Jianyang brocade, five-colored silk, glass beads and bottles, white tin, lead, fishing weights, vermilion, lacquer bowls and dishes, and blue-and-white porcelain. The local specialties brought back to China from Brunei included Borneol, rice-shaped borneol, golden bee-hive tallow, Acronychia pedunculata, and tortoiseshell. In addition to direct trade with Brunei, Chinese merchants also traded with regions surrounding Brunei through it.

The friendly relations between the Song Dynasty and Boni provided favorable condition for the activities of overseas Chinese in Bon. Chinese merchants utilized the northeast monsoon to travel south every autumn and returned to their country the following summer using the southwest monsoon, staying in Boni for nearly a year. Some merchants stayed even longer to engage in trade with the surrounding regions of Boni.

There was no official political exchange between the Yuan Dynasty and Brunei. Yet trade developed significantly between the two countries. Many Chinese merchants went into business in Boni, thereby contributing to the prosperity of the local economy. The trading activities between the two countries focused on areas like Dudu'an (Tanjong Datu), Wanniangang Port and Boni. Dudu'an refers to the estuarine delta region of Sarawak; while Wanniangang was actually the present-day port of Brunei. Boni, located near Pontianak, was the capital of the country. With these three regions on different levels of economic development, Chinese merchants brought different products according to the demands of different regions, providing Dudu'an with fabrics, red and green silk, salt, iron, bronze tripods, colored satins, Wanniangang with iron bars, copper cash, printed homespun, clay bottles, and Pontianak with Chinese products like ingots, red gold and colored satin.

Both the policy of the Yuan Dynasty that bolstered foreign trade and the development of economy and trade between China and Brunei had boosted the population of Chinese immigrants in Brunei. Overseas Chinese engaged in trade and production activities locally while getting along amicably with the local people. In *Dao Yi Zhi Lue* (*A Brief Account of the Islands*), Wang Dayuan of the Yuan Dynasty noted that the people of Boni "especially respect and love the Tang (referring to the Chinese); and when drunk, they carry them back to their homes" - this clearly illustrates the harmonious relationship between the overseas Chinese and the local residents.

The Ming Dynasty witnessed the heyday of friendly relations between the two countries.

In August of the third year of Hongwu of Ming (AD 1370), Emperor

Taizu of Ming sent Shen Zhi, Office Manager of Fujian Branch Secretariat, and investigating censor Zhang Jiaoyuan to lead an embassy for the visit in Boni. In the following year, Muhammad Shah, the Sultan of Boni, dispatched envoys in company with Shen and Zhang to visit China. Emperor Taizu of Ming personally received the visiting envoys and hosted a banquet for them. Upon their return, Emperor Hongwu presented a large number of gifts to the king and the envoys.

During the Yongle years of Ming, the relations between the two countries blossomed. In the third year of Yongle (AD 1405), when Sultan Maharaja Karna of Brunei had dispatched envoys present homage to the Ming court, Emperor Chengzu of Ming sent officials to Brunei, entitling Maharaja Karna as the sultan of Boni and conferring him with seal, imperial mandate, rider tallies, brocades, damask, colored coins and the like. Research shows that in the winter of the fifth year of the Yongle reign (AD 1407), Zheng He's fleet visited Boni when he was on his second voyage to the Western Seas. In the following August, Sultan Maharaja Karna of Boni, with his wife, children, elder brother and sister, relatives and vassals, personally visited Nanjing, the capital of the Ming court. As the first massive embassy visit led by a foreign king since the establishment of the Ming Dynasty, this visit met with a solemn and cordial reception from the Ming court. During their stay in China, Emperor Chengzu of the Ming Dynasty assigned special attendants to accompany them each day, and both sides exchanged a substantial number of gifts, fostering a harmonious and friendly relationship. Unfortunately, the Sultan of Boni fell ill and passed away in October of the same year. Before his death, he left a final wish, hoping that after his passing, "his remains would be interred in China". After his death, Emperor Chengzu suspended his court for three days for mourning, and mandated the Ministry of Works to select coffins and grave goods, interring the Sultan outside of Andemen in Shizigang. An ancestral temple and a monument were erected beside this tomb, with officials dispatched to sacrifice and renovate it in springs and autumns. In memorial of the friendly performance of Maharaja Karna before his death, Emperor Chengzu also gave him the posthumous title of "Gongshun" in accordance with Chinese rite.

After Maharaja Karna's death, Emperor Chengzu immediately mandated the king's son, Xiawang to be the sultan of Boni, and assigned men to escort him back home. In the tenth year of Yongle (AD 1412), Xiawang visited China as a sultan with his mother and wife, visiting his father's tomb before they returned home in the following year. During Xiawang's stay in China, the Ming court also treated him with a warm welcome and the utmost cordiality. Upon the Sultan's return, Emperor Chengzu "granted him a hundred *liang* of gold, five hundred *liang* of ingot, 1,500 strings of copper coins, four pieces of brocade, eighty bolts of fine silk and satin, and one set each of gold-woven and gold-embroidered garments; he also bestowed various items such as utensils, bedding, and curtains. The Sultan's mother and uncles received various gifts as well."

The visits of two Sultans of Boni pushed the friendly relations between China and Boni to climax, laying solid foundation for the constant development of the political relations between the two countries. According to incomplete statistics, from the Hongwu to Hongxi eras (AD 1368-1425), China dispatched envoys to Brunei for four times while the embassy of Boni had visited China for ten times, which revealed the close ties between the two countries. After that, the frequency of envoys sent by Boni decreased. However, even during the height of Brunei's power in the 16th century, the king of Boni continued to send envoys to China to offer tribute.

The friendly political relations between the Ming Dynasty and Boni promoted the development of their bilateral economy. In terms of the maritime transportation between the two countries, in addition to the original tribute trade route via the Malay Peninsula to Guangdong, a new shortcut was established in the Ming Dynasty that connected the Philippines to Fujian. Hence it enhanced the convenience of trade activities between China and Boni. Seafarers in the Ming Dynasty referred to Boni as "Brunei", deeming it the partition of the two courses in the Eastern and the Western Seas. During the early period of the Ming Dynasty, the trade between China and Brunei was dominated by tributary trade. Between Hongwu and Hongxi years, Bruneian tributary delegations visiting China were all accompanied by a certain amount of merchant ships. Through the tribute trade, Brunei brought in China a variety of goods in exchange, including multicolored parrots, hanging birds, peacocks, cranes, rhinoceros horns, bear skins, raw tortoiseshell, tortoise shell tubes, gemstones, pearls, gold and silver artifacts, borneol, rice-shaped borneol, sugar like aromatic substance, Dalbergia odorifera, Aquilaria, sandal, cloves, nutmeg, yellow wax, cowrie shells, and black menservant, among others. Chinese products brought in Brunei were mainly textiles and ceramics. In the late Ming Dynasty, there were many merchants in the tributary teams of Brunei to China. With tribute payment dying out instead of its nominal existence, the non-governmental trade had actually replaced the official tributary trade.

Products involved in the non-governmental trade between China and Brunei were not limited to the native Bruneian specialties: Brunei was one of the major distribution centers and ports for Chinese merchant ships to transport products like spices, cubilose and shark fins back home. With its economy reaping tremendous profit from the maritime trade between China and Southeast Asia, Brunei prospered through maritime trade, which contributed to its growing power and strength.

The amicable economic relations between the Ming Dynasty and Brunei created extraordinary conditions for the overseas Chinese residing in Brunei.

During the early Ming Dynasty, it was the period of governance of the first few sultans of Brunei. It was a time when the overseas Chinese actively participated in the local socio-economic development. During the reign of the third Sultan of Brunei, the Chinese community helped transport 40 ships of stone to build a stone wall and a stone fortress between Kaya Orang and Chermin at the mouth of the Brunei River.

During Brunei's economic prosperity, the sultan of the country substantially bolstered pepper cultivation in the hope of promoting pepper business. He employed Chinese workers from China and built pepper gardens one after another on the hillsides around the city of Brunei. The improvement of farming techniques by oversea Chinese ramped up the yields of pepper, enabling pepper to be the biggest exports of Brunei. The development of pepper production, in turn, drove the continuous influx of Chinese into Brunei. In the 15th to 16th century, there was a dramatic increase in the local population of overseas Chinese. Generally speaking, the productive activities of overseas Chinese and the trade with China were beneficial to the improvement and prosperity of society and economy in Brunei.

However, the rigid policy of sea ban in the Qing Dynasty had severed the Sino-Bruneian relations for a time being. It was not until the 23rd year of Kangxi's reign in the Qing Dynasty (AD 1684), when the sea ban was loosened, that the non-governmental business between the two countries was resumed and developed to some extent. Whereas in the 56th year of Kangxi's reign (AD 1717), the Qing court issued another ban on the navigation in Nanyang (Southeast Asia). And the exchanges between the two countries were only increased gradually after the ban was lifted in the fifth year of Yongzheng's reign (AD 1727). Historical records indicate that in 1775, there was a shipyard run by overseas Chinese in Brunei capable of building sailing ships of 580 tons, which could be launched in May while constructed in March. This is a good demonstration that the shipyard boasted fabulous technology and capability.

In the middle of the 17th century, with the decline of its national strength, Brunei suffered from not only the territorial encroachment of western imperial powers, but also restriction and impact on its maritime trade. The Netherlands and the United Kingdom gradually monopolized the maritime trade between Southeast Asia and China. By the 1870s, Brunei was completely expelled from the trade market between Southeast Asia and China, witnessing a lapse in its economy and a drastic slump in the population of overseas Chinese.

Bibliography

1.**ZHENG, Ziyue**. Geographical Records of the South China Sea Islands[M]. Shanghai: The Commercial Press, 1947.

2.**Institute of History, Chinese Academy of Social Sciences (Ed.)**. Selected Historical Materials on Ancient Sino-Vietnamese Relations [G]. Beijing: China Social Sciences Press (Internally Distributed), 1982.

3.**HAN, Zhenhua (Ed.).** Compilation of Historical Materials on China's South China Sea Islands [G]. Compiled by LIN Jinzhi & WU Fengbin. Beijing: Oriental Press, 1988.

4.**MENG, Wentong**. A Study of Vietnamese History [M]. Beijing: People's Publishing House, 1983.

5.**Nansha Integrated Scientific Expedition Team**, Chinese Academy of Sciences. Monograph on the Historical Geography of the Nansha Islands [M]. Guangzhou: Sun Yat-sen University Press, 1991.

6.**SHI, Dizu**. The South China Sea Islands Have Been China's Territory Since Ancient Times [N]. Guangming Daily, 1975-11-24.

7.**Social Sciences Commission of Vietnam**. Vietnamese History [M]. Translated by Vietnamese Language Teaching and Research Section, Department of Eastern Languages, Peking University. Beijing: Beijing People's Publishing House, 1977.

8.**ZHU, Jieqin**. History of Overseas Chinese in Southeast Asia [M]. Beijing:

Higher Education Press, 1990.

9.**CHEN, Liefu**. Overseas Chinese, Ethnic Chinese, and Persons of Chinese Descent in Southeast Asia M. Taipei: Cheng Chung Book Co., 1979.

10.**HU, Cai**. Contemporary Philippines [M]. Chengdu: Sichuan People's Publishing House, 1994.

11.**TAN, Antonio S. (CHEN, Shouguo)**. The Chinese Mestizos and the Formation of the Filipino Nation [M]. Manila: Kaisa Para Sa Kaunlaran, Inc., 1989.

12.**YU, Yake & HUANG**, Min. Contemporary Brunei [M]. Chengdu: Sichuan People's Publishing House, 1994.

13.**CHEN, Yinglong**. Ancient Sino-Brunei Relations and the Activities of Overseas Chinese [M]. Institute of Overseas Chinese Studies, Jinan University (Ed.). Studies on Overseas Chinese. Guangzhou: Guangdong Higher Education Press, 1988.

14.**LIANG, Yingming**. Chinese Immigration and Cultural Exchange in Modern Malaya [M]. Institute of Asian Studies, Peking University (Ed.). Asian Studies. Beijing: Peking University Press, 1994.

1.郑资约.南海诸岛地理志略［M］.南海诸岛地理志略［M］.上海：商务印书馆，1947.

2.中国社会科学院历史研究所.古代中越关系史—资料选编［G］.古代中越关系史—资料选编［G］.北京：中国社会科学出版社（内部发行），1982.

3.韩振华，主编.中国南海诸岛史料汇编［G］.林金枝，吴凤斌，编.北京：东方出版社，1988.

4.蒙文通.越史丛考［M］.北京：人民出版社，1983.

5.中国科学院南沙综合科学考察队.南沙群岛历史地理研究专集［M］.广州：中山大学出版社，1991.

6.史棣祖.南海诸岛自古就是我国领土［N］.南海诸岛自古就是我国领土［N］.光明日报，1975-11-24.

7.越南社会科学委员会.越南社会科学委员会.越南社会科学委员会.越南历史［M］.北京大学东语系越南语教研室，译.北京：北京人民出版社，1977.

8.朱杰勤.东南亚华侨史［M］.北京：高等教育出版社，1990.

9.陈烈甫.东南亚洲的华侨、华人与华裔［M］.台北：正中书局，1979.

10.胡才.当代菲律宾［M］.成都：四川人民出版社，1994.

11.陈守国.华人混血儿与菲律宾民族的形成［M］.马尼拉：菲律宾华裔青年联合会，1989.

12.俞亚克，黄敏.俞亚克，黄敏.当代文莱［M］.成都：四川人民出版社，1994.

13.陈应龙.古代中国与文莱的关系及华侨的活动［M］//暨南大学华侨研究所.华侨研究.广州：广东高等教育出版社，1988.

14.梁英明.近代马来亚华人移民与文化交流［M］//北京大学研究所.亚洲研究.北京：北京大学出版社，1994.北京大学出版社，1994.

Chapter 6
The Basic Argument for China's Maintenance of its Sovereignty Over South China Sea Islands and Maritime Rights and Interests

Section 1 A Comparative Research on the Legal Basis of the Sovereignty Over Nansha Qundao Proposed by China and Relevant Countries

At Present, countries that claim their sovereignty over all or part of the islands and reefs in China's Nansha Qundao include Vietnam, the Philippines, Malaysia, Brunei and Indonesia. The jurisprudential emphases on which those countries based their claims, though varying with their geographical location and historical process, are nothing more than the six points below.

I. Historical evidence

Historical facts are the most powerful evidence for territorial entitlement. Therefore, all relevant countries invariably present historical evidences as the major legal basis of their claims on the sovereignty over South China Sea Islands.

1. China is the first country to maintain its sovereignty over South China Sea Islands according to historical facts.

Early in the ninth year of Guangxu's Reign in the Qing Dynasty (AD 1883), when Germany conducted surveys in Xisha Qundao and Nansha Qundao, the Qing government demonstrated and lodged complaint on the basis of historical facts that these islands were the territory of China, thereby forcing Germany to halt its investigation.

In 1909, the Japanese merchant Nishizawa Yoshitsugu was driven out by the Chinese government when he attempted to exploit the mineral resources in Dongsha Qundao. The Qing government made representations to the Japanese consul in Guangdong on the basis of historical facts, forcing Japan to admit its unjustifiable act and acknowledge that Dongsha Qundao is the territory of China.

After France provoked the "Incident of the Nine Islets" in the South China Sea in 1933, the Ministry of Foreign Affairs in China issued an order to the Chinese embassy in France on March 20th, 1934, refuting point by point against the arguments in the "Reply on the diplomatic note to the Chinese government" by the French Ministry of Foreign Affairs on September 27th, 1933.

On November 25th, 1975, the *People's Daily* published an article entitled "South China Sea Islands has been Chinese Territory Since the Ancient Times" under the name of "Shi Dizu". In May, 1985, the Ministry of Foreign Affairs of the PRC issued documents like the one entitled *China Holds Indisputable Sovereignty Over Xisha Qundao and Nansha Qundao*, all of which are based on a large amount of historical facts, comprehensively and systematically expounding that the Chinese government was the first to discover, develop and monitor South China Sea Islands (including Nansha Qundao). Therefore, the Chinese government holds indisputable sovereignty over Nansha Qundao.

2. The alleged historical materials used by Vietnam do not actually refer to South China Sea Islands, which indicates the invalidity of Vietnam's claim to South China Sea Islands on this basis.

All of the six so-called historical evidence proposed previously by Vietnam are as follows:

(1) The *Collection of the South's Road Map* (aka. the *Hong Duc Atlas*) compiled by Do Ba in the mid-17th century;

(2) The *Miscellaneous Records on the Pacification of the Frontiers written by the Vietnamese* scholar Lê Quý Đôn in 1776;

(3) *The Complete Map of Unified Dai Nam* drawn in 1838 in the Nguyen dynasty;

(4) *The Regulations of Successive Dynasties by Subject-Matter: Treatise on Geography* (1821) and the *Treatise on Geography of the Royal Viet* (1833), works of Vietnam;

(5) the Dai Nam Comprehensive Encyclopedia compiled in 1910;

(6) Jean Louis Taberd said in his article "Note on the Geography of Cochinchina", published in the *Journal of the Royal Asiatic Society of Bengal* in 1838, that "the king Gia Long... In 1816, he went with solemnity to plant his flag..."

None of the above-mentioned historical evidence presented by Vietnam involves Nansha Qundao (or even Xisha Qundao). Using the device of "place name displacement", Vietnam forcibly relocates Hoàng Sa Island, specifically identified as the Canton Islands off the central coast of Vietnam (historically known as Cát Vong, Bãi Cát Vong, Wailuo Mountain, Lý Sơn Island, etc.), to Xisha Qundao, and even expanded it to Nansha Qundao. The description of "Bac Hai Company" in Lê Quý Đôn's *Miscellaneous Records on the Pacification of the Frontiers* that "Nguyen also established the Bac Hai Company, which had no fixed number of members, consisting of either people from Tứ Chính Village of Bình Thuận Prefecture, or residents of Cảnh Dương Commune. Those who were willing to participate were exempted from the fees for searching for money and other crossing charges, allowed to use private fishing boats to go to places like the Bac Hai Island, Côn Lôn Island, and the islands of Hà Tiên, to collect items such as hawksbills, sea cucumbers, and other marine products. This company was also put in charge of the Hoàng Sa Company. However, they generally found little in terms of marine goods, gold and silver, or heavy cargo." The "Bac Hai Company" mentioned here was the only evidence provided by the white book of Vietnam that they had collected maritime goods in "Trường Sa". But the areas mentioned above were from Bình Thuận Province to Côn Lôn Island, bypassing Cape Cà Mau into Gulf of Siam, reaching Hà Tiên at the border of

Vietnam and Cambodia. This explicitly illustrates that the location of activities described as the "Bac Hai Company" to "Trường Sa" in Vietnamese historical texts refers to the coastal areas in southern Vietnam. Besides, there is not a single trace of historical evidence that proves the arrival of Vietnamese in Nansha Qundao.

All of the aforementioned historical evidences were patched up by the French after their encroachment on Vietnam, who had long been designing to deprive China of South China Sea Islands. This so-called evidence was collected mainly by the officials in the colonies, none of whom were any "sinologist" truly acquainted with history. The major process of their evidence collection was as follows: early in 1898, France received a report from the French Consulate in Haikou about Paracel (the name used by some countries for Xisha Qundao), believing that "the location of these islands is correlated with the interests of Indochina." Since then, the French colonists had searched their heavens for excuses to encroach on Xisha Qundao. On September 24th, 1920, Remy, Captain of the French Navy, stated "there is not a single document in the files of the Navy that can decide the territorial entitlement of Paracel. But I can assure you that it does not belong to France." In 1921, the Commander-in Chief of the French Navy and the Governor-General of Cochinchina respectively expressed that "there is not any intellectual information in the documents of the French Navy that can decide the territorial entitlement of the Xisha Qundao." The Governor-General of Cochinchina had issued an order to search for relevant material in the archive of the Government House, only to find this effort in vain. In Telegraph No. 569 sent to the Saigon Navy on January 23rd, 1921, the Paris Navy asserted that "In 1909, the Chinese claimed their ownership of the Xisha Qundao. This is the only available information at present." Until August 22nd, 1921, the French Prime Minister and Minister of Foreign Affairs still asserted in his letter to Maugras, the French chargé d'affaires in Beijing, that "because the

Chinese government established their own sovereignty in 1909, it is now impossible for us to lodge any claim on these islands at present."

On January 12th, 1929, the Governor-General of Indochina still required in his letter to the Resident-Superior of Annam in Huế, that "the Annam government may have established its sovereignty over these (Paracel) islands... For that, it should search for any single trace of evidence, if not all, in its favor." Under this circumstance, Fol, the Resident-Superior of Annam, found an article entitled "Additional Notice on the Geography of Cochinchina", which was published in the *Journal of the Royal Asiatic Society of Bengal* sponsored by the "Asiatic Society", and translated by the cleric Taberd into English in 1838. It was stated in the article that the Vietnamese emperor Gia Long had once planted a flag in these islands, and that the Nguyen dynasty had mobilized the "Hoàng Sa Company" and the "Bac Hai Company", with the emperor issued order to dispatch men for the measurement of the waterway of Hoàng Sa. But at the same time, Pol also admitted that "Annam seems to have nothing to do with Paracel at present. The fishermen and ship owners in the coastal area of Annam know nothing about the existence of these island, let alone any soul having been there," adding that "as a matter of fact, these islands are the natural extension of Hainan Island".

The Vietnamese attempted to illustrate, by historical evidences, that Nansha Qundao (and even the entire South China Sea Islands) is the territory of Vietnam. However, these evidences do not withstand factual scrutiny and therefore is not valid.

3. The Philippines has also proposed some alleged historical rights that are unsubstantiated.

The first article of the new Philippine Constitution, which came into effect in 1973, states that, in addition to the Philippine archipelago, Philippine territory also includes "all other territories that belong to the Philippines by historical rights or legal ownership". To demonstrate its claim over Nansha Qundao, the Philippines issued Presidential Order No. 1596 in June, 1978, proposing that the so-called "Kalayaan archipelago", which was coined by the Philippines itself, "must be perceived as a region under the Philippine sovereignty for historical reasons". Nonetheless, the Philippines has never presented any fact regarding the historical evidence for the claim above. On December 1st, 1987, the Ministry of Foreign Affairs of the Philippines issued a document, stating the country's position regarding the Kalayaan archipelago that "the ancient Filipinos had been to the Kalayaan archipelago even before the Spanish rule, who used some of the islands as fishery bases. These islands are located adjacent to Palawan Island, making it possible to reach them for the ancestors of the modern Filipinos engaging in navigation industry. However, these islands were then just used as the bases of navigation operations instead of being occupied permanently!" So, what is the specific evidence for this "possible" statement then? Judging from the history of the Philippines, it is impossible for them to offer any evidence. As is objectively pointed out by a Filipino researcher named Diane C. Drigot in his article published in *The Philippine Yearbook of International Law* in 1982[1], "among the countries proposing their claims on Nansha Qundao on the basis of their historical rights, China is the one with the most abundant evidence."

4.Malaysia also purported its historical claim, yet without any evidence.

On December 21st, 1979, Malaysia published a new map that designated its continental shelf and territorial sea, blatantly including the region of the South China Sea south of the line of Siling Jiao (Commodore Reef), Boji Jiao

---

[1] Drigot D C. 1982. Interest in oil as a factor in the Philippine claims and disputes over marine territory in the South China Sea. Philippine Yearbook of International Law, 8, 1982, pp. 39-91. HeinOnline

(Erica Reef), Nanhai Jiao (Mariveles Reef), Anbo Shazhou (Amboyna Bank), Nanle Ansha (Glasgow Shoal) and Xiaowei Ansha (North East Shoal) in the territory of Malaysia. Accordingly, China had lodged protest against this act. Malaysia's explanation regarding this incident was that "the Amboyna Bank and the Swallow Reef have always been part of the Malaysian territory," offering no demonstration about any relevant evidence.

In general, in the face of historical evidence, China is the country with the most abundant facts about its territorial sovereignty.

II. Geographical evidences

Claimants must offer an accurate description about the geographical location, landscapes and ecological environment of the territory they claim.

1.China presented crystal-clear description about the geographical location of Nansha Qundao even in the ancient times.

Normally, Nansha Qundao is located in a certain position of some waterway, or a certain direction in the prefecture it belongs to. In the Song Dynasty, the location of Nansha Qundao was marked thorugh the combination of waterways and navigation schedule. In the Ming and Qing dynasties when "Geng Lu Bu" prevailed, location description was highly precise by using directions and the measurement of *Gengs* (更数, 1 Geng $\approx$ 34 km in Ming Dynasty).

The ancient description of the landscape of Nansha Qundao focused mainly on the peril therein. For example, there were statements like "the water is shallow and filled with magnetic stones", which explicated that the place is a coral reef, noting that "the depth of the ocean here varies, with rushing waters and abundant rocks, causing seven or eight of every ten boats to turn over". In the Yuan Dynasty, Wang Dayuan not only stated clearly in his *Dao Yi Zhi Lüe (A Brief Account of the Islands)* the distribution features of the islands and reefs in Nansha Qundao, but explained the distribution rule of it with Zhu Xi's "hypothesis of geomantic veins".

Regarding the features of the ecological environment in Nansha Qundao, Wu Kangtai of the Three Kingdoms Period explicitly described in his *Fu Nan Zhuan (A Memoir of Fu'nan)* that "in the coral reef, there are rocks at the bottom of the continent with coral born on it". This indicated that Wu had realized that Nansha Qundao is actually a series of coral reefs. Works appearing after that bear accurate records about the sea cucumbers, shellfish, conches, giant clams, flying fish, coconuts growing here as well as the seabirds helping fishermen with their navigation, which conform completely with the ecological characteristics of Nansha Qundao.

2.Vietnam: Upon reviewing the ancient Vietnamese descriptions of Hoàng Sa or Trường Sa, neither the geographical location, terrain characteristics, nor the ecological environment of these two places match those of South China Sea Islands.

Geographical location: In *Hong Duc Atlas,* which claimed itself to be the oldest document of Vietnam, there are two instances of the term "Da Chang Sha (Great Trường Sa)" in the "Map of Cochinchine." One instance appears on the right side of the harbor of Do Dat with the three Chinese characters "Da Chang Sha," and the other is between the Đại Thiep (Đại Chiêm) and the harbor of An Hòa, where there are five Chinese characters reading "Da Chang Sha Yi Xia (Below the Great Trường Sa)". Accordingly, the "Great Trường Sa" refers to the grand beach from Hoi An in coastal area in the middle of Vietnam to Chu Lai along the bank. Besides, the "Map of the Guangnan Circuit (of the Lý dynasty)" is noted in the original manuscript as "redrawn based on the Map of Thien Nam from 1741," which also contains the phrase "a copy of the Map of Thien Nam from the second year of the reign of Cảnh Hưng". In Map 2, "Bãi Cát Vong" is located on the sea between Hoi An and Sa Huynh in the middle of modern Vietnam; in Map 3, there is a long strip with words reading "one day past Trường Sa", located to the right side of the harbors of Dai to Sa Kỳ, near the sea between present-day Sa Huynh and Chu Lai. There has been Vietnamese scholars explaining "one day past" as "requiring over one day to reach here, which means the island is located in the distant sea". In contrast, in the mid-18th century, a voyage of more than a day by sea could take one as far as the Canton Islands in central Vietnam. Another evidence of Vietnam's claim is *the Complete Map of Unified Dai Nam*. On September 28th, 1979, the Ministry of Foreign Affairs of Vietnam stated in a white book that this map "was drawn approximately in 1838". Drawings vary from different versions of maps. On the complete map of Vietnam, the northern part is labeled "Paracels" (Hoàng Sa), and the southern part is labeled "Spratlys" (Quan dao Trường Sa). In the detail view, "Paracels" and "Spratlys" are omitted but enclosed together with a dashed line. This map is a forgery. But with regard to the "Hoàng Sa" and "Quan dao Trường Sa" drawn therein, the northern part of it is no farther than the seaport of Hải Vân and its southern part no farther than the south boundary of Phú Yên, with its width within 1° longitude. Therefore, the range of the said region extends north of Da Nang, south to the vicinity of the large islands in the southern part of Phú Yên Province, east to the longitude of 110°E, and west to the central coastal area of Vietnam, which has nothing to do with Nansha Qundao of China. Published in 1910 when Vietnam had fallen to a French colony, the Dai Nam Comprehensive Encyclopedia noted under the item of "Trường Sa" that it "extends south from the estuary of Việt Yên along the sea, with an ancient name 'Great Trường Sa'. Measuring over a hundred *li* in width, it reaches the coast to its east and some forests to the west," which again matches the view of *Hong Duc Atlas*. Therefore, statements about the location of the Great Trường Sa in all of the ancient Vietnamese records have nothing to do with Nansha Qundao.

Topographic feature: Lê Quý Đôn described the Great Trường Sa Island in his *Miscellaneous Records on the Pacification of the Frontiers* that "An Vinh Commune of Bình Sơn, Quảng Ngãi Province, is located in the near sea where in the northeastern part there is an island with over 110 mountains." As Phan Huy Chú said in his *Regulations of Successive Dynasties by Subject-Matter: Treatise on Geography*," The village of An Vinh, Bình Sơn District, Quảng Ngãi Prefecture, is close by the sea. To the northeast (of the village) there are many islands and miscellaneous rockheads jutting out of the sea, totaling 130 altogether. According to *the Dai Nam Comprehensive Encyclopedia*, Trường Sa is a coastal beach, while the Hoàng Sa Island was having over 130 hills therein. Hence none of these accounts could illustrate that Hoàng Sa is an island formed by coral reefs. While the statement about "over 130 mountains" indicates that the so-called Hoàng Sa Island and Vạn Lý Trường Sa refer to the continental island in the middle of Vietnam.

Ecological environment: Both the *Miscellaneous Records on the Pacification of the Frontiers* and the *Regulations of Successive Dynasties by Subject-Matter: Treatise on Geography* mentioned that "there are countless swallow's nests at the margin of the island". The fact is that swallow's nests can only be found in places with steep cliffs, standing no chance to appear on coral islands. So, the alleged Vạn Lý Trường Sa of Vietnam is not located in South China Sea Islands.

3. Both the Philippines and Malaysia started to claim their sovereignty over Nansha Qundao after the 1970s, failing to offer any geographical evidence.

III. Stipulations in treaties

Certain stipulations in various treaties are the crucial basis of territorial entitlement. In the disputes over the territorial sovereignty of South China Sea Islands, all parties seek to leverage relevant stipulations on which they can set up their legal basis.

The *Continuation of Discussions on Specialized Matters* signed by China and France in 1887, the *Cairo Declaration* published in 1943, the *Potsdam Declaration* published in July,1945, and the Sino-Japanese Peace Treaty signed by the Japanese government and the authorities of Taiwan, China on April 28th, 1952, are all compelling proof of China's claim of sovereignty over South China Sea Islands according to stipulations in relevant treaties.

Vietnam emphasized that on September 7th, 1951, Trần Văn Hữu, the Premier of the Bảo Đại government, led a delegation and declared at the San Francisco Peace Conference, asserting Vietnam's sovereignty over the Hoàng Sa Islands and the Trường Sa Islands, based on which it presented its claims to sovereignty over Xisha Qundao and Nansha Qundao.

The Philippines claimed that the Treaty of Peace with Japan in San Francisco only stipulated Japan's renunciation of sovereignty over the islands in the South China Sea, without specifying to whom the sovereignty is relinquished. Therefore, the Philippines asserts its sovereignty over Nansha Qundao based on the principle of "discovery and occupation of terra nullius".

According to the principle of treaty stipulation, both Vietnam and the Philippines took advantage of the fact that the Article Six of the Treaty of Peace with Japan in San Francisco only stipulated that "Japan relinquish all rights, bases of rights and requirements over Nansha Qundao and Xisha Qundao", without specifying the jurisdiction of these islands after the relinquishment, thereby lodging their own claims for rights. This, however, does not hold water for the following reasons:

(1) Neither China nor Taiwan, China participated in the peace conference in San Francisco. But Zhou Enlai, the Premier of the Chinese government, publicly announced early on August 15th, 1951, that South China Sea Islands is part of China's territory, with Taiwan, China issuing a

similar declaration;

(2) At that time, Gromyko, the head of the delegation of Soviet Union, pointed out that "islands including Xisha Qundao and Nansha Qundao are inseparable territory of China";

(3) On April 28th, 1952, the Sino-Japanese Peace Treaty was signed by the Japanese government and the authorities of Taiwan, China as a bilateral treaty, wherein Japan acknowledged that "Japan has relinquished all the rights, bases of rights and requirements over Taiwan, the Penghu, Nansha and Xisha Qundao".

This treaty did not include regions like North Korea, the Kuril Islands or Sakhalin, indicating that this is a bilateral agreement. At that time, Isao Kawada, the plenipotentiary of Japan, stated that "this provision should only stipulate for the territories belonging to China." It was under this circumstance that in 1952, Okazaki Katsuo, the Minister for Foreign Affairs of Japan, signed the *Standard Atlas of the World*, in which Map No. 15 entitled "Southeast Asia" charted the same borders in the South China Sea as in the map published by China. Also, with "the People's Republic of China" clearly labeled, Map No. 15 also marked Dongsha Qundao, Xisha Qundao, Zhongsha Qundao and Nansha Qundao labelled with Chinese Pinyin.

Other countries around South China Sea Islands claim their sovereignty over Nansha territory without the support of any treaty stipulation, which is an advantage that China should make full use of.

IV. International recognition

International recognition is of huge significance in territorial disputes. The established public opinion has binding force on all parties concerned. Be it the United States, Europe, Japan or other countries in the ASEAN, they are exactly concerned about the said point when they sometimes take a neutral stance on the Nansha disputes.

There are mainly four types of international recognition:

(1) The attitudes held by various international conferences toward the parties concerned on the territorial disputes;

(2) The statements made and attitudes held by the governments and public opinion of various countries;

(3) Relevant records about this issue in publications of various countries, including textbooks;

(4) The marking methods of maps published by countries other than China.

As a matter of fact, both the quantity and the clarity of the four elements mentioned above are all beneficial for China. Countries like Vietnam, the Philippines and Malaysia, when asserting their sovereignty over Nansha Qundao, spare no effort to bypass this sensitive issue. Worse still, Vietnam strains every nerve to distort the fact.

By considering publications and maps as examples, we shall examine the internationally recognized territorial claims of Nansha Qundao.

Admittedly, publications and maps are crucial devices that reveal territorial entitlement. The extensive and continuous demonstration of territorial claims is a significant basis for territorial ownership. Vietnam attempts to use the attached maps in *Hong Duc Atlas*, the *Complete Map of Unified Dai Nam*, and the *Record of Unified Dai Nam* to purport that Hoàng Sa and Trường Sa are Vietnamese territories while regarding the maps put forward by China "utterly worthless". Isn't this just evaluating the same thing by different standards?

First and foremost, the name of "Changsha" in "Wanlichangsha" appeared in Chinese classics at the latest in *Lingwai Daida (Representative Answers from the Region beyond the Mountains)* by Zhou Qufei in 1178 of the Song Dynasty, and has been in use for nearly 700 years, through the Yuan, Ming and Qing dynasties. While the earliest use of the name "Trường Sa" in Vietnamese classics was in *Hong Duc Atlas* in 1630, which was 452 years later than the appearance of "Changsha" in Chinese historical texts.

Secondly, from the "Zheng He Navigation Chart" (published in 1430, 200 years earlier than the *Hong Duc Atlas*), various Chinese maps have consistently referred to Nansha Qundao with names like "Changsha", "Wanli Changsha", and "Shitang".

Numerous foreign maps clearly indicate that Nansha Qundao are Chinese territory, and the number is undoubtedly several times greater than the maps presented by Vietnam. For example, in 1952, the second year after the signing of the Treaty of Peace with Japan in San Francisco, Map 15 in the Standard Atlas of the World, which was signed by Okazaki Katsuo, the then Minister for Foreign Affairs of Japan, marked Dongsha, Xisha, Nansha and Nansha Qundao asChinese territories; moreover, in 1973, the *Atlas of China* published by Heibansha of Japan explicitly marked Nansha Qundao as Chinese waters using historical maritime boundary lines.

The 1974 edition of *The Times Atlas of China* (translated by D.C. Twitchett and edited by P.J.M. Geelan) clearly states on page 115 that South China Sea Islands belongs to China.

In the 1943 edition of the *Rand McNally World Atlas*, on page 122, the map titled "China, French Indochina, Siam, and Korea" clearly labels Xisha Qundao as "Paracel Islands (China)."

In 1978, the famous *Websters Atlas* of the U.S. labeled Xisha Qundao on the map of "South East Asia" as "Paracel Islands (China)".

The Encyclopedia Genre Japonica: Atlas of the World, published by the Japanese publisher Shogakukan in 1978, labels Xisha Qundao and Nansha Qundao (Xinnan Zhudao) in Chinese (with Japanese notes), with Xisha

Qundao and Nansha Qundao plotted on the major part of page 14.

The *Wall Chart of China* published by the Soviet Union in 1957 charted that Xisha Qundao (Octpoba Cenllauoh) belongs to China, meanwhile specifically labeled in an inset at the bottom right of the map that these islands belong to China.

These are only a small fraction of the many maps in discussion, which is an ample indicator that be it in the time-honored stream of history or in the foreign maps in modern times, there are a great deal of maps labeling Nansha Qundao and Xisha Qundao as Chinese territories.

V. National laws

Strictly speaking, if the domestic law of a country conflicts with that of relevant countries, it will not be binding on the relevant countries. But undoubtedly, it is still significantly practicable in unifying and mobilizing the thoughts and action of people of this country. And there is also no deny that this law will be useful in relevant international disputes to some degree.

Legislation, as a form of state action, should include relevant decisions from both central and local legislative and administrative departments. In the 1930s, the Chinese government established the National Committee for the Review of Maritime and Overland Maps composed of General Staff, Ministry of the Interior, the Ministry of Foreign Affairs, the Admiralty, the Ministry of Education, the Mongolian and Tibetan Affairs Commission. This committee was responsible for reviewing land and water maps published across the country. And during its 25th meeting held on December 21st, 1934, it approved a total of 132 Chinese and English place names for the islands in the South China Sea. Among them, there are 96 place names in the Nansha Qundao, with the rest of them belonging to "Dongsha Qundao", "Xisha Qundao" and "Nansha Qundao (present-day Zhongsha Qundao)". On March 22nd, 1935, during the 29th session, it was decided that the political and territorial maps must clearly label Dongsha, Xisha, Nansha, and Tuansha archipelagos. In April, 1935, the Map of Islands in the South China Sea was compiled, which plotted both South China Sea Islands and the names of various islands within it.

In 1947, the Department of Territorial Affairs of the Ministry of the Interior printed "Location Map of South China Sea Islands". In addition to the names of the islands of South China Sea Islands, this Department also plotted 11 intermittent national boundaries from the estuary of Beilun River on the Map, and officially examined and revised the *Comparison Chart of New and Old names of Islands in the South China Sea* at the end of the same year.

In 1946, after the end of World War II, the Chinese government, as one of the victors, dispatched senior officials aboard naval vessels to officially take control of Xisha and Nansha Qundao.

In 1947, the Chinese government decided to place the four archipelagos under the jurisdiction of the Guangdong Provincial Government while temporarily placing them under the control of the Navy Command Headquarters, which established the management offices of Dongsha, Xisha and Nansha.

In 1959, the Chinese government set up "Offices on Xisha, Nansha and Zhongsha Qundao" on Yongxing Dao (Woody Island), which was changed into "the Revolutionary Committee of Xisha, Zhongsha and Nansha Qundao in Guangdong Province" in 1969.

We should deny the opinion of Vietnam that France's acts of aggression against the Xisha and Nansha Qundao are a legacy it should inherit.

In 1956, the authorities of Saigon in South Vietnam took the liberty of placing Nansha Qundao under the direct jurisdiction of Phước Tuy Province. In 1973, the authorities of Saigon of South Vietnam again took the liberty of placing part of the islands in Nansha Qundao under the jurisdiction of Phuoc Hai Village, Hồng Thổ District, Phước Tuy Province.

On May 12th, 1977, Vietnam issued the *Declaration of the Socialist Republic of Vietnam on Territorial Sea, Contiguous Zone, Exclusive Economic Zone, and Continental Shelf*, asserting its sovereign areas as a territorial sea extending 12 nautical miles from the baseline, a contiguous zone of 12 nautical miles, and an exclusive economic zone of 200 nautical miles, as well as the continental shelf extending naturally to the outer edge of the continental margin.

The Philippines is the country acting most strenuously to scramble for the waters of Nansha through domestic legislation. On June 11th, 1978, the Philippines issued the Presidential Decree No. 1596, declaring to "circle out" the so-called "Kalayaan Island Group" in the waters of Nansha Qundao, and placing it under the jurisdiction of Palawan Province. Furthermore, on July 15th, a Presidential Decree No. 1599 was issued, declaring that the Kalayaan Island Group are located within the Philippine Exclusive Economic Zone and asserting that the waters between the "Kalayaan Island Group" and Palawan Island are considered internal waters, prohibiting foreign vessels from entering.

Indonesia announced its exclusive economic zone of 200 nautical miles in 1980, part of which have actually been included in the traditional sea boundary of China.

On May 15th, 1980, Malaysia announced to put its 200-nautical-mile economic zone in effect, which included the continental shelf and territorial waters defined in 1979, thereby encroaching upon a significant portion of China's maritime rights.

To sum up, in terms of establishing the legal basis of the territorial entitlement of Nansha Qundao and maritime rights in the neighboring waters,

China has a compelling advantage in historical and geographical evidence, stipulations in relevant treaties as well as international recognition, while still lagging behind in domestic legislation.

Section 2 The Nature of the Nine-Dash Line in the South China Sea and the Significance of China's Maintenance of its Sovereignty over and Maritime Rights in South China Sea Islands

In the waters of the South China Sea, the Nine-dash Line delineates a vast sea boundary, covering an area of two million square kilometers. This maritime space, together with over 200 islands, reefs, shoals and banks within it, has been explored, developed, managed, and governed by the Chinese government and people over a history of more than 2,000 years. Therefore, China holds undeniable historical rights over this sea area, which plays a significant role in the future survival and development of China.

I. The nature of the dashed lines in the South China Sea

The Chinese refer to the nine-line segments differently in various works, such as the "intermittent line", "traditional sea boundary", "national boundary", "baseline of territorial waters", "line of island ownership", "line of historical waters", "U-shaped line", etc. The connotation of those names can be roughly divided into three categories:

(1) The names of "intermittent line" and "U-shaped line" only express the existence of the nine intermittent lines without defining its nature;

(2) The name of "line of island ownership" only emphasizes the entitlement of the islands in this sea area while ignoring the existence of other titles of China in the discussed maritime space;

(3) Names like "national boundary", "baseline of territorial sea", "line of historical waters" and "traditional sea boundary", though seeking to clarify the nature of these line segments, still entail further discussion after careful discernment.

"National boundary":

According to the present international convention, national boundary, existing only on land with specific mark, is a concept of sovereignty with strong exclusiveness, for which the nine-line segments cannot be dubbed as "national boundary".

"Baseline of territorial sea": According to the definition of territorial sea in Article 2 of the *United Nations Convention on the Law of the Sea*, "The sovereignty of a coastal State extends beyond its land territory and internal waters to an adjacent belt of sea, described as the territorial sea." Furthermore, it stipulates that "the breadth of the territorial sea" shall not exceed "twelve nautical miles, measured from the baselines." Therefore, the nine-line segments are not a baseline of territorial sea.

"Line of historical waters": This is a wording promoted by an array of scholars in both sides of the Taiwan Strait. Also, it is a highly controversial statement approved in 1982 via *the United Nations Convention on the Law of the Sea*, which includes no stipulation on the nature or constituent factor of the line segments, and only illustrates two points regarding their legal status:

(1) The provisions on bays in Article 10, which do not apply to "historic bays";

(2) The delimitation of the territorial sea between States with opposite or adjacent coasts, which do not apply to "historic waters". The exact range of "historic waters" remains a question unsolved in the academic circle of the law of the sea.

"Traditional sea boundary": This name still emphasizes historic title. Although there is no definition of traditional sea boundary in the modern law of sea, it is still an inalienable right as "historical waters". In 1958, in the documents prepared by the United Nations Secretariat for the First United

Nations Conference on the Law of the Sea, the concept of "historic bays" was proposed, suggesting that a country's historic rights include not only "historic bays" but also "historic waters." The latter refers to marine areas that are not bays, such as archipelagic waters, the waters located between an archipelago and the mainland, as well as straits, estuaries, and other similar maritime areas. However, this proposal was not adopted by the conference. The rights associated with "historic waters" are equivalent to those of internal waters. If the term "historic waters" is applied to the dashed line in the South China Sea, it may lead to disputes with more countries regarding navigation, aviation, and other related issues. Therefore, the term "traditional sea boundary" was suggested, which indicates that the rights included in this line are stipulated by the historical tradition of China that encompasses the following content: The rights of generations of Chinese to discover, develop, manage, and operate all islands, reefs, shoals, and banks within the boundaries of this territory; the rights to explore and utilize the resources within this range; this "traditional sea boundary" has, both historically and in modern times, not hindered the navigation and aviation rights of other countries. Therefore, using the term "traditional sea boundary" to define it in terms of island ownership and resource exploration and utilization rights aligns more closely with historical realities and can be more widely accepted by other countries.

II. The Background and process of the generation of the Nine-Dash Line in the South China Sea

On December 1st, 1947, the Chinese government released *Location Map of South China Sea Islands*, which was compiled and drawn by the Department of Territorial Affairs of the Ministry of the Interior, and printed by the Bureau of Survey of the Ministry of National Defence. This was the first time that the specific dashed line in the map, which is still in use, was officially promulgated.

China boasts a history of over 2,000 years in the discovery, development, management, and operation of the islands and adjacent waters in the South China Sea. Throughout this long historical development, China has been the most powerful country in the region surrounding the South China Sea Other countries around the South China Sea have either been incorporated into Chinese territory or have maintained long-term friendly relations as vassals. Compared with other countries, China has led by a large margin in terms of national strength, level of productivity forces, and navigation equipment and technology.

However, in the advent of the stage of imperialism, the countries around the South China Sea were reduced to colonies or semi-colonies of the imperial powers one after another. Against this backdrop, since the 20th century, the imperialists of France and Japan successively began to invade in the South China Sea.

Notably, in April, 1933, France dispatched vessels to encroach on some islands and reefs in Nansha Qundao, creating the "Incident of Nine Islets" that astonished the world. This incident immediately led to fierce protests from the Chinese government and its people. On June 7th, 1933, the Chinese government set up "the National Committee for the Review of Maritime and Overland Maps" composed of the General Staff, the Ministry of the Interior, the Ministry of Foreign Affairs, the Admiralty, the Ministry of Education and the Mongolian and Tibetan Affairs Commission, which was responsible for the examination of the land and water maps published all over China. In its 25th session held on December 21st, 1934, the Committee examined and approved 132 "Chinese and English names of the islands in the South China Sea", and published them in the first proceedings of the Committee released in January, 1935. This map has included all of China's maritime boundary extending south to Zengmu Tan (James Shoa), west to Qianwei Tan (now known as Wan'an Tan, aka Vanguard Bank), east to Haima Tan (Seahorse

Shoal) and north to Dongsha Qundao, and names them as Dongsha Qundao, Xisha Qundao, Nansha (now known as Zhongsha) Qundao, and Tuan Sha (now known as Nansha) Qundao, respectively. On March 22nd, 1935, the Committee held its 29th conference and stipulated that future administrative boundary maps must indicate the aforementioned four archipelagos.

On September 28th, 1945, U.S. President Truman issued a "Presidential Proclamation," declaring that in order to conserve and utilize the natural resources of the seabed and continental shelf, the continental shelf adjacent to the U.S. coast, extending to a depth of 100 fathoms (600 feet or 183 meters), and covering an area of 700,000 square miles of seabed adjacent to the U.S. continental coast, is under U.S. jurisdiction and control.

This practice triggered the emulation from other coastal countries. On October 25th, 1945, Mexico declared its right to develop the continental shelf extending offshore to a depth of 200 meters. In 1947, Chile and Peru announced their jurisdiction and control over the marine areas extending 200 nautical miles off their coasts, which, however, does not affect the rights of free navigation in the high seas. Subsequently, Latin American countries advocated for the establishment of a 200-nautical-mile area of sovereignty and jurisdiction through several international conferences and policy declarations. In this context, in November, 1947, the Second United Nations General Assembly passed a resolution to establish the International Law Commission, prioritizing the law of the sea as the priority on its agenda.

Therefore, it was absolutely common and natural for the Chinese government to clarify its maritime jurisdiction and control range, in the name of the Ministry of Civil Affairs, with the 11-dashed line in December 1947, which was based on the effort made by the former "National Committee for the Review of Maritime and Overland Maps". As a major victor in World War II, China announced its establishment of jurisdiction and control zone in the South China Sea according to its historic title, yet inferior to the extensive range declared by the U.S. president. Besides, ever since the announcement, maps in China and abroad have all referred to China's maritime boundary in the South China Sea as the 11-dashed line, which has never met with any protest from any state concerned, and even been approved and recognized by some countries involved. This indicates that this line of range is set up on fairly profound legal basis.

III. The significance of the intermittent range line on the maintenance of China's sovereignty over and maritime rights in Nansha Qundao

The intermittent range line epitomizes China's territorial sovereignty and maritime equities in the waters of Nansha Qundao. Without this, we will lose the basis for all of our rightful claims over Nansha Qundao.

1.Claims on the sovereignty of islands

Taiping Dao (Taiping Island) is the only island in the Nansha waters that does not need any supply of subsistence from the outside world (like water) and is habitable for human beings. Some of the islands and reefs, though already equipped with man-made structures, are only livable by humans when fresh water, vegetables and other supplies are transported from the mainland. Moreover, among over 230 islands and reefs that have been named, quite a few of them are reef flats and shoals still hidden under water at high tide. Such reefs, shoals and underwater banks are, according to the stipulation of the principle about islands in the modern law of the sea, do not meet the conditions for asserting territorial claims. Especially in the case of Zengmu Ansha (James Shoal), it is clearly stated in our elementary school textbooks as well as various newspapers and magazines that this is the southernmost territory of China. And a great number of encyclopedias, dictionaries, textbooks, newspapers, magazines and even maps in foreign countries note that "Zengmu Ansha is the southernmost territory of China". The sole evidence of this statement is the traditional sea boundary in discussion. The highest point of Zengmu Ansha is 21 meters away from the sea level, for which there has undoubtedly been not inhabitant before. Furthermore, most of the islands and reefs in Nansha Qundao are located on the Sunda Shelf. So, China may lose the basis of sovereignty claim on those islands according to the principles of continental shelf.

2.Maritime equities

China's maritime equities in the waters of Nansha Qundao are mainly shown in the four aspects as follows:

(1) The right to manage, conserve, exploit and develop all of the biological and non-biological resources encompassed in the ocean and its subsoil;

(2) The priority to conduct scientific research;

(3) The right to supervise and protect the maritime environment;

(4) The right to control the navigation and air traffic in this water.

As an inheritance of traditional rights, since Chinese fishermen have historically engaged not only in fishing but also in collecting benthic marine treasures such as sea cucumbers and shells, which involves the seabed, China enjoys the rights to manage, conserve, explore, and develop biological and non-biological resources within the traditional boundary line of the South China Sea. Since it was suggested at the Far East Observatory Conference held in Hong Kong in the 1930s that a meteorological station establish in the South China Sea, and requests were made in the 1950s and 1980s to set up meteorological and hydrological observation stations in the same area, China has priority rights to conduct scientific research in this region. In order to preserve the biological and non-biological resources in the waters of Nansha Qundao, China must carry out surveillance and preservation of marine environment within the traditional sea boundary of the South China Sea, and investigate and prosecute illegal actions that violate the environmental law and lead to major marine environmental accidents.

That said, both historically and currently, all countries can navigate and fly in the South China Sea, so China should not impose traffic controls on the South China Sea like it does in internal waters or territorial seas. Still, according to international maritime law, China enjoys the rights to regulate navigation and air traffic within a 12-nautical-mile territorial sea and contiguous zone of our islands and reefs.

IV. The conception to fight for China's territorial sovereignty over and maritime equities in Nansha Qundao and its neighboring waters using the intermittent range line

The 11-dashed line, as a traditional sea boundary, fully presents China's equities in this water as follows: China's traditional fishing practices and collection of marine treasures in this area should be fully carried out, with protection and support from the state in terms of production conditions and material supplies; scientific research activities should be further strengthened, and research results should be published at various domestic and international scientific forums. Additionally, efforts should be made to enhance popular science education, spreading knowledge about Nansha Qundao to all segments of society at home and abroad, especially the youth, as part of patriotic education; rescue operations for major maritime accidents in the Nansha waters should be strengthened to demonstrate China's presence; the surveillance and management of accidents detrimental to the environment of the Nansha water should be strengthened. Besides, the most important thing for China is to exert full sovereignty over the islands, reefs, shoals and banks within this range line. Any attempts by any country to encroach upon our islands and reefs should be met with resolute actions, and those that have illegally occupied islands and reefs should be publicly declared to be acts of aggression against China's territory, holding them accountable for all consequences of their actions.

This intermittent boundary line, as China's traditional sea boundary in the South China Sea, should have its geographical coordinates and connection scheme clarified as soon as possible. It is the foundation for China to negotiate with relevant countries to solve the issue of the delineation of their maritime boundary. Should there be any overlap between this line and other provisions of relevant countries stipulated by international maritime laws (e.g. the principle of continental shelf and the 200-nautical-mile exclusive economic zone), the dispute should be solved via negotiation. When China's traditional sea boundary overlaps with the entitlement lines of relevant countries, there are two possible solutions: (1) Establishing the median line between China's traditional sea boundary and the other party's entitlement line as the dividing line between the maritime areas of both parties; (2) If the previous solution is not feasible, all islands and reefs within the overlapping area of the two lines shall be considered China territory, and the maritime area shall be designated as a jointly developed zone between China and the relevant countries. The biological resources in this area should have specific percentages set for the catch limits of both parties, provided that their production capacity is fully protected. For the exploration and development of non-biological resources, both parties should negotiate to determine the investment scale, production volume, and profit-sharing methods of each side.

Section 3 An Analysis on the "Argument" of the Philippines for Sovereignty Claims over Nansha Qundao

The Philippines lodged its earliest sovereignty claim on Nansha Qundao in August 1933, when former Senator los Reyes of the Philippines thought that the nine small islands in the South China Sea which were occupied by France should belong to the Philippines, and tabled his proposal to Governor-General Murphy of United States in the Philippines. At that time, the coast surveys of the United States in the Philippines believed that the nine islets captured by France lie 200 miles outside of the maritime boundary of the Philippines stipulated by the *Treaty of Paris*, for which they are not within the territory scope of the Philippines. It is said that in 1938, the Philippine President Quezon attempted to persuade the Japanese government to occupy Nansha Qundao in joint force.

On May 11th, 1956, Cloma, a Filipino, arrived in Nansha Qundao with his brothers and a crew of 40 men, hoisting the flag of the Philippines on various islands (including Taiping Dao), declaring its "official entitlement" of Nansha Qundao, and renaming the occupied islands as the "Kalayaan Island Group". Subsequently, Cloma wrote to the Vice President and Minister of Foreign Affairs Garcia of the Philippines, noting that he had occupied Nansha Qundao. Cloma included islands like Nanwei Dao, Taiping Dao, Hongxiu Dao (Namyit Island), Nanhai Jiao (Mariveles Reef), Haikou Jiao (Investigator Northeast Shoal), Yuya Ansha (Investigator Shoal) in the alleged "Kalayaan Island Group", and proclaimed according to the "right of discovery and occupation" that he was the prince of the "kingdom of freedom", hence being called "maniac" by the journalistic circles of the Philippines.

Yet the Philippines treated Cloma's deed with tremendous support. During Cloma's so-called "expedition" to Nansha Qundao in 1956, Vice President Garcia joined the banquet for the "expedition team" on March 1st, proclaiming in December that "except from the seven island groups internationally known as Nansha Qundao..., most of these islands have never been occupied or inhabited.... Due to their adjacency to the western boundary of the Philippines' and their historical and geographical connection with the Philippine Archipelago, these islands are of essential strategic value for the national defence and security of our country," for which Nansha Qundao should be placed under the jurisdiction of the Philippines.

In 1971, President Marcos of the Philippines claimed in a conference for national security that apart from Nansha Qundao, there are 53 islands under the jurisdiction of the Philippines. He also noticed that, "these islands are deemed as terra nullius which may well be acquired through approaches acknowledged by international law, such as taking them by occupation and effective management."

The Philippines dispatched its navy to occupy Mahuan Dao (Nanshan Island) and Zhongye Dao (Thitu Island) in August, 1970 and April 1971 respectively, after which it captured and renamed islands like Feixin Dao (Flat Island), Xiyue Dao (West York Island), Nanzi Dao (Southwest Bank) and Nanyao Dao (Loaita Island). Subsequently, the Philippines joined hands with foreign oil company for the exploration of oil and gas resources.

I. Untenable "arguments"

1. The "principle of discovery and occupation" promoted by the Philippines is utterly ignorant of the fact

In February, 1957, the Minister of Foreign Affairs of the Philippines announced in his letter to Cloma that Nansha Qundao "is newly surfaced and not included on maps, and they are unoccupied, so the Filipinos naturally have the right to explore economically and cultivate the land". In February, 1974, the Philippine government forwarded its letters to the authorities of Taiwan and the Saigon government of South Vietnam to Chinese representative at the United Nations, stating that Nansha Qundao is "terra nullius and does not belong to any country." Such an argument based on "the principle of discovery and occupation" is held regardless of facts. There is even no need to trace back to ancient history: just in January 1935, the first issue of the "Bulletin of the National Committee for the Review of Maritime and Overland Maps" published the "Location Map of South China Sea Islands"; and in 1947, Department of Territorial Affairs of the Ministry of Internal Affairs of the Nanjing National Government compiled the "Map of the Locations of Nansha Qundao", both of which clearly marked all the islands that the Philippines claimed to have "discovered" more than 20 years before Cloma's so-called "exploration" and "expedition" of the "Kalayaan Island Group". As for occupation, the Chinese government retrieved all of the islands and reefs in Nansha Qundao and Xisha Qundao occupied by Japan in May, 1947 after World War II.

2. The "principle of the occupation and effective management of terra nullius" was put forward by the Philippines as an excuse of invasion

In 1971, the Philippine President Marcos proclaimed that, "These islands are deemed as terra nullius which may well be acquired through approaches acknowledged by international law, such as taking them by occupation and effective management." However, Nansha Qundao has been Chinese territory since ancient times. Early before Marcos' announcement of the said principle, China had actually occupied the Taiping Dao, the major island of Nansha Qundao. How can one claim that these islands are terra nullius? To occupy the territory of another country is aggression, and "effective administration" is a manifestation of this aggressive act; therefore, it is always illegal.

3. The Philippines proclamation that "the Kalayaan Island Group is not Nanhai Qundao" is a clumsy trick of changing territorial entitlement by renaming

In July, 1971, after the Philippines occupied several islands and reefs in Nansha Qundao of China, the Philippine President Marcos said in a press conference, "The Philippines has not made any claim on the Nansha Qundao... Our troop is not on the Spratly but other islands." In February, 1974, the Minister of National Defence Enrile of the Philippines said, "The islands occupied by the Philippines do not belong to the Xisha Qundao. And we believe that they are outside of the Nansha Qundao." It sounded as if the Philippines had discovered a "new world" in the waters of the South China Sea. It was in this way that they thought it possible to separate the islands they occupied from Nansha Qundao. However, according to Juan Alegrado's words, the Freedomland "is home to 53 islands, islets, coral reefs, shallow shoals, banks and beaches, which are located in the South China Sea, extending over an area of 65,000 square kilometers, generally between 110°55' to 118°00' east longitude and 7°30' to 10°55' north latitude." The historical scope line of China's South China Sea is between 3°40' to 21°04' north latitude and 108°00' to 118°00' east longitude, which overlaps with the majority area of the free land mentioned above. The Philippines, on one hand, regards Taiping Dao, Zhongye Dao (Thitu Island), Shuangzi Jiao (North Danger Reefs), Nanyao Dao (Loaita Island), Xiyue Dao (West York Island), Mahuan Dao (Nanshan Island), Feixin Dao (Flat Island), etc., which have long been Chinese territory, as the so-called "Kalayaan Island Group", while proclaiming that the Kalayaan Island Group is not Nansha Qundao on the other hand. This tactic of changing territorial entitlement by simply using a different name is indeed a rare practice in the history of world boundaries.

4. To lodge a territorial claim according to geographical adjacency runs

counter to the basic norms of international conduct

In the international disputes over territory, geographic factors like geology, topographic structure and adjacency cannot be used as a basis for determining sovereignty. Neither will geographical strategy justify the unilateral assertion of sovereignty or claims to sovereignty over an island or a group of islands for the simple reason that they are located in a place of strategic importance. Early in May, 1950, President Quirino of the Philippines claimed that if the Spratly (present-day Nansha) Islands are occupied by enemies, "the national security of our country will be threatened", for which he advocated that this island groups "should belong to the closest country to it, i.e., the Philippines." In February, 1957, García, the Vice President and Minister of Foreign Affairs of the Philippines declared that Nansha Qundao is ought to be Philippine territory in that the Philippines is the closest country to it. Yet the territorial sovereignty of a country is not determined by geographical distance. The unity of national sovereignty does not lie in the unity of physical geography. The territory of a country is usually composed of non-contiguous spatial parts separated even by other countries or the high seas, etc., which is a common international phenomenon. Therefore, to lodge a territorial claim according to geographical adjacency runs counter to the basic norms of international conduct.

II. The territory of the Philippines has been defined by international law and even the laws of the Philippine itself

According to Article 3 of the treaty signed in Paris by the U.S. and Spain, the territorial boundaries of the Philippines is as follows: "Island groups called the Philippine Archipelago ceded by Spain to the U.S., including the islands within the following boundaries: this boundary runs from west to east along or near latitude 20°N, passing through the navigable waterway at the center of the Bashi Channel from Greenwich along longitude 118° to 127°E, thence due along longitude 127°E to the intersection at latitude 4°45'N, thence due to its intersection with 119°35'E, thence due along longitude 119°35'E to latitude 7°40'N, thence, due to its intersection with 116°E of Greenwich, thence due along the parallel of 10°N with its intersection with 118°E of Greenwich, thence to the point of beginning from 118°E of Greenwich." This boundary does not, undoubtedly, include Nansha Qundao of China.

In 1900, the U.S. and Spain signed the Treaty for Cession of Outlying Islands of the Philippines, which not only reaffirmed the provisions of the 1898 Treaty of Paris but also ceded the Kalayaan islands, Sulu Archipelago, Sibutu, and their associated islets to the U.S. Similarly, Nansha Qundao is not included in the island groups above.

On June 16th, 1961, the Philippines issued Republic Act No. 3046m proclaiming that its territory extends from 21°7'N (Ivatan Island, the northernmost part of Batan Islands) to 4°24'N (in Prances Reef) in the south, and from 116°55'E (located in Bank) in the west to 126°36'E (located in Pusan Point) in the east. Despite the alternation of specific latitude of the Philippine territory, Nansha Qundao is still not within this range.

On March 7th, 1955, the Philippines submitted a declaration to the International Legal Commission of the United Nation about the range of the territorial sea of the Philippines, claiming that, "the Philippines believes that the sea between each island in this island group (Nansha Qundao), however its area and size, is the necessary accessory of the Philippine territory that constitutes its internal waters and is under its exclusive sovereignty. Meanwhile, based on the Treaty of Paris signed on December 10th, 1898, the treaty on November 7th, 1900 between the United States of America and the Kingdom of Spain, the Convention between the United Kingdom and the United States on July 6th, 1932, Section 6 of Act No.4003 of the Commonwealth of the Philippines, and Article 2 of the Philippine Constitution, all of the other waters repeatedly mentioned in the said documents are all deemed as the territorial waters of the Philippines. The purpose is to protect the fishing rights of the Philippines, safeguard its fishery resources, enforce taxation and anti-smuggling laws, ensure national defense and security, and protect the rights and interests that the Philippines considers essential to its national welfare and security, including the unbiassed granting of the right of innocent passage to vessels from friendly countries through these waters." This declaration did not include any record that Nansha Qundao is Philippine territory.

On June 17th, 1961, the Philippines issued Republic Act No. 3046 entitled "The Law of the Determination of the Baseline of Territorial Sea of the Philippines", with provisions as follows:

The national territory referred to in the Philippine Constitution includes all lands ceded to the United States as stipulated in the Treaty of Paris signed on December 10, 1898, the scope of which is outlined in Article III of the aforementioned treaty. This territory also includes all islands as provided in the treaty signed between the United States and Spain on November 7, 1900, and the treaty signed between the United States and Great Britain on January 2, 1930. The Philippine government, with its constitution published, has jurisdiction over all of its territory.

Hence the waters within the range of the territory as stipulated in the treaties above have always been viewed as part of the territorial island groups of the Philippines.

Hence all of the waters surrounding and connecting various islands of the Philippines, however their width or area, have always been regarded as the necessary appendage of the land territory of the Philippines, constituting part of the Philippine inland or internal waters.

Hence the waters out of the islands on the outer edge of the Philippine Archipelago while within the Philippine territory stipulated by the treaties above, still constitute the territorial sea of the Philippines.

Hence the baseline defining the Philippine territorial sea is determined by the straight line connecting the proper points of the islands on the outer edge of the Philippine Archipelago.

Hence the baseline in discussion shall be clear and defined and illustrated in specific clarity for the information of the concerned.

This law did define the baseline and range of the Philippine territorial sea clearly, explicitly and unequivocally. Whereas it also demonstrated with tremendous clarity that Nansha Qundao is not within the territorial sea of the Philippines.

Nansha Qundao is not included within the territorial waters of the Philippines as defined by international law and Philippine laws and regulations. Thus, the following "arguments" put forward by the Philippines for its claim over Nansha Qundao are untenable: Depending merely on the personal "discovery and occupation" of Cloma on May 15th, 1956, President Marcos of the Philippines declared that Nansha Qundao is an island group "left on the sea with controversy". On June 11th, 1978, the Philippines, by issuing Presidential Decree No. 1596, named the islands it occupied as "the Kalayaan Island Group", and placed them under the jurisdiction of Palawan Province; on July 15th, the country published Presidential Decree No. 1599, announcing that the so-called Kalayaan Island Group is located in the exclusive economic zone of the Philippines, for which the entrance of foreign vessels is prohibited. This is a purely unilateral practice that cannot provide any legal basis; therefore, it is deemed illegal.

Section 4 A Review on the "Arguments" of Vietnam About the Sovereignty Issue of Xisha Qundao and Nansha Qundao

Since time immemorial, Xisha Qundao and Nansha Qundao have been the territory of China, over which the People's Republic of China enjoys an indisputable sovereignty. This is not only proved by a wealth of historical materials, documents, maps, cultural relics and abundant legal basis, but also acknowledged by many countries around the world and widespread global opinion. However, as the old China was plagued by enduring impoverishment and long-standing debility, the "Treasure Island" (Taiwan) of China was occupied by French and Japanese imperialists. After the victory in the War of Resistance Against Japan, the Chinese government took over these islands from the Japanese army, thereby reclaiming and consolidating its sovereignty. At that time, France did not protest against China's actions, implicitly acknowledging China's sovereignty. After World War II, especially since the 1960s, due to the discovery of rich oceanic resources like oil and gas around Xisha Qundao and Nansha Qundao, countries around this two island groups stirred up disputes over China's sovereignty over those islands, leading to the severe situation that "the islands of China are encroached on, the waters of China are divided and the resources of China are deprived." Among them, Vietnam is the country that "has occupied the most islands and reefs of Nansha Qundao, divided the largest area of the South China Sea, and exhibits the most rampant and arrogant actions that infringe upon China's maritime rights in the South China Sea". They have successively published four white papers (including the white paper from the Saigon authorities in South Vietnam) and a multitude of signed articles and propaganda pamphlets, tirelessly collecting "evidence", coining public opinion, deceiving both the international community and their own people, and repeatedly inciting anti-

China and anti-Chinese sentiments. Since China proposed the policy of "sovereignty belongs to China, disputes can be shelved, and we can pursue joint development" and the normalization of relations between the two countries and parties in November 1991, Vietnam has continued to maintain its stubborn stance, exhibiting extreme sensitivity and causing repeated frictions and incidents, which have become a serious obstacle to the normal development of bilateral relations. Therefore, in order to safeguard the sacred sovereignty of China, we must refute the "legal basis" and "historical and geographical evidence" brought up by Vietnam.

I. The untenable "legal basis"

1.The "legal basis" put forward by Vietnam is without a trace of legal force

Since the first White Book cast by the Saigon authorities of South Vietnam in 1975, wishing to perpetrate the notion that Xisha Qundao and Nansha Qundao "have been Vietnamese territory since ancient time", the Hanoi authorities have cast three successive white books to patch up 19 pieces of repeated "supporting materials" in total. Taking the Hanoi white book in September 1979 as example, all 14 articles, from Article VI to XIX are all materials proving the encroachment of the French colonial authorities, Saigon authorities of South Vietnam and Hanoi authority on China's Xisha Qundao and Nansha Qundao since 1933. As is known to all, the aggression of the French colonists soon encountered intensive protest and opposition from the Chinese government and its people. According to international law, aggression cannot serve as a legal basis for rights and claims. Therefore, the materials they cited regarding the jurisdiction over Xisha Qundao and Nansha Qundao by the French colonial authorities and the Vietnamese authorities that succeeded them are devoid of legal effect.

2. Xisha Qundao and Nansha Qundao are not "terra nullius" over which

France has no "priority"

The Hanoi authorities pointed out that France had once occupied Xisha Qundao and Nansha Qundao in the name of its "jurisdiction in the name of Vietnam". While in fact, Xisha Qundao and Nansha Qundao are part of Chinese territory since ancient times. Before the "key dates" when France occupied the nine islets of China's Nansha Qundao on the pretext of "terra nullius" on July 25th, 1933 (i.e. "Incident of Nine Islets"), and announced its "occupation" of China's Xisha Qundao on July 3rd, 1938, the said two island groups have always been under the effective jurisdiction and control of generations of Chinese governments, without experiencing any disputes on their sovereignty between China and any other foreign government. According to international law, terra nullius could be lands either being uninhabited, never occupied, under no jurisdiction of any country, or once belonging to a certain country but abandoned by the previous occupant (Wheaton, *Elements of International*, 1906, p264, cited from Zhao Lihai, Legal Issues on South China Sea Islands). How could Xisha Qundao and Nansha Qundao possibly be terra nullius while having been Chinese territory for thousands of years? Besides, the French government has admitted, throughout its history, that Xisha Qundao and Nansha Qundao are Chinese territory. In the 1887 Convention Respecting the Delimitation of the Frontier between China and Tonkin, France explicitly admitted that all of the island groups in the South China Sea were under the jurisdiction of China. Later in 1920, the Nanko Enterprise of Japan, coveting the guano (phosphorite) on China's Xisha Qundao, sent a request letter to the Admiralty of France in Saigon inquiring about whether Xisha Qundao was the territory of French Annam. At that time, the head of the French Navy replied that, "To the best of my knowledge, although there are no records to verify, I can confidently assert that the Xisha Qundao do not belong to France." In 1921, the French Premiere and Minister of Foreign Affairs Briand admitted that, "due to the fact that the Chinese government established their own sovereignty in 1909 (i.e., Li Zhun's patrol on the South China Sea), it is now impossible for us to lodge any claim on these islands at present." (cited from the magazine *Reviews on Foreign Affairs*, April, 1934, p. 774). In 1929, the French colonial authorities, in the attempt to fabricate evidences to encroach on China's Xisha Qundao, ordered its officials to consult relevant documents, which was proved to be in vain. Therefore, the French Governor-General in Indochina could do nothing but admit that, "According to various reports, the Xisha Qundao should be deemed as the territory of China." Until July, 1931, the colonial department of France wrote to Governor-General Gougal in Indochina that if the foreign activities of occupying China's Xisha Qundao "are rejected, and under the condition that our legal approaches have been exhausted, France will admitted China's sovereignty over the Paracel." A French navigator at that time also stated, "It seems at present that Annam has nothing to do with the Xisha Qundao." However, on December 4th, 1931, France proposed territorial claim over Xisha Qundao in the name of the protectorate of Vietnam, which was immediately met with strong protest and definite refuse from the Chinese government. At that time, the French Ministry of Foreign Affairs noted the Chinese Embassy in France that Vietnam had a "Prior right" over Xisha Qundao, of which the basis is that in 1816, Emperor Gia Long of Vietnam "occupied the Hoàng Sa Islands", and in 1835, Emperor Minh Mạng sent men for "temple constructions and stone tablets" there. Just as the French government made territorial claim over China's Xisha Qundao, the 172nd issue of the Vietnamese magazine Nam Phong published an article titled "France Wants Xisha Qundao for Us Vietnamese" in 1931, reflecting the lack of awareness Vietnamese academic community regarding this matter. On July 27th, 1932, the Chinese Ministry of Foreign Affairs instructed its embassy in France to protest against France's territorial claims over Xisha Qundao. On September 29, it formally notified the French government, stating that the Guangdong provincial government had long approved Chinese nationals to develop resources in Xisha Qundao, thereby exercising sovereignty over the islands. It also expressed doubts about France's claim that Vietnam had previously controlled the islands and demanded clarification on the locations of "temple constructions and stone tablets" (the former Nationalist Government, *The Communique of the Foreign Ministry*, July to September, 1933, pp. 203-209). On March 20, 1934, the Chinese government again instructed its embassy in France to notify the French government, pointing out that France's claim that Vietnam occupied the islands in 1816 prior to China's occupation in 1909 was inaccurate. It noted that "in 1816, Annam was still under Chinese rule, making any possibility of occupying Chinese territory implausible. Furthermore, there are no historical records or documents in Chinese history that indicate the islands were ever occupied by Annam, and the accounts in Vietnamese history are therefore inaccurate. In 1909, when Li Zhun erected a flag and fired cannons, it was merely a commemorative ceremony to reaffirm the island's name. In fact, the islands had been occupied by China long before, dating back to the Han Dynasty during General Ma Yuan's southern expeditions, which is well-documented in Chinese history. Furthermore, regarding more recent practices, any merchants wishing to cultivate the islands must obtain approval from the Guangdong authorities, a consistent procedure in place since the 10th year of the Republic (1921) and still upheld today, further proving that the islands are Chinese territory and that the Chinese government has always maintained actual administrative authority over them"(Document No. 483-1 of the Ministry of Foreign Affairs of the Nationalist Government in March, 1934, "Document of Xisha Qundao", Vol. II). With regard to this notification from the Chinese government in categorical terms, the French government made no reply, which is an adequate indication that the French government was devoid of arguments to justify itself, hence unable to persist in its unreasonable claim.

Soon after attempting to occupy China's Xisha Qundao, France again ventured to seize Nansha Qundao of China. On July 25, 1933, France declared in the *Journal Officiel de la République Française* that the French government had dispatched naval forces to occupy nine islands in the South China Sea, declaring that these islands "will henceforth be under French sovereignty." While France considered these small islands to be "terra nullius," it acknowledged that only Chinese people were living on the islands at the time of their occupation. However, in the eyes of both Eastern and Western colonialists, indigenous residents were never regarded as human beings, and the territories they occupied were uniformly treated as "terra nullius." The aforementioned acts of robbery by France immediately met with strong resistance from Chinese fishermen on Nansha Qundao, who cut down the flagpoles and flags erected by the French and dug up the markers buried by them.

The Chinese government and the public were extremely outraged by France's aggressive actions. On August 4th, 1933, the Chinese government formally notified the French government, stating that it "reserved its rights regarding the French government's declaration until the facts were thoroughly verified." Subsequently, a formal protest was lodged, condemning the French government's occupation of Nansha Qundao. The "Incident of Nine Islets" sparked anger among the Chinese people, with labor unions, agricultural associations, commercial groups, and other mass organizations sending telegrams to denounce France's aggressive actions and demanding the swift recovery of lost territory.

On July 3rd, 1938, taking advantage of China's struggle against Japanese aggression, France suddenly occupied China's Xisha Qundao. In response to this act of aggression, Gu Weijun, the Chinese ambassador to France, immediately lodged a protest with the French government.

These facts demonstrate that France's occupation of Xisha and Nansha

Qundao in the 1930s was entirely an act of aggression and is invalid under modern international law. The claim that France "replaced Vietnam in administering" Xisha and Nansha Qundao has no legal basis whatsoever.

3.The spirit of the *Cairo Declaration* and the *Potsdam Proclamation* must not be distorted or tampered with

Three days after France occupied China's Xisha Qundao on July 3rd, 1938, the Japanese Ministry of Foreign Affairs issued a statement on July 6th, 1938: "According to the declarations made by Britain and France in 1900 and 1921, Xisha Qundao is part of the administrative region of Hainan Island; therefore, the current claims of Annam or France regarding Xisha Qundao are indeed unjust" (Hong Kong South China Morning Post, July 7th, 1938). Soon after, Japan occupied China's Hainan Island as well as all the islands in the South China Sea, including Xisha and Nansha Qundao. On April 9th, 1939, the Japanese Governor-General of Taiwan announced in a government bulletin that Xisha and Nansha Qundao had been incorporated into Japanese imperial territory and were under the jurisdiction of Kaohsiung County in Taiwan. Japan's stance and its occupation of Xisha and Nansha Qundao provided significant legal grounds for our post-war recovery of these islands.

From November 22nd to 26th, 1943, representatives from China, Britain, and the United States met in Cairo, and on December 1, they announced the *Cairo Declaration*, signed by U.S. President Franklin D. Roosevelt, British Prime Minister Winston Churchill, and Chinese leader Chiang Kai-shek. The *Cairo Declaration* declared that the three nations aimed to strip Japan of all islands it had gained or occupied since the beginning of World War I in 1914, and to restore territories stolen from China, such as Northeast China, Taiwan, and the Penghu Islands. Japan had recognized before the war that Xisha Qundao and other islands in the South China Sea belonged to China, and it temporarily occupied them during the war, announcing their incorporation under Kaohsiung County. According to the provisions of the *Cairo*

Declaration, these islands should rightfully be returned to China.

On July 26th, 1945, the *Potsdam Proclamation*, issued by China, the United States, and Britain, urged Japan to surrender and reiterated that "the conditions of the *Cairo Declaration* must be implemented," once again stipulating that Japan should return the territories it had occupied in China.

After Japan's surrender, it withdrew from Xisha and Nansha Qundao on August 26th, 1945. The French government, recognizing its untenable position, did not send troops to take over, clearly having abandoned its territorial claims over Xisha and Nansha Qundao. At that time, the Supreme Allied Command issued orders for Japanese troops north of latitude 16°N in Vietnam (including Xisha Qundao) to surrender to the Chinese theater commander. Consequently, North Vietnam was under the military occupation of China. The Chinese theater commander instructed the Japanese troops stationed in Nansha Qundao to surrender to the Chinese forces at Yulin Port on Hainan Island. Later, in March 1946, when the Chinese government handed over the territory of northern Vietnam to France, the French did not make any claims over Xisha and Nansha Qundao.

The Chinese government, in contrast to France, received the territories that had been stolen from China by Japanese invaders in accordance with the provisions of the *Cairo Declaration* and the *Potsdam Proclamation*. In November and December 1946, the Chinese government appointed Xiao Ciyin and Mai Yunyu as commissioners to receive Xisha Qundao and Nansha Qundao respectively. They boarded four naval vessels, namely "Yong Xing", "Zhong Jian", "Tai Ping", and "Zhong Ye", to carry out the reception and held a ceremony on the islands, erecting monuments reading "Monument' of the Navy Recapture of Xisha Qundao" and "Taiping Island", etc. The Chinese Navy, along with officials from the Ministry of Internal Affairs and Guangdong Province, conducted mapping and investigations of the two groups of islands. Subsequently, the Chinese government once again placed the two groups of islands under the jurisdiction of Guangdong Province. Starting from March 15th, 1947, they were temporarily placed under the jurisdiction of the Navy Command. On December 1st of the same year, the Ministry of Internal Affairs renamed 159 islands, reefs, shoals, and sands in Xisha and Nansha Qundao, and marked China's traditional maritime boundaries in the South China Sea with a dashed line on Chinese maps, which was officially implemented. During this period, the actions of the Chinese government to receive Xisha and Nansha Qundao and consolidate its sovereignty were not challenged by the French colonial authorities or any other country. This fully demonstrates that China's sovereignty over Xisha and Nansha Qundao is entirely legitimate.

However, Vietnam has deliberately distorted and misinterpreted the spirit of the *Cairo Declaration* and the *Potsdam Proclamation* to justify its aggressive actions. It claims that these documents only specify the return of Northeast China, Taiwan, and the Penghu Islands to China, without mentioning Xisha and Nansha Qundao. In fact, the original text of the *Cairo Declaration* includes the phrase "for example" before Northeast China, Taiwan, and the Penghu Islands, and the word "etc." afterward, making it clear that the *Cairo Declaration* intended to provide examples and was not necessary to list all "territories that Japan had stolen from China." However, Vietnam intentionally omitted the word "etc." when quoting, distorting and misinterpreting the original intent of the *Cairo Declaration*. This despicable tactic of swapping reality for fiction is truly astonishing.

4.The actions and statements of the Vietnamese government violate the principle of "estoppel" in international law

In order to occupy China's Xisha and Nansha Qundao, Vietnam has used the 1951 San Francisco Peace Treaty, which was not recognized by China, the Soviet Union, Vietnam, and other countries at that time, as a formal "legal basis." This fully exposes their approach that disregards historical facts and international credibility, as well as their contradictory position.

People will not forget that prior to 1974, Vietnam had solemnly and officially recognized in its government statements, diplomatic notes, as well as in newspapers, maps, and textbooks, that Xisha Qundao and Nansha Qundao have been China's territory since ancient times On June 15th, 1950, Nguyen Van Quyen, Deputy Minister of Foreign Affairs of the Democratic Republic of Vietnam, met with Charge d'Affaires Li Zhimin of the Chinese Embassy in Vietnam, and solemnly stated: "According to the materials from Vietnam, Xisha Qundao and Nansha Qundao are supposed to be the territory of China from a historical standpoint." At that time, Le Loc, Deputy Director of the Asian Department of the Vietnamese Ministry of Foreign Affairs, further elaborated on the materials from the Vietnamese side and added, "Historically, Xisha Qundao and Nansha Qundao have belonged to China since the Song Dynasty." On September 4th, 1958, the Chinese government issued a statement declaring that the territorial sea of the People's Republic of China is 12 nautical miles wide, and explicitly stated, "This regulation applies to all territories of the People's Republic of China, including... Dongsha Qundao, Xisha Qundao, Zhongsha Qundao, Nansha Qundao, and other islands belonging to China." On September 9th, *Nhân Dân*, the newspaper of the central organ of the Communist Party of Vietnam reported and acknowledged the detailed content of the Chinese declaration in a prominent position on its front page. On September 6th, Premier Phạm Văn Đồng of the Vietnamese government noted Premier Zhou Enlai of the Chinese State Council solemnly that "the government of the Democratic Republic of Vietnam admits and agrees with the declaration of the government of the People's Republic of China about the decision on territorial sea on September 4th, 1958," and that "the government of the Democratic Republic of Vietnam shows respect to this decision." The notification of Phạm Văn Đồng clearly demonstrated that the heads of the

Vietnamese government admit that Xisha Qundao and Nansha Qundao are the territory of China. In the event of foreign invasion into Xisha Qundao, the Vietnamese government had clearly admitted that Xisha Qundao belongs to China. On May 9th, 1965, the Vietnamese government issued a statement about the definition of the "operational area" of the U.S. army in Vietnam, pointing out that, "The U.S. President Johnson designated the entire territory of Vietnam and the surrounding waters extending about 100 nautical miles off the Vietnamese coast, as well as part of the territorial sea of Xisha Qundao of the People's Republic of China, as the operational area for the U.S. armed forces". This was considered a "direct threat to the security of the Democratic Republic of Vietnam and its neighboring countries." Furthermore, on May 13th, 1969, the Vietnamese newspaper *Nhan Dan (People)* reported that "on May 10th, a U.S. military aircraft violated the airspace over Yongxing Dao and Dong Dao (Lincoln Island) in Xisha Qundao of Guangdong Province, China." Similar reports continued to appear in Vietnamese media. The official maps and textbooks published in Vietnam have clearly recognized Xisha Qundao and Nansha Qundao as Chinese territory. In 1960, a world map compiled by the Geographic Department of the General Staff of the Vietnam People's Army marked Xisha Qundao and Nansha Qundao with their Chinese names and noted that they belonged to China. In 1974, in the geography textbook for the ninth grade in common schools in Vietnam, it was stated in a text titled "The People's Republic of China", "From the Nansha and Xisha Qundao to Hainan Island, Taiwan Island, the Penghu Islands, and the Zhoushan Islands... these islands take on a bow shape, forming a 'Great Wall' to protect the Chinese mainland."

Now, while the Vietnamese government is forced to acknowledge the aforementioned "official materials belonging to the state" and "documents with legal value," it nonetheless openly fabricates lies with sophistry. It is argued that Vietnam's past actions were motivated by a need to seek China's support for its struggle against American aggression. The Vietnamese authorities should be well aware that China's support for Vietnam's national liberation struggle was entirely for just purposes, without any conditions attached, and never made any selfish demands. Vietnam had no need, and did not exchange territorial sovereignty for "deals" with China. Moreover, when the Vietnamese government solemnly recognized in 1956 and 1958 that Xisha and Nansha Qundao belonged to Chinese territory, Vietnam had not yet begun its struggle against American aggression; the Vietnamese government's statements fully reflected their own position. The seriousness of Vietnam's flip-flopping lies in the fact that, according to international law, statements made by a country's head of government or minister of foreign affairs, especially those concerning territorial sovereignty, are legally binding. Once they make a recognition or acknowledgment, they must adhere to it and cannot retract their statement; otherwise, it constitutes a violation of the principle of "estoppel" under international law, and they will bear all the international responsibilities that arise from it. Since the Vietnamese government has clearly acknowledged China's sovereignty over Xisha and Nansha Qundao, it has a legal obligation not to dispute China's sovereignty over these two islands and has no justification for encroaching on certain reefs of Nansha Qundao that belong to China. Their inconsistent positions and various sophistries fundamentally violate the principle of "estoppel" in international law and are completely untenable.

II. The mis-attributing "evidences of historical geography"

Similarly, Vietnam, cannot provide any credible evidence in terms of historical geography. By conducting a brief analysis of the place names "Hoàng Sa" and "Trường Sa" in ancient Vietnamese texts, along with what they boast as the most original and direct records - *the Collection of the South's Road Map, Miscellaneous Records on the Pacification of the Frontiers*, and the *Complete Map of Unified Dai Nam* — we can see that their so-called "historical geographical evidence" largely relies on the devices of name displacement and misrepresentation. They claim that China's Xisha Qundao and Nansha Qundao are their territory name "Hoàng Sa" and "Trường Sa" respectively, which is a mins0attribution fundamentally untenable.

1. Regarding the place names of "Hoàng Sa" and "Great Trường Sa" in Vietnamese ancient texts

The Vietnamese white papers and the numerous articles they have published create confusion regarding place names by forcefully linking Xisha and Nansha Qundao, which are 350 nautical miles apart. They claim that "for many centuries, the Hoàng Sa Islands and Trường Sa Islands have often been combined in maps and documents, sharing common names such as Hoàng Sa, Great Trường Sa, or Vạn Lý Trường Sa." This "combination," however, often leaves them feeling guilty and weak, leading them to fabricate the claim that Vietnam's "Hoàng Sa Islands" refers to the islands internationally known as the Paracels, while the "Trường Sa Islands" refer to the islands internationally known as the Spratlys. They further state that "Vietnamese historical texts often mention the 'Great Trường Sa Island', referring to both the Paracels and Spratlys, and more generally to all islands and territories belonging to Vietnam."

Above all, it should be pointed out that the "Hoàng Sa" and "Great Trường Sa" mentioned in Vietnamese historical records do not "refer to all islands and territories belonging to Vietnam".

It is recorded in *the Miscellaneous Records on the Pacification of the Frontiers (Vol. II)* that, "Outside of various harbors of Thanh Quang, there are rocky mountains rising, with each harbor serving as a fortification, varying in width. At the northern village of An Nieu Commune (安裊社) in the southern provincial administration prefecture(南布政州), there is a mountain named Culao Gu（㕦劳轱）, which can be reached by sea in about four watches. Outside the harbor of Da Nang of Điện Bàn Prefecture, there are the famous Hoan Tra (丸茶) and Hoan Lo (丸鲁), which can be reached by sea in about half a watch. Outside of Đại Chiêm of Thang Hòa Prefecture, there is a large mountain called Culao Cham（㕦劳针） with three peaks facing each other. Two of these peaks are lofty and lush, with dwellings, fields, villages, and flowering citrus trees, and there are sweet springs atop them; while one peak is small and dry, reachable by sea in about two watches. Outside the harbor of Dai in An Vinh Commune of Bình Sơn County, Quảng Ngãi Prefecture, there is a mountain named Culao Ung(㕦劳蕹), where there used to be the Tu Chinh Ward (四政坊) and village fields, reachable by sea in about four watches. Beyond that is Dao Trường Sa Lon, which was once bustling with marine products and foreign goods. The Hoàng Sa Company was established to collect goods there, with a journey taking three days and nights to reach, and it is located near Bac Hai Island. At the harbors of Tan Quan , Thi Phu , Tre Tram, and Nac Man of Quy Nhơn Prefecture, there are plenty of hills, islands and swallow's nests, for which the government establishes Thanh Chau Company for their collection. Outside of the sea of Bình Thuận Dinh, there is a mountain named Côn Lôn, which is several miles in width and abounding with swallow's nests. Beyond there is a mountain called Culao Van, which abounded with marine products and foreign goods in the past. Thus, the government establishes Hai Mun Company to collect them. At the harbor of Gia Định Prefecture, there is a mountain named Great Côn Lôn in the outer sea of Hà Tiên Town, with dwellings on it." Only from the records in the *Miscellaneous Records on the Pacification of the Frontiers*, it can already be seen that the islands and banks along the coast from Thanh Quang to Hà Tiên have their own names, which cannot be roughly referred to as "Hoàng Sa" and "Great Trường Sa". The ambiguous and vague "historical evidence" provided by Vietnam are of no legal value.

Secondly, the term "Great Trường Sa" mentioned in ancient Vietnamese texts does not, evidently, refer to China's Nansha Qundao, but rather to islands and banks in the sea near the middle of Vietnam.

The *Abridged Chronicles of Viet* is the earliest ancient Vietnamese text mentioning "Great Trường Sa". This book (Vol.II) mentions in its record about the conquest of Chiem Thanh by Lý Thánh Tông in 1069 that, "On the second day... in the second month of spring in the first year of Than Vu (Earth Rooster), Lý Thánh Tông dispatched men like Hoang Jianin Dai lieu ban (Meritorious Officials) to assault the seaport of Nhat Le and seized it. On the sixth day, the troop reached Great Trường Sa; and on the seventh day, they arrived at the seaport of the southern border."

In the *Complete Annals of Dai Viet* (Chapter 2 of the Basic Annals: The First Annal of Lý- Thai Tong) of Ngô Sĩ Liên, both Lý Thái Tông's conquer of Chiem Thanh in 1044 and "the Great and Minor Trường Sa" are mentioned as follows: "On the day of *kuimao* in the first month of the spring in the third year of Thong Thuy (*jiashen*), the Emperor personally led a campaign against Chiem Thanh... On the day of *jiachen*, the army departed from the capital. On the day of *yisi*, the army reached the seaport of Da'e ('Great Evil') when the winds and waves calmed down, which was favorable for crossing. So, the name of Da'e was changed to Da'an ('Great Peace'). Upon arriving at Ma Co Mountain, there were purple clouds embracing the sun. As they passed the Ha Nao Bay, a cloud enveloped the Emperor's boat and followed its movements. On this day, they set up camp at the seaport of Tru Nha. They set out the next day, passed the Great and Minor Trường Sa in just one day by taking advantage of the wind, and arrived at the seaport of Tu Dung

It is recorded in the *Recent Chronicles of O Prefecture (Vol. I, Article about the harbor of Minh Linh),* the regional treatise of Huế, that "A three day voyage from Nhat Le to this place (the harbor of Minh Linh) - of which the traveling distance is pretty much the same both by maritime and overland route alike - will take one to a place named Great Trường Sa." In the article about the harbor of Nhuyen (堧), "The place from the harbor of Viet and that of Tu Dung is named Great Trường Sa; while this harbor (the harbor of Nhuyen) is called Minor Trường Sa."

Actually, the record about the Great and Minor Trường Sa in *The Miscellaneous Records on the Pacification of the Frontiers* follows the statement in *The Recent Chronicles of O Prefecture* that "there is a harbor called Minh Linh (明灵) in the Minh Linh Prefecture... One can reach this place by navigating two days from the harbor of Nhat Le, of which the distance is pretty much the same via maritime and overland route alike. And this place is called Great Trường Sa." Also, the book said that "there is a harbor named Viet in Vũ Xương County", "there is harbor of Tu Dung in Tu Dung County", "there is a harbor called Nhuyen in Kim Tra County... The place starting from Viet to Tu Dung is called Great Trường Sa; while this harbor (Nhuyen) is called Minor Trường Sa."

Later historical and geographical books provide definite notes about the terms "Great Trường Sa" and "Great and Minor Trường Sa" mentioned in the ancient Vietnamese texts above. *The Imperially Ordered Annotated Text Completely Reflecting the History of Viet (the Major Chronicle: Vol. III)*, an official book published in 1884 by the Nguyễn dynasty, cited Lê Quý Đôn's *Miscellaneous Records on the Pacification of the Frontiers* in the note of "Great and Minor Trường Sa", "The place extending along the coast from southern Nhat Le to Minh Linh is called Great Trường Sa, while the area from Viet to Tu Dung is called Minor Trường Sa." Phan Huy Chú also stated in his *Treatise on Geography of the Royal Viet (Vol.I)* that, "The area from the harbors of Viet to Tu Dung is named Great Trường Sa, and the northern harbor is called Minor Trường Sa." Another official publication of the Nguyen dynasty named the *Dai Nam Comprehensive Encyclopedia (Vol. VII)* also recorded in the chapter about "Situation" of Quảng Trị Province that, "...

Moreover, there is this place named Great Trường Sa that extends southward along the coast, resembling a sandy city that stands guard, truly a place of scenic beauty and strategic importance. "The note under the section on "Great Trường Sa" mentions that, "The area extending south from the estuary of Việt Yên along the coast was anciently called Great Trường Sa, stretching over a hundred *li*. To the east, it meets the sea; to the west, it connects with dense forests. The people cherish their towering hills, where the white sands rise in layered mounds, making it, alongside Thừa Thiên Prefecture, a sprawling sand city.""

Besides, present day Vietnamese scholars have made specific statements about "Great and Minor Trường Sa" as well as "Trường Sa" in historical texts. As Thái Văn Kiểm explains, "As for the term Trường Sa, it was seen in the *Hong Duc Atlas* drawn on April 6th of the 21st year of Hongde (i.e. April 25th, 1490) of Lê Thánh Tông's reign (1470-1498). There is a land on this map, with words reading 'One-day Trip from Trường Sa'. This certainly does not refer to an archipelago, but the coast from the seaport of Nhat Le (Quảng Bình), passing the seaports of Hai Phong and Việt **Yên** (Quảng Trị), all the way to Tam Giang - Cau Hai Lagoon (Thừa Thiên). The coast here boasts endless white sand that takes one a day to walk on it (one-day trip). In the *Dai Nam Comprehensive Encyclopedia*, volumes about Quảng Bình, Quảng Trị and Thừa Thiên have all mentioned the long beach above, which also enjoys names like Trường Sa, White Sand (anciently known as Great Trường Sa). The *Recent Chronicles of O Prefecture of Duong Van An* also mentions Trường Sa, defining it as the long white sand zone located in the entire coastal area of Bình Trị Thiên[2]. In the introduction of the *Territory of Vietnam Through the Ages*, Professor Đào Duy Anh listed "Hoàng Sa Archipelago" as a "special issue" that entails further discussion, without affirming that

---

[2] *The Specific Examination on Hoàng Sa and Trường Sa*, (Viet.) Nguyen Nha, etc., the Commercial Press, 1978, pp.217-218.

"Hoàng Sa Archipelago" is Xisha Qundao of China. In his statement of the conquest of Chiem Thanh by Lý Thái Tông in 1044 that "he crossed both the Great and Minor Trường Sa and reached directly in the estuary of O Long", Prof. Đào cited the note of the *Miscellaneous Records on the Pacification of the Frontiers* about "Great and Minor Trường Sa". This shows that Prof. Đào admitted that "Great and Minor Trường Sa" refer to the islands and banks from the harbor of Nhat Le to the harbor of Minh Linh, and from Viet to Tu Dung. (*The Specific Examination on Hoàng Sa and Trường Sa*, p.291)

Needless to say, Vietnamese scholars, in ancient and modern times alike, believe that both the term "Great and Minor

Trường Sa" and "Great Trường Sa Island" refer to the islands, banks and sand zones of the coastal area of Quảng Bình, Quảng Trị and Thừa Thiên of Vietnam, which have nothing to do with Xisha and Nansha Qundao of China.

2.On records in the *Collection of the South's Road Map*

The Vietnamese white papers and monographs do not provide any substantial evidence from historical or geographical perspectives to prove their claims that "Hoàng Sa" (China's Xisha Qundao) and "Trường Sa" (China's Nansha Qundao) have long been "territories of Vietnam." Their much-admired "oldest" and most significant "Vietnamese document" is The *Collection of the South's Road Map*) by Do Ba from the 17th century, which includes a regional map of Quảng Ngãi (collected in the *Hong Duc Atlas*). This map includes a marginal note labeled "Illustration Commentary," stating,

"At the village of Kim Ho, on both banks of the river stand two mountains each containing a gold deposit exploited under governmental control. On the high sea, a 400-ly long and 200-ly wide archipelago called Bãi Cát Vong (摆葛鑕) emerges from the deep sea facing the coastline between the harbor of Đại Chiêm and the harbor of Sa Vinh. During the Southwest monsoon season, commercial ships from various countries sailing near the coasts often wreck on the insular territories. The same thing happens during the North-East monsoon season to those ships sailing on the high sea. All the people on board wrecked ships in this area would starve. Various kinds of wrecked cargoes are amassed on these islands. Each year during the last month of winter, the Nguyễn rulers send to the islands an 18-junk flotilla in order to salvage them. They obtain big quantities of gold, silver, coins, rifles and ammunitions. From the harbor of Đại Chiêm the archipelago is reached after a journey of one-and-a-half day, while one day suffices if one embarks from Sa Kỳ. This long strip of bank is also known for its tortoiseshell."

Off the harbor of Sa Kỳ, there is a mountain abundant in guava wood, known as the Du Troung, which is under governmental control.""

The *Introduction of The Collection of the South's Road Map)*, i.e. the textual illustration of The *Collection of the South's Road Map)*, has similar records with "Illustration Commentary" in the section about "the landscape and attractions of various harbors in Thanh Ngai and Quang Thuan":

"Outside the harbor of Chau Mi , there is a long bank called Bãi Cát Vong, approximately four hundred *ly* long and twenty *ly* wide, floating in the sea. Whenever merchant vessels from various countries enter from the harbors of Đại Chiêm to Sa Vinh and are caught by the southwest storm, they drift here; those caught by the northeast storm also drift here, causing all their goods and treasures to sink to the sandy bottom. Every winter, the king sends eighteen ships to collect the treasures. The journey from Đại Chiêm to here takes a day and a half, from the harbor of Sa Vinh to here takes half a day, and from the harbor of Chau Mi to this archipelago takes two days and two nights."

"Outside the sea of Sa Kỳ, in the harbor of Chau Hong, there is a mountain abundant in guava wood, known as Du Truong Son."

The cited texts above from the *Collection of the South's Road Map* of Do Ba indicate that the "Trường Sa" mentioned therein is not a proper noun, but rather a general term referring to the long sandy belt stretching approximately 400 *li* north-south and 20 *li* east-west along the coasts of Thang Hòa and Quảng Ngãi. This includes the continuous sandbanks and islands collectively known as "Bãi Cát Vong (摆葛鑌)", or Hoàng Sa Bank.

Referring to Do Ba's map, from north to south, there is a river drawn south of Hà ĐôngCounty of Thang Hòa Prefecture (now Tam Kỳ in Quảng Nam Province), whose mouth is at the harbor of Đại Chiêm. In Duy Son County (now Duy Xuyên County in Quảng Nam Province), there is a "Kim Ho Commune" depicted, east of which are "Hóa Hợp Shoal" and "the harbor of Hóa Hợp." Between Binh Som County (now part of Bình Sơn County and Nghĩa Hành County in Quảng Ngãi Province), there is another river whose mouth is at the harbor of Quy Hai. Between Chuong Ngai County and Mo Hoa County (now part of Mo Duc County and Đức Phổ County in Quảng Ngãi Province), there are the harbors of Dai and Tieu, while between Mo Hoa County and Bồng Sơn County in Quy Nhơn Prefecture (now part of Bồng Sơn County and Hoai An County in Binh Dinh Province), there is a harbor called My Tho. Another seaport in Bồng Sơn County is the harbor of Sa Vinh, with Phủ Lý County (now Phu My and Phù Cát Counties in Binh Dinh Province) to its south. In the off shore area between south of the harbor of Đại Chiêm and the harbor of Hóa Hợp, there are representations of inner and outer islands or sandbanks; and in the near sea between the south of the southern Quy Hai and the harbor of Tieu, there is also another island or sandbank depicted. Though no mark of "Bãi Cát Vong" is given on the map, the texts therein still indicate that these series of islands and banks are exactly the "Bãi Cát Vong" in Do Ba's eyes. The location of it corresponds exactly to the offshore islands around Champa, Tong Island, and Canton Islands. Ancient cartographers would not have overlooked these offshore islands while recording China's Xisha Qundao in the ocean. According to Do Ba, from the harbor of Đại Chiêm to the harbor of Sa Vinh, there are two routes divided by "Bãi Cát Vong" into the inner and outer ones, merging into one at Sa Vinh. The route he mentioned can only be an offshore one since the navigation from the harbors of Đại Chiêm to Sa Vinh does not pass through China's Xisha Qundao, nor be divided into two separate lines by it. Places like Sa Kỳ, Du Truong Son, Chau Mi and Chau Hong mentioned in the "Illustration Commentary" and "Introduction" of Do Ba are all not drawn out in his map.

Some place names therein can also be found in the maps of the *Treatise on Giao Chau: Three Prefectures of Quảng Nam*. The map presents, from north to south, the harbor of Han in Hà Đông County, the harbor of Đại Chiêm between Le Duong County and Duy Xuyên County, the harbor of Hóa Hợp between Duy Xuyên County and Bình Sơn County, the harbor of Chau O in Bình Sơn (i.e., the harbor of Chau Hong in Do Ba's word), the harbor of Chau O between Bình Sơn and Chuong Ngai counties (i.e., the harbor of Chau Mi in Do Ba's word), and the harbor of Dai Than Xich Phien between Chuong Ngai and Moc Hoa counties. The "Bãi Cát Vong" is drawn in the open sea between the harbors of Hóa Hợp, Chau O and Chau Mi, almost paralleling the Hoan Son Tra outside of the harbor of Han (now Sơn Tràpeninsula of Da Nang), which is a further indication that it is an offshore island. "Bãi Cát Vong", corresponding to the present-day Canton Islands, is but a part of the Trường Sa in Do Ba's word.

The *Map of the Quảng Nam Circuit* re-drawn by Dumouriez presents from north to south a series of harbors along the coastal area from Hà Đông, Duy Xuyên, Bình Sơn, Chuong Ngai and Moc Hoa counties as follows: the harbors of Đại Chiêm, Hóa Hợp, Yet Huyen, Sa Kỳ , Tieu, Dai, and Ma Ac (the aforementioned My A). In this map, from the harbor of Đại Chiêm to the offshore area south to the harbor of Ma Ac, there is a peanut-shaped boundary line of the "Bãi Cát Vong". Also, an island named "Du Truong Son" is drawn among the sea between the harbors of Sa Kỳ and Tieu in Chuong Ngai County. The boundary of "Bãi Cát Vong" is the same as Do Ba's description of its location, i.e., the islands and sand banks from Champa Island, Zongdao Island to Canton Islands in the present day. The "Du Truong Son" in the map, according to the Vietnamese scholar Hoàng Xuân Hãn, "is no doubt the present-day Culao Re", namely the Lý Sơn Island in Canton Islands. It is included in the boundary line of "Bãi Cát Vong".

In the *Map of Thien Nam* redrawn in 1741 (including *The Map of the Quảng Nam Circuit in the Lê Dynasty*), harbors like Sa Kỳ, Tieu, Dai and My A are also drawn from north to south along the coast of Bình Sơn, Chuong Ngai, Moc Hoa, Bồng Sơn counties. Directly opposite the harbor of Sa Kỳ is a depiction of "Youchang Mountain," namely "Du Truong Son", along with a long strip of boundary line. The northern starting point is not indicated on the map, but there is a section from the south of Bình Sơn County to the area between the harbors of Tieu and Dai, labeled "One-day Trip to Trường Sa". This is apparently part of the aforementioned "Bãi Cát Vong", which is a "Trường Sa" costing a one-day trip to pass. The term "Trường Sa" here is not a name of an island, but a general reference to the islands and sand banks in this area.

We can see from the aforementioned maps by scholars like Do Ba provided by Vietnam, that "Trường Sa", namely "Bãi Cát Vong", refers to the offshore islands and sandbanks north from the harbors of Đại Chiêm and Sa Vinh, which correspond to the islands and sand banks from present-day Champa Island, Tong Island, to Canton Islands. According to Do Ba, "from the harbor of Đại Chiêm the archipelago is reached after a journey of one-and-a-half day", "while one day suffices if one embarks from Sa Kỳ", and "from the harbor of Chau Mi the archipelago is reached two days and two nights". But considering the ancient navigation technology, it would have been impossible to reach China's Xisha Qundao from any port in Vietnam in half a day, a day and a half, or even two days and two nights, let alone to reach Nansha Qundao of China. This shows that the "Bãi Cát Vong" in Do Ba's words refers to some offshore island of Vietnam. Furthermore, from a geological perspective, the "Bãi Cát Vong" described by Do Ba has a length of 400 *li* from north to south and a width of 20 *li* from east to west, indicating a geographic shape that is long in the north-south direction and narrow in the east-west direction. This is in stark contrast to Xisha Qundao, which is long in the east-west direction and short in the north-south direction. Therefore, "Bãi Cát Vong" cannot be Xisha Qundao, let alone Nansha Qundao, which is way larger.

3. On records in the *Miscellaneous Records on the Pacification of the Frontiers*

Lê Quý Đôn's Miscellaneous Records on the Pacification of the Frontiers is often vaunted by Vietnam as "one of their extremely eloquent evidence" and "unprecedentedly informative material" proving that China's Xisha Qundao and Nansha Qundao are the "Hoàng Sa" and "Trường Sa" in their words. The second volume of this book contains two relatively concentrated accounts, which both the Saigon authorities and the Hanoi authorities, as well as the papers and monographs published by Vietnamese scholars, usc as the "basis" for their arguments. Below is a transcript of the relevant passages, along with a brief analysis to see what this "compelling evidence" actually illustrates.

When making an overview on the offshore islands in the coastal area of mid-southern Vietnam, Le said, "Outside the various harbors in Thanh Quang, there are mountain rocks rising, with each harbor serving as a town, varying in width. At the northern village of An Nieu Commune in the southern provincial administration prefecture, there is a mountain named Culao Gu, which can be reached by sea in about four watches. Outside the harbor of Dai in An Vinh Commune of Bình Sơn County, Quảng Ngãi Prefecture, there is a mountain named Culao Ung that reaches over 30 *ly* in width. There used to be four government offices and village fields, reachable by sea in about four watches. Beyond that is Dao Trường Sa Lon, which was once bustling with marine products and foreign goods. The Hoàng Sa Fleet was established to collect goods there, with a journey taking three days and nights to reach, and it is located near Bac Hai Island… At the harbor of Gia Định Prefecture, there is a mountain named Côn Lôn in the outer sea of Hà Tiên Town, with dwellings therein."

When describing the islands in the outer sea of An Vinh Commune of Bình Sơn County, Quảng Ngãi Prefecture, Lê Quý Đôn wrote, "The village of An Vinh, Bình Sơn District, Quảng Ngãi Prefecture, is close by the sea. To the northeast (of the village) there are many islands and miscellaneous rockheads jutting out of the sea, totaling 130 altogether. It takes a day or several watches to sail between each rockhead where there are sometimes springs atop. The archipelago contains a long Hoàng Sa Chu (Golden Sandy Island) of approximately more than 30 ly long, with wide, even surface and freshwater streams transparent to the bottoms. The island has countless swallow's nests and other kinds of birds that are bold and unafraid of people. …Ships from various countries encountering winds often wreck on this island. In the past, the Nguyễn had created a Hoàng Sa Company of 70 men, made up of people from An Vinh village. Every year they take turns in going out to the sea, setting out during the first month of the lunar calendar in order to receive instructions regarding their mission. Each man in the company is given six months' worth of dry food. They row in five fishing boats and it takes them three days to reach the islands. They are free to collect whatever they wish, to catch the birds as they see fit and to fish for food. They (sometimes) find the wreckage of ships which yield such things as bronze swords and copper horses, silver decorations and money, silver rings and other copper products, tin ingots and lead, guns and ivory, golden bee-hive tallow, felt blankets, pottery and so forth. They also collect turtle shells, sea urchins and striped conches in large quantities. This Hoàng Sa Company does not come home until the eighth month of the year. They go to Phú Xuân (present-day Huế) to turn in the goods they have collected in order to have them weighed and verified, then get an assessment before they can proceed to sell their striped conches, sea turtles and urchins. Only then is the Company issued a certificate with which they can return. These annual collections sometimes can be very fruitful and at other times more disappointing, it depends on the year."

It is well-known that the Miscellaneous Records on the Pacification of the Frontiers was a "work of haste" left by Lê Quý Đôn during his 6-month military life in Ngiem Hiep Town of Huế when he followed the army of Trinh from February to August, 1776. Having never published, this book circulated in the world in the form of transcript, for which it is full of ambiguity and misrepresentations by the later generations, with its content rendered in tremendous miscellaneity. For example, the preceding text mentioned above about the islands and sand banks "outside of the harbor of Dai of An Vinh Commune, Bình Sơn County, Quảng Ngãi Prefecture" mentioned the terms "Culao" and "the Great Trường Sa Islands"; whereas the subsequent text discussing the issue at length only mentioned "Hoàng Sa Chu (Golden Sandy Island)", without further discussion of "Culao" and "Great Trường Sa Islands". Another case in point is that the latter text cited mentioned both "Hoàng Sa Company" and "Cat Liem Company". In fact, "Hoàng Sa Company" is a Chinese title, while "Cat Liem Company" is a variant of the Vietnamese Chu Nom "Cat Hoàng" or "Cat Vong" (meaning yellow sand). The name was altered to avoid using the character "Hoàng" due to the taboo associated with Nguyen Hoang. Thus "Hoàng" was written as "Liem," which essentially refers to "Hoàng Sa Company". This was an apparent falsification by people in the Nguyễn dynasty. And the list of similar examples goes on and on. Therefore, the content of the *Miscellaneous Records on the Pacification of the Frontiers*, when employed, shall go through careful identification.

The first paragraph cited above in the work of Lê Quý Đôn mentioned that the navigation to "Great Trường Sa Islands" takes "a three-day trip", while "Hoàng Sa Chu (Golden Sandy Island)" in the subsequent text "can be reached after a three-day trip at sea", both of which are of similar distance. Moreover, both places are home to marine products and foreign goods, and are significant operative spots of Hoàng Sa Company, indicating that the "Dao Trường Sa Lon" in the former text is the same place as the "Hoàng Sa Chu" in the words of the later generations. Furthermore, looking from their locations, "Culao" is located in "the outer sea of An Vinh Commune, Bình Sơn County, Quảng Ngãi Prefecture," while the "Golden Sandy Island" is described as an island in "near the coast and northeast offshore in An Vinh Commune, Bình Sơn County, Quảng Ngãi Prefecture." The locations being the same, these three places must refer to the same place. Therefore, we believe that what Lê Quý Đôn referred to as "Culao", "Great Trường Sa Islands," or "a Golden Sandy Island" refers to one single location.

So, where is this place now? Many scholars in China and Vietnamese ones like Hoàng Xuân Hãn believe, after examination, that "Culao", or "Culao Re", refers to the present-day Lý Sơn Island or Lý Island. Lý Sơn Island is located in northeast Bình Sơn County, composed by several peaks and craters, each resembling an independent isolated island. And this looks like the scene described by Lê Quý Đôn as "miscellaneous rockheads jutting out of the sea, totaling 130 altogether". However, overlooked from the north, the island is all flat as what is described as "flat and vast", and is "over 30-ly in length". With swallow's nests, and marine products like turtle shells, striped conches, sea urchins, this island is also located within the dangerous zone of offshore navigation in the ancient times. Therefore, this place matches Lê Quý Đôn's description in terms of navigation distance, natural landscape and products.

In the first volume of *A Geographical Description of Vietnam* by Qing Dynasty scholars (written by Sheng Qingfu in the ninth year of Guangxu, 1883, revised by Lü Diaoyang in the 19th year of Guangxu, 1893), there are accounts similar to those of Lê Quý Đôn in the section on "Guangyi Province",

"The village of An Vinh Commune in Bình Sơn County is located near the coast, with islands to the northeast. The mountains overlap, with more than 130 ridges (original note: referring to Wailuo Mountain). Between the mountains lies the sea, about a day's journey or several watches apart. At the foot of the mountains, there are sweet springs, and among them is a Golden Sandy Island (original note: referring to Yezi Tang), which is approximately 30 *li* long, flat and expansive, with clear and pristine water, where many merchant ships anchor..."

Lü's notes clearly point out that the "over 130" islands in the northeastern sea of the village of An Vinh Commune in Bình Sơn County refer to "Wailuo Mountain" frequently mentioned in Chinese historical accounts; and the "Golden Sandy Island" in these islands refers to "Yezi Tang (Coconut Pond)". Zhang Xie of the Ming Dynasty mentioned in his *Dong Xi Yang Kao (Studies on the Oceans East and West)* that "Wailuo Mountain appears as a gateway from a distance, while up close it slopes from east to west, with Yezi Tang inside." *Liangzhong Haidao Zhenjing (Two Guides about Navigation Routes)* also mentioned that "Wailuo Mountain slopes from east to west, with Yezi Tang inside." Nguyễn Thông's A *Brief Revision of the Comprehensively Reflected Chronicles of Viet History (Vol. IV, Lam Ap)* recorded that the island of Lý Sơn is also known as "Ngoai Culao", "commonly known as 'Ngoai Lao'", and "written by Chinese people as Wailuo". The Chu Nom "岣崂" is written in central Vietnamese as "Culao", meaning island or mountain. "Ngoai Culao" and "Ngoai Lao" are traslated

as "Wailuo Mountain" or "Wailuo" in Chinese historical records, referring to the island of Lý Sơn. The "Hoàng Sa Chu", or Wailuo Mountain, refers to the "Yezi Tang" in the north of the island of Lý Sơn - being the same place.

The "Culao Rong", "Dao Trường Sa Lon" or "Hoàng Sa Chu" in Lê Quý Đôn's words, with its specific reference respectively, are naturally not China's Xisha Qundao or even Nansha Qundao. Judging by the first cited text of Lê Quý Đôn, he originally intended to expound that "outside of various harbors of Thanh Quang", the offshore sand banks and islands were formed by the "rocky mountain rising" within. The navigation distance between them and the Vietnamese coast takes several watches or a day, or three days and nights at the farthest. Since the Hoàng Sa Company "use private fishing boats", which are small fishing vessels operated by human power with no cooking facilities and large freshwater storage equipment, they can only fish in nearshore waters. Their speed is very slow, and in three days and nights, they can only reach islands not far from the Vietnamese coast, making it impossible to reach the distant Xisha and Nansha Qundao in the open sea. According to Lê Quý Đôn's record, the islands including "Hoàng Sa Chu" are "miscellaneous rockheads jutting out of the sea, totaling 130 altogether". However, all of the islands in China's Xisha Qundao, even taking into account the ones that come up out of the water in low tides, add up to only 35, which is a number way smaller than 130. Counting all of the islands in Xisha and Nansha Qundao altogether, the number will only be 50, less than over 130. Therefore, Lê's statement does not refer to Xisha and Nansha Qundao of China. He added that "Hoàng Sa Chu is more than 30 ly long, with wide, even surface". But in China's Xisha and Nansha Qundao, no big island as Lê's description can be found at all. Yongxing Dao (Woody Island), the largest island in Xisha and Nansha Qundao, is only 1.95 kilometers long and 1.35 kilometers wide, which cannot be counted as a large one and is poles apart with "Hoàng Sa Chu". Neither Xisha nor Nansha Qundao produce any swallow's nest, which does not conform with Lê's record that "there are countless swallow's nests at the margin of the island" in Hoàng Sa Chu. All of the above indicates that Lê's record has nothing to do with China's Xisha Qundao and Nansha Qundao in the slightest. Therefore, Vietnamese authorities are just attempting in vain to fabricate "evidences" for their intrusive deeds with mis-attributions.

The Vietnamese white papers and relevant writings often cite "Hoàng Sa Company", as recorded in Lê Quý Đôn's the *Miscellaneous Records on the Pacification of the Frontiers*, as the "legal basis" for the Vietnamese government to exercise development, jurisdiction, and establish sovereignty. However, anyone who has read the *Miscellaneous Records on the Pacification of the Frontiers* knows that the "Hoàng Sa Company", as did the "Bac Hai Company", "Hai Mon Company", and "Thanh Chau Company", was a labor organization established by the Nguyen feudal dynasty to exploit its people. The mission of "Hoàng Sa Company" was only to collect "marine products and foreign goods" for the feudal rulers of the Nguyen court. This book also recorded the team of workers such as painters, gunsmiths, metalworkers, and matmakers who were conscripted to perform labor for the Nguyen dynasty in order to gather other items. It was recorded in Volume VI of the book that "there is a team of mat weavers in Yafan Commune of Phủ Lý Commune, Quy Nhơn Prefecture, producing 30 pairs of edge-sewn mats annually; similar team exists in Phu An Prefecture, producing 50 pairs of broad mats, one pair of connecting mats, and one pair of narrow mats each year." "The villages named Phan Xa and Hoang Giang in Khuong Loc County are skilled in gun-making, and the Nguyen dynasty conscripted 60 people from Phan Xa to form two teams of left and right gunsmiths." "In Huế, there are two teams of metalworkers, each with 30 people, and there is a foundry located on the southern bank of the Phú Xuân River." There is also records in Volume IV of this book about "Hoàng Sa Company" set for gold exploitation: "At the hill in Nam Pho Coummue of Phu Vinh County... gold is also produced at its foot... The Hoàng Sa Company was summoned, and 65 laborers were hired to dig and wash for gold. Working for four months, they only obtained four taels and five coins, which did not cover the cost of labor and food, so they ceased their operations." It is evident from the above that the companies established by the Nguyễn dynasty, including the "Hoàng Sa Company", were neither a political power nor a navy, and thus had no jurisdiction to establish Vietnam's sovereignty. The Hanoi authorities' white paper from April, 1988 also stated that the activities of the Hoàng Sa Company's "continued uninterrupted from the Nguyen dynasty (1558–1777) to the Tây Sơn dynasty (1778–1802)," with which they attempted to prove the "continuous" jurisdiction of the Vietnamese government. However, they could not provide any information to demonstrate the Hoàng Sa Company's activities during the Tây Sơn dynasty, while the Nguyen dynasty's *Record of Unified Dai Nam* (Vol. VI) clearly states that "at the beginning of the Gia Long reign, the old system was emulated, and the Hoàng Sa Company was established, which was soon abolished." Since Minh Mạng's reign, the "Hoàng Sa Company" had been abolished, and ceased their labor to collect marine products and foreign goods. Thus the evidence provided by Vietnam collapse of itself.

The white book of Saigon even clings to the record in the *Miscellaneous Records on the Pacification of the Frontiers* that "the shores of the Hoàng Sa Islands are not far from Lien-chou Prefecture in Hainan Province, China. (For that reason) our ships sometimes meet with fishing boats from our Northern neighbor (China) on the high sea. They often see the hall officer of Wen-ch'ang District, Ch'iung-chou Prefecture (Hainan

Island, China), An official document of Huế says, "In the eighteenth year of Ch'ien-lung (1753), ten soldiers from An Binh Commune belonging to the Cat Liem Company, Chương Nghĩa County, Quảng Ngãi Prefecture, Annam, set out during, the seventh month to go to the Van Ly Trường Sa to collect sea products. Eight of the ten men went ashore for the collection of products, and two remained on the ship to watch it. A typhoon soon developed which caused the anchor cord to split, and the two who remained in the ship were washed into the port of Ch'ing-lan. After investigation the Chinese officer found the story to be correct and consequently had the two Vietnamese escorted home to their native village. Lord Nguyễn Phúc Chu subsequently had the Governor of Thuận Hóa Province, the Count of Thuc Luong, write a courtesy note as a reply". Providing this, Saigon attempted to prove that China had acknowledged that Vietnam "had exercised its legal rights over these islands", claiming that "this ironclad evidence proves that in the past, the Chinese government acknowledged and respected Vietnam's sovereignty over the Xisha Qundao and Nansha Qundao, never showing any intention to contest sovereignty over this island region. "This is an argument that calls white black. The aforementioned materials show that the Vietnamese boatmen not only "meet with fishing boats from our Northern neighbor (China)" in the high sea, but "often see" the hall officer of Wen-ch'ang District, Ch'iung-chou Prefecture patrolling the area. This precisely proves that the Chinese people and government have already exercised development and jurisdiction over these islands. The "event" found by Lê Quý Đôn in an official document about what happened in the 18th year of Qianlong (1753) was that "soldiers from An Binh Commune belonging to the Cat Liem Company" go to the Chinese territory "Wangli Changsha" (Lê clearly separated "Hoàng Sa Chu" and "Wanli Changsha" in the same paragraph, of which the latter one is a Chinese name known to the world) to "collect" and "search" for the articles in the shipwreck. Such petty theft cannot serve as a "legal basis" for the Vietnamese government to exercise sovereignty. Besides, when the Chinese officer found their story "to be correct", the two Vietnamese were "escorted back to their native village", which was essentially a deportation. Furthermore, the king of Nguyen ordered the local governor of Thuận Hóa to "write a courtesy note as a reply". According to the white book of Saigon, it was an act to "extend appreciation". While the whole process of this incident is a definite prove that the Chinese government had exercised its sovereignty, which was acknowledged by the Vietnamese ruler.

Most of the ancient Vietnamese texts about "Hoàng Sa" and "Trường Sa" after the *Miscellaneous Records on the Pacification of the Frontiers* follow this book, or employ some tricks of altering place names. The records in the original version of the *Miscellaneous Records on the Pacification of the Frontiers* do not refer to China's Xisha or Nansha Qundao. And since we have clarified this work, there is no need for further debate on subsequent derivative ones.

4.On the *Complete Map of Unified Dai Nam*

The white books of Vietnam and relevant writings in the country fail to provide any substantial or direct evidence regarding their sovereignty over Nansha Qundao. Therefore, Vietnam resorted to a map titled the *Complete Map of Unified Dai Nam* as a stopgap. The white book of Saigon said, "In about 1838, the *Complete Map of Unified Dai Nam* published by Phan Huy Chú called the Nansha Qundao 'Vạn Lý Trường Sa', clearly referring to it as part of Vietnamese territory." The white book published by the Hanoi authorities in 1982 also mentioned that *the Complete Map of Unified Dai Nam*, which was drawn in about 1838, recorded that "Hoàng Sa" and "Vạn Lý Trường Sa" belong to the "Vietnamese territory". However, there are a mass of doubts regarding important issues such as the origin and creation date of this map, about which the Vietnamese side has been evasive, unable to provide a coherent explanation. A vague "historical evidence" like this can by no means be used by Vietnam as the legal basis for its territorial sovereignty.

Saigon falsely claimed in its white book that according to the *Chronicle of Dai Nam*, the famous *Detailed map of the Dai Nam*, which was "a picture book drawn" in Hoàng Sa from the 16th year (1836) to the 17th year (1837) of Minh Mạng's reign, and "was composed of materials collected during the investigation, was completed in around 1838". This, however, is a sheer piece of fabrication. There is not a single letter in the *Chronicle of Dai Nam* mentioning the drawing process of the *Complete Map of Unified Dai Nam* or *the Detailed map of the Dai Nam*. This map cannot even be found in the officially edited *Record of Unified Dai Nam,* either in its general map or the ones of individual province. They continued to trumped up, "In around 1838, the map called the *Complete Map of Unified Dai Nam* was published by Phan Huy Chú ", meaning that the map was drawn by Phan as his work. However, the *Regulations of Successive Dynasties by Subject-Matter: Treatise on Geography*, which was published in 1821, was almost a copy of the preceding *Treatise on Geography of the Royal Viet* published in 1833. Regarding this, the Vietnamese scholar Vu Long Te states, "The *Complete Map of Unified Dai Nam* does not originate from the *Treatise on Geography of the Royal Viet* which is first published in 1833 (absolutely not 1834), and the reason for that is simple: Emperor Minh Mạng did not use the title 'Dai Nam' until 1838"(cited from "Issues on the Toponymy of the Archipelagos of Hoàng Sa and Trường Sa", published in *The Specific Examination on Hoàng Sa and Trường Sa*). In order to fill the aforementioned leap holes and conform to the fabricated fact that the title "Dai Nam" was enacted in 1838, the white books of Saigon and Hanoi said in vague terms that this map "was approximately drawn in 1838". Nonetheless, they failed to provide any supporting reason for this statement. Vu Long Te revealed in one of his articles that "this map (the

Complete Map of Unified Dai Nam) is a copy that Mr. Chu Ngoc Thoi, the assistant to the Vice Premier in charge of national development planning and congressional liaison, collected a long time ago and generously offered for our use." This indicates that the *Complete Map of Unified Dai Nam*, which was demonstrated by the white books of Saigon and Hanoi later, is merely an unsubstantiated copy, produced by Chu Ngoc Thoi, the bureaucratic politician, to serve the political demand of Saigon authorities, who sought to unlawfully occupy China's Xisha Qundao and Nansha Qundao. Its reliability is highly questionable and should not be regarded as credible evidence.

When comparing the *Complete Map of Unified Dai Nam* with the map attached in the *Record of Unified Dai Nam*, one will soon discover that the *Complete Map of Unified Dai Nam*, which the Vietnam authorities claim to be drawn in 1838, is far superior in cartographic technique to the illustrations in the *Record of Unified Dai Nam*. This can only indicate that the *Complete Map of Unified Dai Nam* is a forgery created after 1910.

Yet the essential problem is, it can be clearly seen from this accurately drawn map that unlike China's Xisha Qundao and Nansha Qundao that are 500 kilometers from each other, "Hoàng Sa" and "Vạn Lý Trường Sa" are located close together. The white book of Saigon had to admit that these two island groups are "not drawn in the right position" in the map. This serves as strong evidence that the "Hoàng Sa" and "Trường Sa" drawn in the unidentified *Complete Map of Unified Dai Nam* are not China's Xisha or Nansha Qundao in any way.

5.On the materials provided by Bishop Taberd

The Vietnamese white book never grows tired of saying that in 1816, the first Nguyễn emperor Gia Long "took formal possession of" the islands of Hoàng Sa, and "the Vietnamese flag was planted in a formal ceremony on the Paracels". They are largely based on the material left by a French Catholic reverend Louis Taberd, who had once lived in Vietnam. In *the Journal of the Royal Asiatic Society of Bengal, India*, Bishop Taberd published an article entitled "Note on the Geography of Cochinchina" in September, 1838, which reads, "The *Pracel* or *Parocels*, is a labyrinth of small islands, rocks and sand-banks, which appears to extend up to the 11th degree of north latitude, in the 107th parallel of longitude from Paris. Some navigators have traversed part of these shoals with more fortunate than prudent, but others have suffered in the attempt. The Cochin Chinese called them Con Vang. Although this kind of archipelago presents nothing but rocks and great depths which promises more inconveniences than advantages, the king Gra Lone thought he had increased his dominions by this sorry addition. In 1816, he went with solemnity to plant his flag and take formal possession of these rocks, which it is not likely anybody will dispute with him." Vietnamese scholars still added another material by Taberd - that is, his book the *Record of the World: the History of All Nations and the Overview of Their Religions, Customs and Manners* published in 1833. It is recorded in the book that "Emperor Gia Long attached great importance to adding the eccentric flower on his crown, because he thought it imperative to go overseas in person for the occupation of these islands (referring to the Xisha Qundao). Therefore, in 1816, he planted the Cochinchina flag there with solemnity."

When citing the materials by western colonists like Taberd, the white book of Saigon says, "It must be emphasized that all of the works cited were published before the French had controlled Vietnam, which were thus not designated for the maintenance of France's claim over these islands." This is truly an instance of trying to conceal an obvious truth! Anyone who has the slightest acquaintance with Vietnamese history will know that at the end of the 17th century, the French king Louis XVI had, according to the proposal of Bishop Pedro, generated the "French Oriental Empire Plan" to transform Vietnam into a French colony, and took a series of practical measures to invade in Vietnam. Subsequently to Pedro, missionaries, merchants and explorers arriving in Vietnam all promoted this invasive project proactively. It is no wonder that some colonists, in order to convert Vietnam into a colony of France in the future, deliberately distorted facts and favored Vietnam in the materials they left behind. A typical case in point is that Bishop Taberd has coined that Vietnamese Emperor Gia Long occupied the Xisha Qundao in 1816.

According to Taberd, "Emperor Gia Long attached great importance to adding the eccentric flower on his crown", which seems like a reasonable description of a queen from a western country, while a bit too ridiculous to portray a Vietnamese emperor in the oriental world. Even more ludicrously, Taberd had imposed the flag-raising ceremony commonly used by Western colonialists when occupying or discovering a piece of land onto Emperor Gia Long. At that time, oriental monarch like the king of Vietnam had not yet developed such an etiquette habit as the western colonists, for which he could not have held any "official ceremony" of flag raising. Half of the modern Vietnamese territory came from the invasion of the Nguyen dynasty and the preceding kings of Nguyen. Around 1816, Vietnam had invaded in quite a few places of Cambodia and Laos. While there is no any record about the flag raising ceremony held in these invaded places in the Vietnamese historical texts. This suffices to prove that the story depicted by Taberd is purely imaginary.

According to Taberd, Emperor Gia Long of Vietnam had "personally led his soldiers in a military operation" in the Xisha Qundao. But this is exceptionally ridiculous, because the official records detailing the actions of Vietnamese emperors, the *Chronicle of Dai Nam*, and its supplement, *Quoc Su Di Bien*, surprisingly have no mention whatsoever of such a significant event as the emperor's personal expedition. If it were true, it was impossible that there is no record about it in the *Chronicle of Dai Nam*.

If Taber's materials are accurate, the Xisha Qundao occupied by Emperor Gia Long in 1816 are not, in fact, China's Xisha Qundao. In the *Note on the Geography of Cochinchina* cited above, Taberd mentioned that Xisha Qundao are located in the 107th parallel of longitude from Paris, i.e., 109°10' E longitude of Greenwich. Though he did not explicitly state in the text that this archipelago extends from a certain latitude north to 11°N, the accompanying map in the *Dictionarium Anamitico-Latinum*, compiled by the same Taberd and published in 1838, indicates that the latitude of the Xisha Qundao starts at 17°N, with a longitude of approximately 110°E. In this view, the latitude of the Xisha Qundao as mentioned by Taberd is from 11°N to 17°N, and their longitude is from approximately 109°E to 110°E (with Paris corresponding to 107°E - 108°E). This set of coordinates has no overlap with the latitudes and longitudes of China's Xisha Qundao (15°47'N - 17°08'N, 111°10'E - 112°55'E). According to Taberd's coordinates, it is possible he was referring to Pulloeseccade Terra, which has coordinates of 11.2°N and 108.9°E, a barren land almost entirely composed of rocks, rising to 27 meters. In 1816, the islands occupied by Emperor Gia Long certainly included some islands around the southern end of the Xisha Qundao at approximately 11°N, specifically Pulloeseccade Terra (also known as Bình Thuận Island). The Vietnamese, using the method of name substitution, have imposed what Taberd described onto China's Xisha Qundao, which is a clear case of mis-attribution.

The aforementioned materials from Taberd were glorified in the Saigon White Paper, but the subsequent Hanoi White Paper lacked the courage to resurrect this "treasure" and instead relied on the account from the *Chronicle of Dai Nam*, which records that in the 15th year of Gia Long's reign (1816), the emperor "ordered the naval forces and the Hoàng Sa

Company to measure the waterway," as the "historical basis" for Vietnam's claim of sovereignty over Xisha Qundao. The "measurement of the waterway", a kind of survey as it was, cannot serve as the legal basis of territorial claim. In the 19th century, some individuals from Western countries such as Britain and Germany conducted unauthorized surveys of certain islands in Xisha and Nansha Qundao of China, citing navigational safety as their reason. These acts, as did their measurements of China's extensive coastline, do not indicate that these islands and coastlines belong to them. The sovereignty over these islands and coastlines rightfully belongs to China, which is a fact recognized by countries around the world, including those involved in the said surveys. The conclusion in the Hanoi White Paper's that "Emperor Gia Long occupied the Hoàng Sa Islands in 1816", based on the "measurement of the waterway", is completely untenable.

Taberd's materials were originally of no value and had not received any attention from scholars for nearly a century. It was only in 1929 that the French colonial authorities, in their attempt to occupy China's Xisha Qundao, picked up this seemingly plausible material as a basis. It was immediately met with a stern rebuttal from the Chinese side. It is now even more futile for Vietnam to echo this sentiment by resurrecting Taberd's materials as a basis for territorial claims over China's Xisha Qundao.

Bibliography

1. **South China Sea Integrated Science Expedition Team, Chinese Academy of Sciences.** *Comprehensive Survey and Research Report on the Nansha Islands and Adjacent Sea Areas (Volumes 1 & 2)* [R]. Beijing: Science Press, 1989.

2. **Zeng Bingguang and Chen Jing.** *History, Current Status and Prospects of Fisheries Development in the Nansha Sea Area* [Z]. Unpublished Materials of the South China Sea Integrated Science

Expedition Team, Chinese Academy of Sciences, 1991.

3. **South China Sea Integrated Science Expedition Team, Chinese Academy of Sciences, ed.** *Collected Papers on Marine Environment Research of the Nansha Islands and Adjacent Sea Areas (Part 1)* [G]. Wuhan: Hubei Science and Technology Press, 1991.

4. **Han Zhenhua.** "A Study of the Ancient 'Paracel'" [M]. In *Collected Essays on Historical and Geographical Research of the South China Sea Islands*, by Han Zhenhua. Beijing: Zhonghua Book Company, 1981.

5. **Li Baotian and Wang Yingjie.** "Origins of the Territorial Dispute over the Nansha Islands" [M]. In *Special Collection on Historical Geography of the Nansha Islands*, edited by South China Sea Integrated Science Expedition Team, Chinese Academy of Sciences. Guangzhou: Sun Yat-sen University Press, 1991.

6. **Foreign Affairs Office of the Revolutionary Committee of Guangdong Province.** *Partial French Archives on the Xisha Islands Issue* [A]. 1976.

7. **Chen Hongyu.** *Sovereignty over the South China Sea Islands and International Conflicts* [M]. Taipei: Youshi Culture Enterprise Co., 1987.

8. **On the 1898 *Treaty of Paris* (US-Spain), 1900 *Treaty on the Cession of Outlying Islands of the Philippines* (US-Spain), and 1930 *Treaty between the US and UK on the Boundary between North Borneo and the Philippines*, see:** Zoilo M. Galang, ed., *Encyclopedia of the Philippines*, Vol. 16: *History* (Manila: n.p., 1957), 20 ‑ 22.

1.中国科学院南沙综合科学考察队.南沙群岛及其领近海区综合调查研究报告上下卷［R］.北京：科学出版社，1989.

2.曾炳光，陈静.南沙海区渔业开发研究的历史、现状和前景［Z］.中国科学院南沙综合科学考察队内部资料，1991.

3.中国科学院南沙综合科学考察队.南沙群岛及其领近海区海洋环境研究论文集（一）［G］.武汉：湖北科学技术出版社，1991.

4.韩振华.古"帕拉塞尔"考［M］‖韩振华.南海诸岛史地考证论集.北京：中华书局，1981.

5.李宝田，王英杰.南沙群岛领土归属争端的由来［M］‖中国科学院南沙综合科学考察队.南沙群岛历史地理研究专集.广州：中山大学出版社，1991.

6.广东省革命委员会外事办公室.法国有关西沙群岛问题的部分档案［A］.1976.

7.陈鸿瑜.南海诸岛主权与国际冲突［M］.台北：幼狮文化事业公司，1987.

8.关于 1898 年美西《巴黎和约》和 1900 年美西《关于菲律宾外围岛屿割让的条约》以及 1930 年美英《关于划定北婆罗洲与美属菲律宾之间的边界条约》，参见佐伊洛·姆·加兰编《菲律宾百科全书》第 16 卷历史部分第 20、21、22 页.